D1174085

Science

GRAPHIS NEW MEDIA 1

A Compilation of New Media Design

Edited by • Clement Mok

Publisher and Creative Director: B. Martin Pederson

Art Directors: Clement Mok, Joshua Michels

Writer: David Livingstone Fore

Editorial Assistant: Hallie Warshaw

Digital Production: Michael Conti, Beth O'Rourke

Graphis U.S., Inc. New York, Graphis Press Corp. Zürich (Switzerland)

opposite:

Magnet Interactive Studios, Chuck Seelye, art director (see page 54 for further credits)

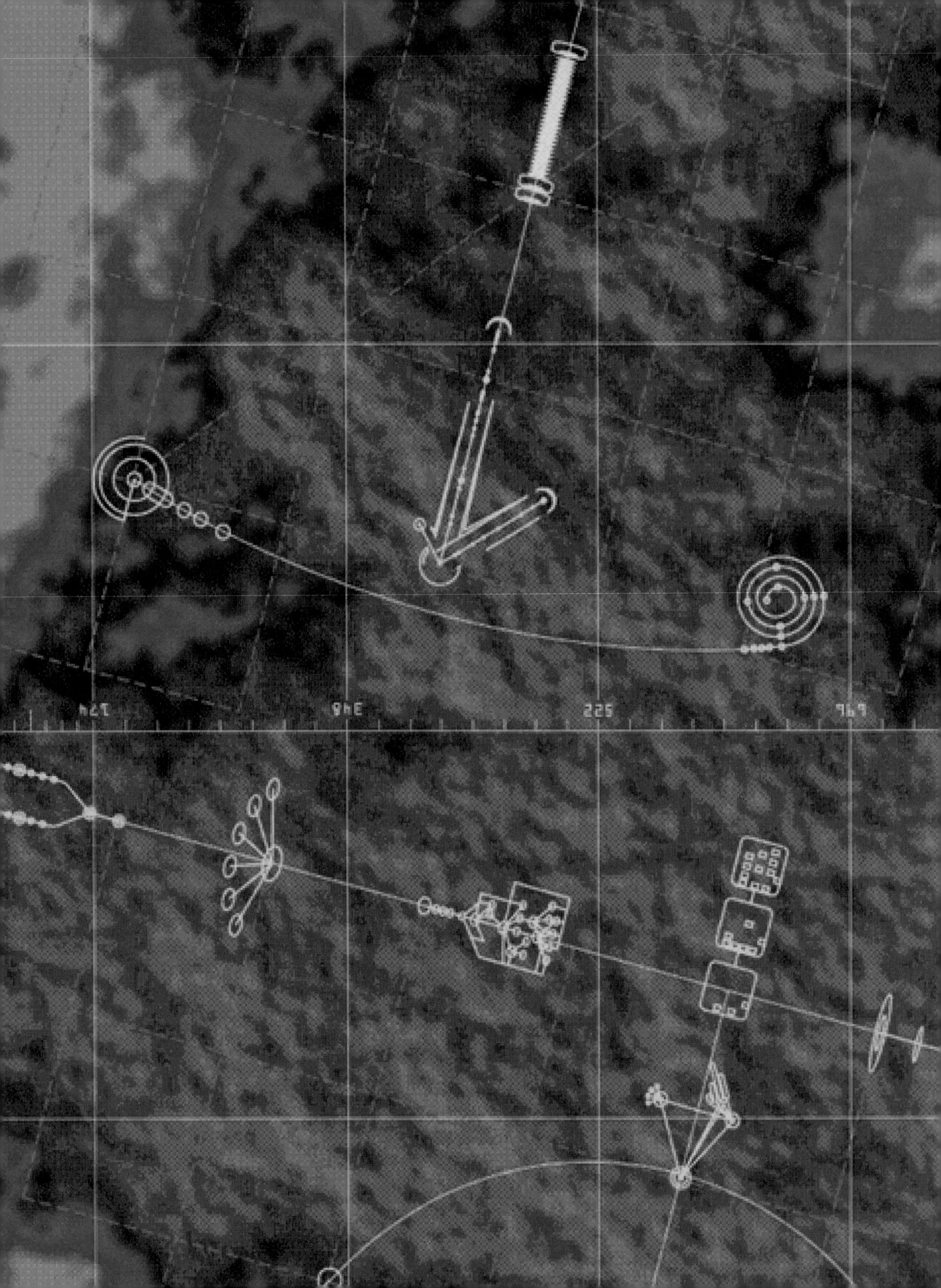

CONTENTS

OPPOSITE: IDEO, PETER SPREENBERG, ART DIRECTOR (SEE PAGE 84 FOR FURTHER CREDITS)

GRAPHIS PUBLICATIONS

GRAPHIS, THE INTERNATIONAL BI-MONTHLY JOURNAL OF VISUAL COMMUNICATION
GRAPHIS SHOPPING BAG, AN INTERNATIONAL COLLECTION OF SHOPPING BAG DESIGN
GRAPHIS MUSIC CD, AN INTERNATIONAL COLLECTION OF CD DESIGN
GRAPHIS BOOK DESIGN, AN INTERNATIONAL COLLECTION OF BOOK DESIGN
GRAPHIS DESIGN, THE INTERNATIONAL ANNUAL OF DESIGN AND ILLUSTRATION
GRAPHIS STUDENT DESIGN, THE INTERNATIONAL ANNUAL OF DESIGN AND COMMUNICATION DESIGN BY STUDENTS
GRAPHIS ADVERTISING, THE INTERNATIONAL ANNUAL OF ADVERTISING
GRAPHIS BROCHURES, A COMPILATION OF BROCHURE DESIGN
GRAPHIS PHOTO, THE INTERNATIONAL ANNUAL OF PHOTOGRAPHY
GRAPHIS ALTERNATIVE PHOTOGRAPHY, THE INTERNATIONAL ANNUAL OF ALTERNATIVE PHOTOGRAPHY
GRAPHIS NUDES, A COLLECTION OF CAREFULLY SELECTED SOPHISTICATED IMAGES
GRAPHIS POSTER, THE INTERNATIONAL ANNUAL OF POSTER ART
GRAPHIS PACKAGING, AN INTERNATIONAL COMPILATION OF PACKAGING DESIGN
GRAPHIS LETTERHEAD, AN INTERNATIONAL COMPILATION OF LETTERHEAD DESIGN
GRAPHIS DIAGRAM, THE GRAPHIC VISUALIZATION OF ABSTRACT, TECHNICAL AND STATISTICAL FACTS AND FUNCTIONS
GRAPHIS LOGO, AN INTERNATIONAL COMPILATION OF LOGOS
GRAPHIS EPHEMERA, AN INTERNATIONAL COLLECTION OF PROMOTIONAL ART
GRAPHIS PUBLICATION, AN INTERNATIONAL SURVEY OF THE BEST IN MAGAZINE DESIGN
GRAPHIS ANNUAL REPORTS, AN INTERNATIONAL COMPILATION OF THE BEST DESIGNED ANNUAL REPORTS
GRAPHIS CORPORATE IDENTITY, AN INTERNATIONAL COMPILATION OF THE BEST IN CORPORATE IDENTITY DESIGN
GRAPHIS TYPOGRAPHY, AN INTERNATIONAL COMPILATION OF THE BEST IN TYPOGRAPHIC DESIGN

GRAPHIS PUBLIKATIONEN

GRAPHIS, DIE INTERNATIONALE ZWEIMONATSZEITSCHRIFT DER VISUELLEN KOMMUNIKATION
GRAPHIS SHOPPING BAG, TRAGTASCHEN-DESIGN IM INTERNATIONALEN ÜBERBLICK
GRAPHIS MUSIC CD, CD-DESIGN IM INTERNATIONALEN ÜBERBLICK
GRAPHIS BOOKS, BUCHGESTALTUNG IM INTERNATIONALEN ÜBERBLICK
GRAPHIS DESIGN, DAS INTERNATIONALE JAHRBUCH ÜBER DESIGN UND ILLUSTRATION
GRAPHIS STUDENT DESIGN, DAS INTERNATIONALE JAHRBUCH ÜBER KOMMUNIKATIONSDESIGN VON STUDENTEN
GRAPHIS ADVERTISING, DAS INTERNATIONALE JAHRBUCH DER WERBUNG
GRAPHIS BROCHURES, BROSCHÜRENDESIGN IM INTERNATIONAL ÜBERBLICK
GRAPHIS PHOTO, DAS INTERNATIONALE JAHRBUCH DER PHOTOGRAPHIE
GRAPHIS ALTERNATIVE PHOTOGRAPHY, DAS INTERNATIONALE JAHRBUCH ÜBER ALTERNATIVE PHOTOGRAPHIE
GRAPHIS NUDES, EINE SAMMLUNG SORGFÄLTIG AUSGEWÄHLTER AKTPHOTOGRAPHIE
GRAPHIS POSTER, DAS INTERNATIONALE JAHRBUCH DER PLAKATKUNST
GRAPHIS PACKAGING, EIN INTERNATIONALER ÜBERBLICK ÜBER DIE PACKUNGSGESTALTUNG
GRAPHIS LETTERHEAD, EIN INTERNATIONALER ÜBERBLICK ÜBER BRIEFPAPIERGESTALTUNG
GRAPHIS DIAGRAM, DIE GRAPHISCHE DARSTELLUNG ABSTRAKTER TECHNISCHER UND STATISTISCHER DATEN UND FAKTEN
GRAPHIS LOGO, EINE INTERNATIONALE AUSWAHL VON FIRMEN-LOGOS
GRAPHIS EPHEMERA, EINE INTERNATIONALE SAMMLUNG GRAPHISCHER DOKUMENTE DES TÄGLICHEN LEBENS
GRAPHIS MAGAZINDESIGN, EINE INTERNATIONALE ZUSAMMENSTELLUNG DES BESTEN ZEITSCHRIFTEN-DESIGNS
GRAPHIS ANNUAL REPORTS, EIN INTERNATIONALER ÜBERBLICK ÜBER DIE GESTALTUNG VON JAHRESBERICHTEN
GRAPHIS CORPORATE IDENTITY, EINE INTERNATIONALE AUSWAHL DES BESTEN CORPORATE IDENTITY DESIGNS
GRAPHIS TYPOGRAPHY, EINE INTERNATIONALE ZUSAMMENSTELLUNG DES BESTEN TYPOGRAPHIE DESIGN

PUBLICATIONS GRAPHIS

GRAPHIS, LA REVUE BIMESTRIELLE INTERNATIONALE DE LA COMMUNICATION VISUELLE
GRAPHIS SHOPPING BAG, UNE COMPILATION INTERNATIONALE SUR LE DESIGN DES SACS À COMMISSIONS
GRAPHIS MUSIC CD, UNE COMPILATION INTERNATIONALE SUR LE DESIGN DES CD
GRAPHIS BOOKS, UNE COMPILATION INTERNATIONALE SUR LE DESIGN DES LIVRES
GRAPHIS DESIGN, LE RÉPERTOIRE INTERNATIONAL DE LA COMMUNICATION VISUELLE
GRAPHIS STUDENT DESIGN, UN RÉPERTOIRE INTERNATIONAL DE PROJTS D'EXPRESSION VISUELLE D'ÉDUTIANTS
GRAPHIS ADVERTISING, LE RÉPERTOIRE INTERNATIONAL DE LA PUBLICITÉ
GRAPHIS BROCHURES, UNE COMPILATION INTERNATIONALE SUR LE DESIGN DES BROCHURES
GRAPHIS PHOTO, LE RÉPERTOIRE INTERNATIONAL DE LA PHOTOGRAPHIE
GRAPHIS ALTERNATIVE PHOTOGRAPHY, LE RÉPERTOIRE INTERNATIONAL DE LA PHOTOGRAPHIE ALTERNATIVE
GRAPHIS NUDES, UN FLORILÈGE DE LA PHOTOGRAPHIE DE NUS
GRAPHIS POSTER, LE RÉPERTOIRE INTERNATIONAL DE L'AFFICHE
GRAPHIS PACKAGING, LE RÉPERTOIRE INTERNATIONAL DE LA CRÉATION D'EMBALLAGES
GRAPHIS LETTERHEAD, LE RÉPERTOIRE INTERNATIONAL DU DESIGN DE PAPIER À LETTRES
GRAPHIS DIAGRAM, LE RÉPERTOIRE GRAPHIQUE DE FAITS ET DONNÉES ABSTRAITS, TECHNIQUES ET STATISTIQUES
GRAPHIS LOGO, LE RÉPERTOIRE INTERNATIONAL DU LOGO
GRAPHIS EPHEMERA, LE GRAPHISME – UN ÉTAT D'ESPRIT AU QUOTIDIEN
GRAPHIS PUBLICATION, LE RÉPERTOIRE INTERNATIONAL DU DESIGN DE PÉRIODIQUES
GRAPHIS ANNUAL REPORTS, PANORAMA INTERNATIONAL DU MEILLEUR DESIGN DE RAPPORTS ANNUELS D'ENTREPRISES
GRAPHIS CORPORATE IDENTITY, PANORAMA INTERNATIONAL DU MEILLEUR DESIGN D'IDENTITÉ CORPORATE
GRAPHIS TYPOGRAPHY, LE RÉPERTOIRE INTERNATIONAL DU MEILLEUR DESIGN DE TYPOGRAPHIE

PUBLICATION NO. 264 (ISBN 1-888001-06-2)

141 LEXINGTON AVENUE, NEW YORK, N.Y. 10016 USA

PRINTED IN SINGAPORE BY CS GRAPHICS PTE LTD.

NEW MEDIA

INTRODUCTION

Take a seat.

Boot up the machine.

Settle in.

Choose something.

Make a choice and *Cézanne's Nudes in a Landscape* emerges from the darkness. Make another choice to examine the contours of the brush strokes.

Make a choice and board a warship, meet its crew, and search from fore to aft for a stowaway.

Make a choice and flip through a catalogue of dingbats, fuzzy fonts, video, and clip art. Make another choice and make your own font.

Make a choice and watch Charles Bukowski discuss the sorry state of poetry as he guzzles red wine.

Make a choice and four spidery lines in blue, green, red, and gold shoot out from the Y-axis of a graph to describe the decline and fall of U.S. interest rates, the Japanese Yen, the Dow Jones Purchasing Managers Index, and five socially responsible mutual funds.

Make a choice and erase a field of stars with the arm of a child to reveal a collage of nervous beauty and unexplored possibility.

This is New Media. Digital technology and creative verve have supplied designers with an arsenal of tools that endows us with outlandish powers for arranging visual space. The dimensions of sound, motion, and time invite us to explore areas previously beyond the realm of print; the interactivity of New Media, meanwhile, promises a new era of collaboration between designers and viewers. This book presents a harvest of the finest design ideas in New Media developed over the past several years. ■ But what are we talking about when we talk about New Media? Most of us have a healthy skepticism when regarding anything that sports a label proclaiming its newness: New Modernism, Post-Modernism, New Journalism, Neorealism, the New Society, New Wave, Next Wave, the New Criticism, New Math, the New Left. What was truly new about any of these things? ■ History is driven by people who hope for progress, but who commonly fall back upon comfortable associations which help them to understand their journey, and ward away the terror of the unfamiliar. When the

"THEIR VERY DESIGN DEMANDS A WIDER AND DEEPER VISION, AND COMPELS US TO JUDGE THEM IN TERMS OF THE AWESOME POWERS AND FRUSTRATING LIMITATIONS OF THE MEDIA THEMSELVES. IN THE END, THERE IS NO SENSE IN FAULTING A POEM BECAUSE IT FAILS AS A SCULPTURE."

Pilgrims stumbled up the shores of the New World during the cruel winter of 1620, they were met by people who spoke a strange tongue, who had never heard the gospel of the New Testament. These native people dressed in clothes the travelers could never have imagined, and offered to share outlandish foods the newcomers had never eaten before. After a long ocean journey from England in search of the New Jerusalem, the settlers had only to walk a short distance into the immense forests to know their peril, for they could neither identify many of the plants and animals they came upon, nor find their way. And since they were not entirely sure of where they were headed, they stayed put and hunkered down. ■ So, faced with the awesome novelty and unexplored potential of their new home, they gave their strange new world the name of the familiar old one: New England. Demonstrating as much hope for a fresh start as they did a desire for old comforts, these pioneers were able to define what was new by what they already knew.

Similarly, many of us are unsure what to make of these gleaming, spinning disks we slip into our computers, and we are left tongue-tied. We assign them to the "New Media" folder, and wait for a more fitting category to come along. Yet there is precious little that is new about New Media. The first records of humanity were informed by efforts to communicate beyond sightline and earshot, to pass on word about hunting grounds or to express contempt for mortality. Like much of the work currently being done in New Media, these efforts have blended word with image, movement with music. What is novel about reading poetry as you listen to somebody else read it aloud? What is new about blending animation with music, or graphing multiple sources of financial information, or playing complex games with unseen opponents, or viewing a painting up close? Disregarding the absence of a nifty interface and clickable hotspots, most elements of New Media are represented in all the old media —not to mention a few elements that New Media typically lack. The packaging might change and the vocabulary might shift, but there remains nothing new under the sun. ■ Still, while it is true that New Media designers are impelled by urges familiar to designers of other media—to manifest their visions, to make their voices heard above the din, to entertain friends and strangers, to reach out beyond the grave, to provide data, to sell something, to upset the apple cart—there is something ... well ... *different* about these full-animation CD-ROM games, interactive portfolios, documentaries-on-a-disk, personal digital assistants, and World Wide Web sites. It's not all hype. Some of the best designers in the world are working in New Media, and they are raising intriguing aesthetic and technical questions, the answers to which have significance for all media. ■ The projects spotlighted in this book are all wonderful in their own quirky ways, though their special qualities are sometimes concealed at first glance. For some, the graphic design harmonizes perfectly with the identity of the client. Others sport wily navigation schemes that allow users to find what they want with a minimum of delay. There are projects that layer information in an elegant manner, offer audacious content, project a shrewd cinematic quality, or render three-dimensional animations with grace and abandon. Much of the work eschews linearity, yet is rich in content. The best manage to describe random pathways of thought and complex informational strata in ways unimaginable just a few years ago. ■ And what of their beauty? Are these projects visually stunning? No, not all of them. The printed renderings of some New Media projects fall flat—they might seem visually inelegant or typographically unsophisticated when placed beside work expressly designed for print. But we will miss out on something if we rely solely on print-oriented standards of style and beauty to gauge the worth of New Media work. Their very design demands a wider and deeper vision, and compels us to judge them in terms of the awesome powers and frustrating limitations of the media themselves. In the end, there is no sense in faulting a poem because it fails as a sculpture. ■ The projects represented here range from fully animated game environments to World Wide Web sites, from multimedia annual reports to interactive desktop catalogues of fine art that double as high-powered research tools. They are as varied in purpose as they are in style, so this book has been arranged to reflect these distinctions: Promotions, Titles, Tools, and Prototypes. ■ Representing the design of New Media work on the printed page is problematic, for these projects can be as dynamic as they are ephemeral. Consequently, captions document the intent of the designers and elucidate certain transient elements of their work. An iconographic system also shows at a glance some of the structural and navigational elements of the projects. These icons are described in the following two pages. ■ Commentaries by two people who see New Media from widely disparate points of view introduce this volume. Stuart Malin has spent much of his career in cybernetics—from designing robotics to World Wide Web sites. Moira Cullen has projected her many corporeal experiences onto the printed page. Together, their views represent a 360-degree vista of New Media, and in that way their differences reach around and almost touch. ■ Given the challenges of rendering the work of New Media designers in print, it is fair to ask whether the purpose of this book is defeated by itself. The answer is simple: the immense portability and storage capacity—as well as the tactile pleasures and beauty—of books remain unparalleled. What we have here are snapshots of time-bound phenomena not unlike the photographic studies of time and motion by Eadweard Muybridge in the 19th Century. With that in mind, I hope this book will serve as a valuable reference to the diversity and inventiveness of work produced by New Media designers today, as well as an inspiration for New Media design in the future. ■ Still, there's nothing like the real thing. So once you have closed this book, take a seat. Boot up the machine. Settle in. Choose something.

—*Clement Mok*

"MUCH OF THE WORK ESCHEWS LINEARITY, YET IS RICH IN CONTENT. THE BEST MANAGE TO DESCRIBE RANDOM PATHWAYS OF THOUGHT AND COMPLEX INFORMATIONAL STRATA IN WAYS UNIMAGINABLE JUST A FEW YEARS AGO."

Hand
indicates that users can navigate or choose action

Web Site **Animation** **Video** **Music** **Voice over**

Solid red lines with directional arrows
indicate movement

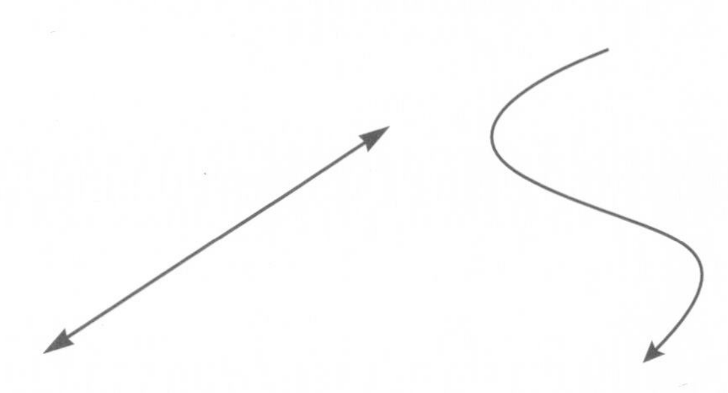

Dotted red lines
are navigational and structural links

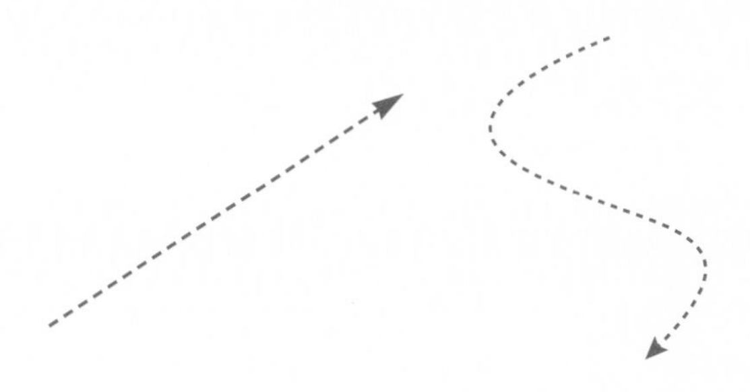

Magnifying Glass
indicates that viewers can gain microscopic and macroscopic views by zooming in or out

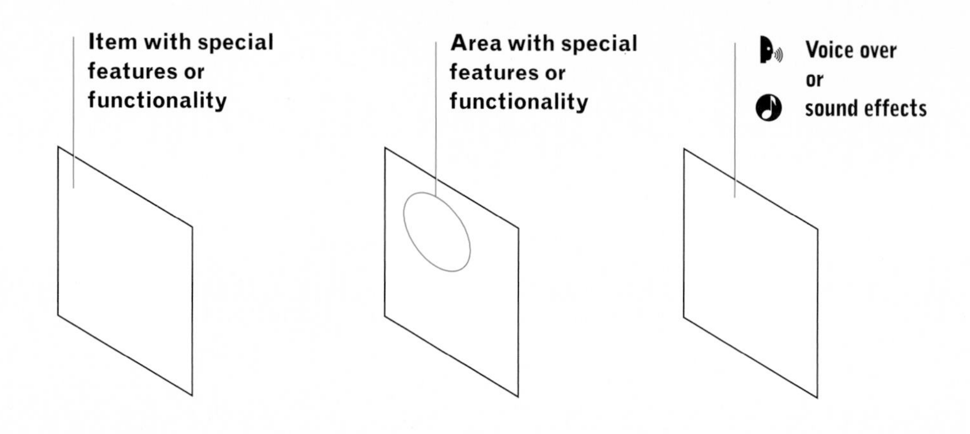

Multiple directional red arrows
indicate movement of a scrollable screen

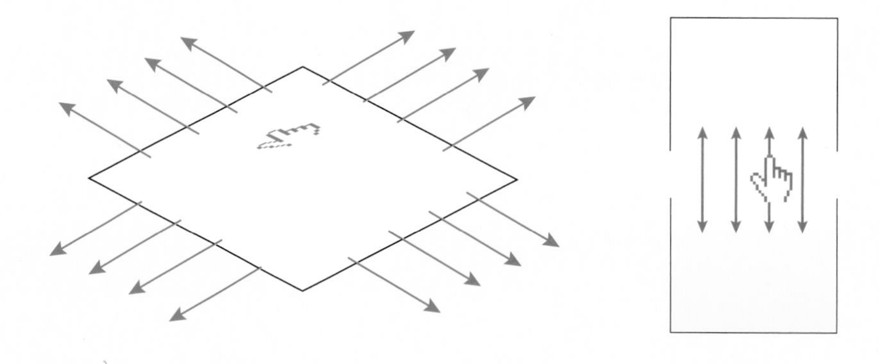

Isometrics with dotted red lines
indicate a screen flow sequence

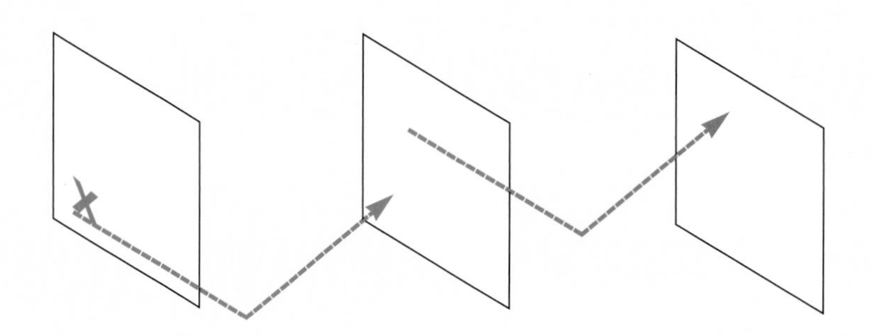

Isometrics
indicate certain hierarchical structures and groupings of screens

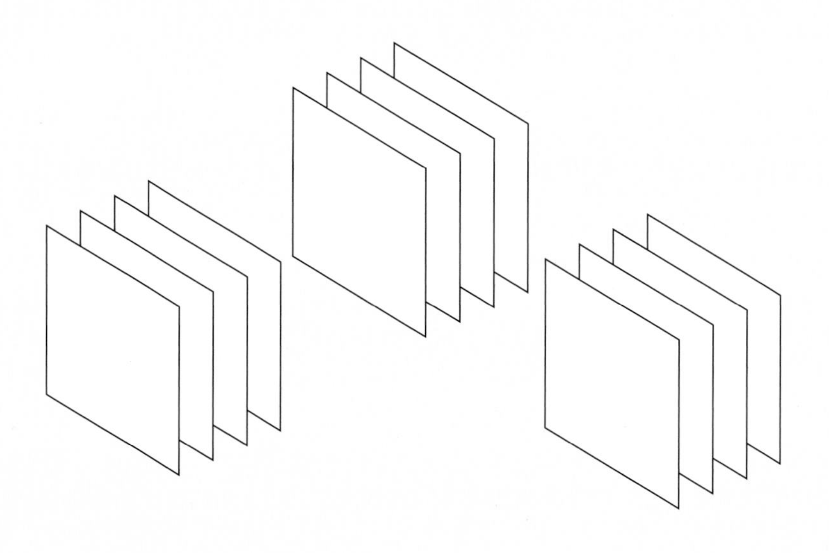

NEW MEDIA

COMMENTARIES

Life In The Click Lane

We live in a new reality. All of the social theorists and futurists say so. They say the very fabric of our social structures is being stretched, perhaps even torn, by the transition to the so-called Information Economy. Interactive media seem to embody or embrace much that this new reality represents. I, for one, do not feel traumatized by interactive media. As tool-using beings, we have many times made the transition to the use of new tools, even though the development and acquisition of new protocols and skills are required to adroitly accomplish this task. This is true both for individuals in the course of a lifetime, as well as collectively over historical time. We have

"AS TOOL-USING BEINGS, WE HAVE MANY TIMES MADE THE TRANSITION TO THE USE OF NEW TOOLS, EVEN THOUGH THE DEVELOPMENT AND ACQUISITION OF NEW PROTOCOLS AND SKILLS ARE REQUIRED TO ADROITLY ACCOMPLISH THIS TASK."

adapted well to indoor plumbing, electric lights, and stereos as well as to airports, highways, and skyscrapers. In light of this, what can be so difficult about interactive media? We are, after all, quite accustomed to media as the interface between two human beings. We've already adjusted to the temporal and spatial displacement that these media provide. What, then, is so different about media that act not as conduits of communication, but as proxies for that communication?

■ Interactive media engage us because they are embodiments of the capacity for human interaction. The technology is shifting the very nature of communication. Our only dilemma is that we have failed to adequately alter our understanding of this change in nature, yet we have easily, and quite unconsciously, made the transition in regard to our expectations. In general, we know what to do when we are confronted with a computer display—we reach for the mouse (or other pointing device) and click. This is life in the click lane.

This is not an oblique and accidental acknowledgement of the hideous "Information Super Highway" metaphor. Rather, it is a pointed reference to the "fast lane" in which the pace of daily life seems ever-accelerating and is always on the verge of being out of control. We race from event to event regretting only the space between events—can't we make it "productive," too? "Fast" is the progenitor of "click." When we click, we want the result—NOW! If we are bored, we click—the remote for the TV, the mouse for a link in Web space. Our minds are restless. We seek immersion—32-bit video at full-frame rates, with surround, powered subwoofer, wavetable, synthesized sound—and "engulf me," is our silent plea. This is our reality. ■ How do we measure time in "MST"—"MTV Standard Time"? Is it the linear progression of time that matters, or the speed at which our perception of time proceeds? Quite likely it is the latter. When the stimulation level drops below threshold, again the Pavlovian response: click. This creates for us a fluid world of disjoint content. What is in a transition anymore? Does a fade or a wipe mean anything beyond a jump-cut, or has even the very transition itself become just another component of this sequential disjoint reality? The space between has been objectified. ■ **Click.** A convenient excuse to change themes. How long has it been since I was last here composing this stream? Does it matter? Once set in type, the printed page waits patiently and obediently while one pauses. ME? I've met my deadline for this essay, allowing the pre-press process to begin. Until now, just another hole to fill, a location in the "meta-map" of this book, pregnant with all possibility, the space is filled. Clement breathes a sigh of relief. (Self-reference, by the way, is the origin of consciousness. The observer observed. Watch the Web become "alive" with dynamic pages.) The wave equation collapses. Reality sets. Jelled. My interaction with the word processor comes to an end. Yet yours continues. Odd how interactive this process is—words in print—for something on the surface so seemingly static. Paper, that which stands as the perfect representation of non-interactivity, is in its deeper reality quite interactive. Haven't you yet had the urge to pencil in a note, to write the publisher demanding explanation of this, or to send me an e-mail message? Ah, e-mail—a world in which we accelerate the pace of dialogue—a half-duplex dialogue that accepts and revels in discontinuity. Interactive? Media? Damn straight. Click to send. ■ **Click.** But what you are reading is an encapsulation frozen in time, a static experience. No matter how often you read this essay, your experience remains the same, right? Balderdash! Your experience changes because you change. The artifact remains invariant, the perception evolves. Static? No, not at all. It is no less interactive than e-mail. The problem is that we have become lazy—who re-reads? ■ **Click.** What makes us believe that these new "interactive media" are any more interactive than other prior, presumedly static media? I suggest in the grand tradition of the Western Scientific Method, the difference is that new media embody behavior that is intrinsic and "of an other." While my assertion that your reaction to this printed piece will change over time (I hope it will, for your sake more than mine), the source of that change is within you—except, of course, if you subscribe to the deconstructionist point of view. But why come back and re-read this when you can? ■ **Click.** Something new. Something fresh. Something unanticipated. Where are we now? Excitement! Exploration! Discovery! An unfolding! ■ **Click.** Are we doing something dangerous when we try to render hyperspace meta-comprehensible? I find what I am looking for, thank God. But where is the surprise, the opportunity for serendipidity? Is Yahoo interactive? "Certainly!" we are quick to reply. Input begets output, but the output is anticipated. Yet the outcome of your reading this is uncertain. Which is more interactive? Which embeds intrinsic behavior? ■ I submit that the locus of interactivity when you use a meta-index is within you. Its behavior is predictable. While it may change over time, it is a static behavior in a more profound sense of "having a behavior." ■ **Click.** My four-year-old son truly enjoys the Brøderbund Living books, the pages of which have been reinstantiated within the belly of the information beast. These books have intrinsic behavior—click on an object in the scene and be surprised by the resulting animation. Or allow the computer to "read" the story, animating the scene. Not only does the story unfold, so does the storyteller. We come to know the storyteller all too well. The surprise drains and the behavior becomes stale. ■ **Click.** The cynic in me says that we are made lazy by interactive media. We abdicate the opportunity to be the locus of the interaction. We allow someone to do the work for us—accepting his or her notion of an experience on a CD-ROM, for example. We partake of the experience vicariously. Are we experiential vampires, sucking the life from the CD-ROM until it no longer surprises? Whose experience, the philosophers among us ask, is "more" authentic? ■ **Click (before we have to think too hard).** The world of *Myst*. I've been seduced. It hardly matters that I can't succeed at *Myst*. The experience envelops like a warm and trusted lover. I am subdued. I am a prisoner. I click all that I want and can not escape. Have you ever thought of *Myst* as a virtual prison? To how many hours have we been sentenced? Enthralled: the seductress as jailkeeper. Don't get me wrong, I admire *Myst*, and I love it even more than I admire it. But I am a victim. *Myst*ers Anonymous. ■ **Click.** You can leave this book on your coffee table. Your friends, guests, clients, family members, competitors, and random passersby can pick it up, find this essay, and read. "What do you think?" they might ask. If I've accomplished what I set out to do, you'll have an opinion. Even if I've been too obtuse, you'll have an opinion, too. But if I am really successful, you'll engage in a discussion. You will interact! This static, lifeless artifact will have engendered true human-to-human interaction. But if you left a CD-ROM on the coffee table instead? If your guest inquired as to what it is, wouldn't your first instinct be to let them experience it for themselves? ■ **It's all about locus. Click.** "But what of MUDs and IRC?" you Internet-savvy technophiles chortle. My only response is http:\\www.idr.com\chortle

"WHAT MAKES US BELIEVE THAT THESE NEW "INTERACTIVE MEDIA" ARE ANY MORE INTERACTIVE THAN OTHER PRIOR PRESUMED-STATIC MEDIA? I SUGGEST... THAT THE DIFFERENCE IS THAT THESE NEW MEDIA EMBODY BEHAVIOR."

Stuart Malin is the founding partner of Informed Decision Resources, a consulting firm that specializes in helping clients plan strategic use of the Internet and World Wide Web.

Print The Light Fantastic

Glowing screens like beacons in the night beckon safe passage to distant digital shores. The hiss of connection, the slide of a disk—with one click we engage, then slip through the portal to alternate realities beyond. Before us unfolds a space of immeasurable bounds—*terra luminata*—a pulsing stream of words, pictures, colors, and sounds reduced to binary signals electrified, recombined, and refracted as light. ■ We embark on a self-directed journey where destinations are determined by choice and chance as each decision prompts a direction or yields a command. Left, right, up, down, advance or "home"—we click along at varied speeds wending our way from islet to icon through the sprawl of vanity pages, past history to education, resources and reference, to shopping and games and other commercial conceits. With each stop we encounter a world apart, singularly configured according to its content with graphic dialects,

> **"PRINT IS STATIC AND STATIONARY; A CHANGE-UP REFLEXIVE RHYTHM THAT SLOWS THE PACE ENOUGH FOR US TO PAUSE FROM THE IMMERSIVE, INTERACTIVE PUSH AND PULL AND PONDER WHAT WE'VE LEARNED OR WHERE WE'VE BEEN."**

customized contours, and navigational controls. ■ Seeking enlightenment, entertainment, or community, we arrive with expectation and demand delight. But unlike the voyagers of yore, our thrill lies not in discovering age-old continents but in constructing new environments and shaping dynamic transactional forms. For our driving quest is the pursuit of immediacy: the interaction and instant access afforded by media that respond to preference with a promise to circumvent the inefficiencies of a cumbersome material world. ■ In the afterglow, we sense that we have traveled. But how far? To where? Can we return? Alternately, we witness and participate in the experimentation and creative expression fueling the media that transport us.

Still, technology presses on in search of further frontiers, more memory, and maximum speed. ■ How can we document our experiences or archive the artifacts of this nascent realm? Disks can be copied but their cultural coherence cannot. Destinations often vanish as quickly as they appear, just as products born on competing platforms or developed in more contemporary formats are incompatible with those of generations before. ■ Suddenly, we recognize that digital things are not only fluid but fragile, that impermanence is a liability as well as a lure, and that even a medium lauded for longevity is vulnerable to obsolescence and the vagaries of real-time. ■ Yet for tens of thousands of years, communication, not duplication, has been the charge. Hieroglyphs, pictograms, and cave paintings at Lascaux were ancestral attempts to express experience in a tangible form. But neither papyrus nor stone could preserve events entirely. Nonetheless, primal media displayed that even absent sound and motion's fury, substance and transcendent meaning could be graphically portrayed. ■ Meanwhile, the screen's translucent membrane divides a diptych world—part material, part cyber-real—with counterpoints of connection yet to be drawn. And paper, that venerable pre-electronic fibrous material, surfaces to chronicle New Media's mutable, transient forms. ■ "Paper?" you ask. But "paper" experience is ersatz and incomplete. Besides, as a container its structure is rigid, its hierarchies too flat, and its formats far too linear for today's layered, free-flowing exchange. Moreover, as a medium, it is perishable; it creases and yellows and crumbles with age. Print is doomed. Like paper currency, it is sure to be supplanted electronically, or so some believe. ■ But the beauty of print is that it is flat and linear and all that electronic media cares not to be. It is tactile and physical, the antidote for disembodied senses that have been tweaked electronically. The sheen of its surface; a pungent hint of ink; deep, varied color, the weight and dimension of the page are hot triggers for cognition and sensual memory. Print is static and stationary; a change-up reflexive rhythm that slows the pace enough for us to pause from the immersive, interactive push and pull and ponder what we've learned or where we've been. And it is flatly spatial; we can analyze the interface of electronic excursions, deconstruct the architecture, identify connective axes, convey the quantity of options, the depth of decisions, and the sequence of layers. We can trace a path of understanding and read the poetry of visual form. Print allows for another perspective, a view of the assembled mosaic that is absorbed only when we cease to move. ■ Indeed, there is more to the design of experience than instant access and speedy information grabs. For all that print affords, it lacks what its electronic counterparts provide. In combination, the two are complementary, not competing, channels for understanding that tenuous balance between the foreign and the known. With technology's advance, media are linked inextricably. Bound by shared content, their essence embedded on exchangeable files, each is reactivated for print or display by a single luminous beam. ■ Doubtless, in time our ability to choreograph multiple media exchanges will evolve. And with luck, our streak through the white glare of digital space will generate a brilliant paper trail.

"NONETHELESS, PRIMAL MEDIA DISPLAYED THAT, ABSENT SOUND AND MOTION'S FURY, SUBSTANCE AND TRANSCENDENT MEANING COULD BE GRAPHICALLY PORTRAYED."

Moira Cullen is a design writer, educator, and strategist whose career traverses the worlds of dance, photography, fashion, marketing, and design. She publishes widely, is an assistant professor of graduate communications design at the Pratt Institute in New York, and is currently director of programs at the American Institute of Graphic Arts.
Photo of Moira Cullen by Reven T.C. Wurman.

N E W M E D I A

INTERNET CONCEPT MAP

The spawn of New Media appears numberless, and this year we have witnessed the awesome growth of yet another: the Internet. Specifically, it is the flashy and chatty, zippy and smart, mouse-clicking, Yahoo-hollering, HTML-speaking, surfboard-totting, URL-delivering, omnipresent World Wide Web that is making most of the ruckus. This *enfant terrible* of New Media was walking before it could climb out of its crib, conquering nations before it got its thumb out of its mouth. ■ The blinding speed with which the Internet spun this Web has been the source of much creativity, a few fortunes, a lot of hype, hours of lost productivity, and a heap of confusion. Who can say they really understand where everything fits together, how to get from Point A to Point B, how they got misdirected, waylaid, or found? Hugh Dubberly's Internet Concept Map should help be-webbed 'Net surfers. It does a terrific job providing the kind of context that is typically missing from most discussions of the 'Net, no matter how erudite and earnest. Lost? Get out the map. Where's the map? Turn the page.

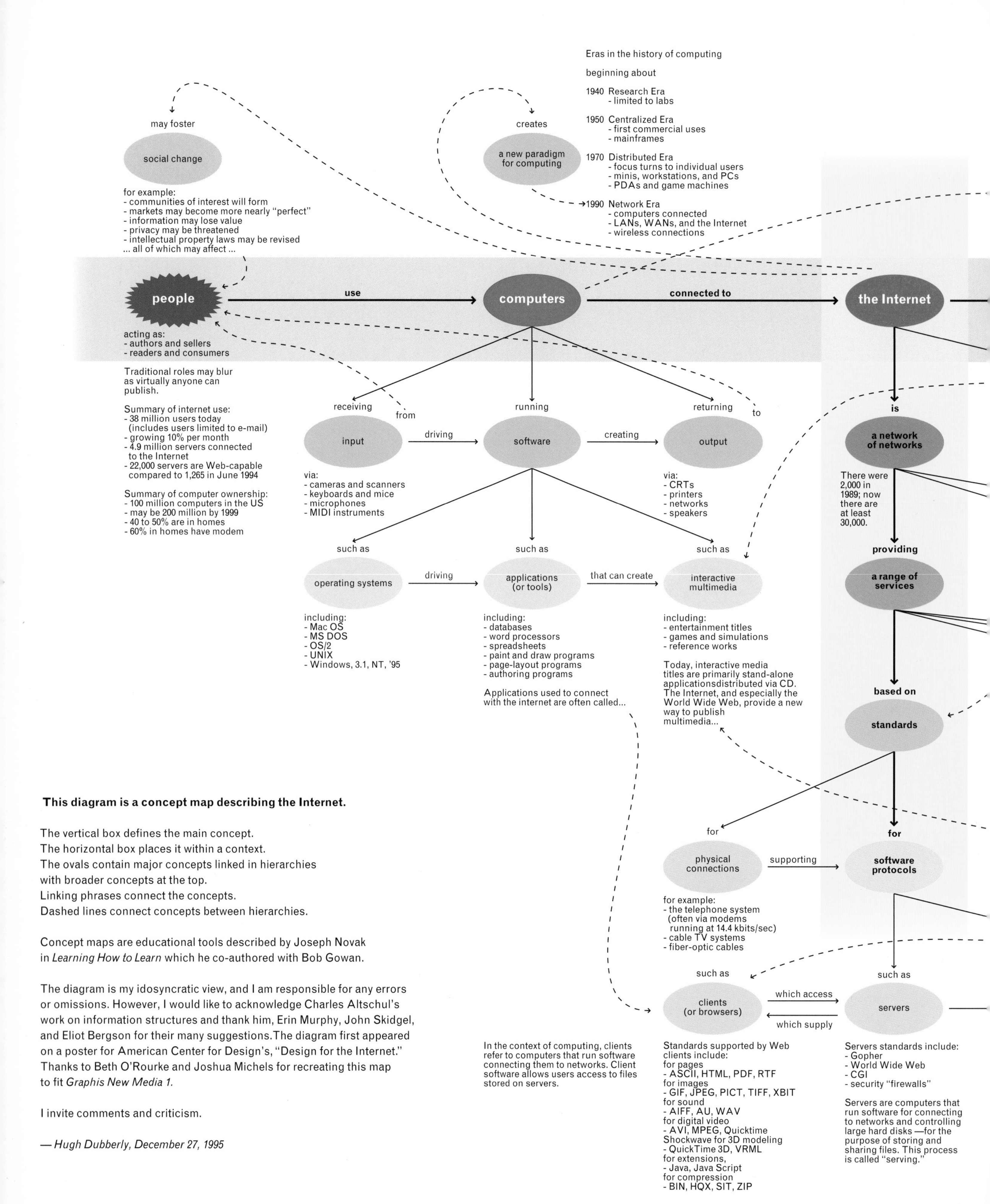

This diagram is a concept map describing the Internet.

The vertical box defines the main concept.
The horizontal box places it within a context.
The ovals contain major concepts linked in hierarchies with broader concepts at the top.
Linking phrases connect the concepts.
Dashed lines connect concepts between hierarchies.

Concept maps are educational tools described by Joseph Novak in *Learning How to Learn* which he co-authored with Bob Gowan.

The diagram is my idosyncratic view, and I am responsible for any errors or omissions. However, I would like to acknowledge Charles Altschul's work on information structures and thank him, Erin Murphy, John Skidgel, and Eliot Bergson for their many suggestions. The diagram first appeared on a poster for American Center for Design's, "Design for the Internet." Thanks to Beth O'Rourke and Joshua Michels for recreating this map to fit *Graphis New Media 1.*

I invite comments and criticism.

— Hugh Dubberly, December 27, 1995

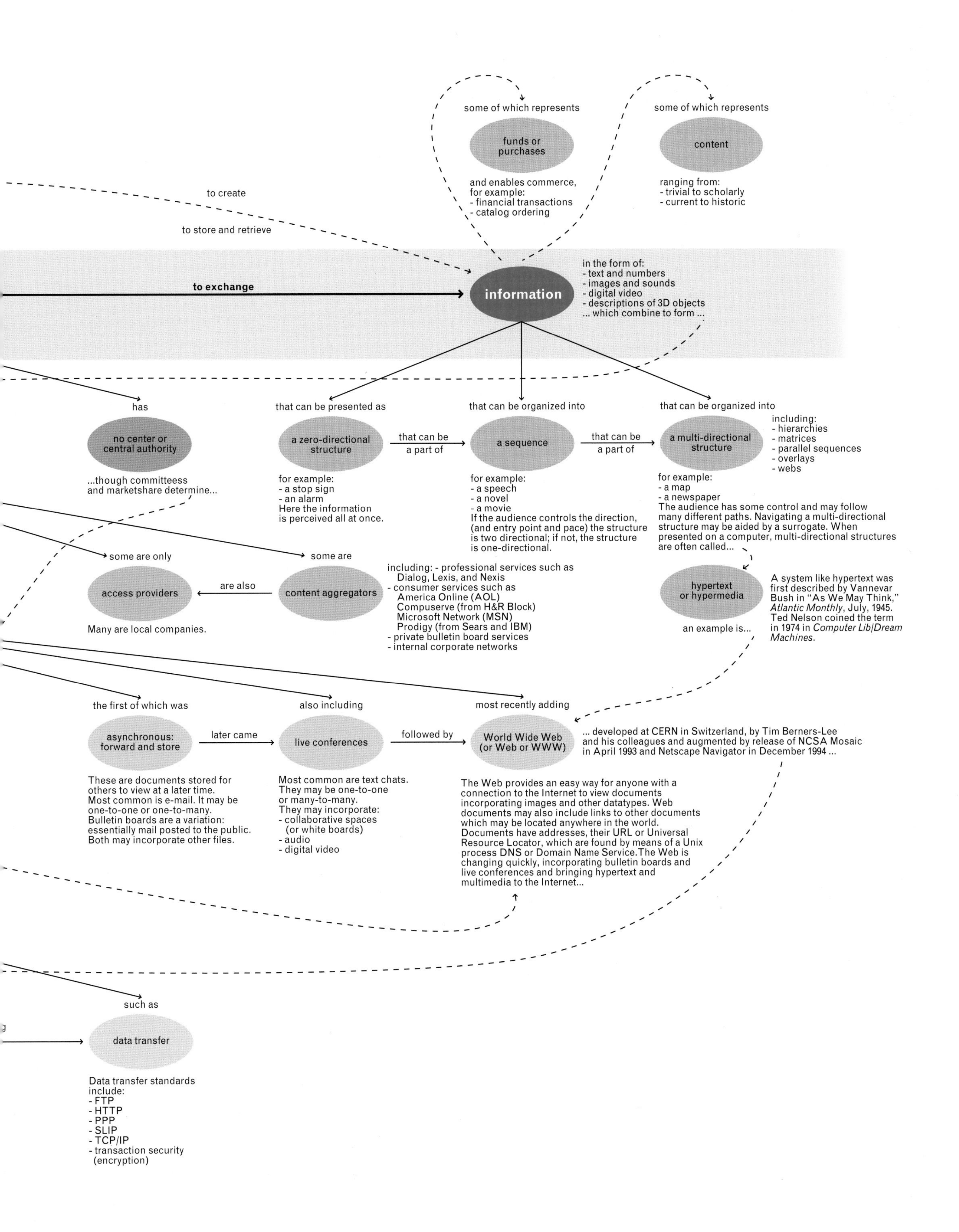

some of which represents
funds or purchases
and enables commerce, for example:
- financial transactions
- catalog ordering
some of which represents
content
ranging from:
- trivial to scholarly
- current to historic
to create
to store and retrieve
to exchange
information
in the form of:
- text and numbers
- images and sounds
- digital video
- descriptions of 3D objects
... which combine to form ...
has
no center or central authority
...though committeess and marketshare determine...
that can be presented as
a zero-directional structure
for example:
- a stop sign
- an alarm
Here the information is perceived all at once.
that can be a part of
that can be organized into
a sequence
for example:
- a speech
- a novel
- a movie
If the audience controls the direction, (and entry point and pace) the structure is two directional; if not, the structure is one-directional.
that can be a part of
that can be organized into
a multi-directional structure
including:
- hierarchies
- matrices
- parallel sequences
- overlays
- webs
for example:
- a map
- a newspaper
The audience has some control and may follow many different paths. Navigating a multi-directional structure may be aided by a surrogate. When presented on a computer, multi-directional structures are often called...
some are only
access providers
Many are local companies.
are also
some are
content aggregators
including: - professional services such as Dialog, Lexis, and Nexis
- consumer services such as
America Online (AOL)
Compuserve (from H&R Block)
Microsoft Network (MSN)
Prodigy (from Sears and IBM)
- private bulletin board services
- internal corporate networks
hypertext or hypermedia
an example is...
A system like hypertext was first described by Vannevar Bush in "As We May Think," Atlantic Monthly, July, 1945. Ted Nelson coined the term in 1974 in Computer Lib/Dream Machines.
the first of which was
asynchronous: forward and store
These are documents stored for others to view at a later time. Most common is e-mail. It may be one-to-one or one-to-many. Bulletin boards are a variation: essentially mail posted to the public. Both may incorporate other files.
later came
also including
live conferences
Most common are text chats. They may be one-to-one or many-to-many. They may incorporate:
- collaborative spaces (or white boards)
- audio
- digital video
followed by
most recently adding
World Wide Web (or Web or WWW)
... developed at CERN in Switzerland, by Tim Berners-Lee and his colleagues and augmented by release of NCSA Mosaic in April 1993 and Netscape Navigator in December 1994 ...
The Web provides an easy way for anyone with a connection to the Internet to view documents incorporating images and other datatypes. Web documents may also include links to other documents which may be located anywhere in the world. Documents have addresses, their URL or Universal Resource Locator, which are found by means of a Unix process DNS or Domain Name Service. The Web is changing quickly, incorporating bulletin boards and live conferences and bringing hypertext and multimedia to the Internet...
such as
data transfer
Data transfer standards include:
- FTP
- HTTP
- PPP
- SLIP
- TCP/IP
- transaction security (encryption)

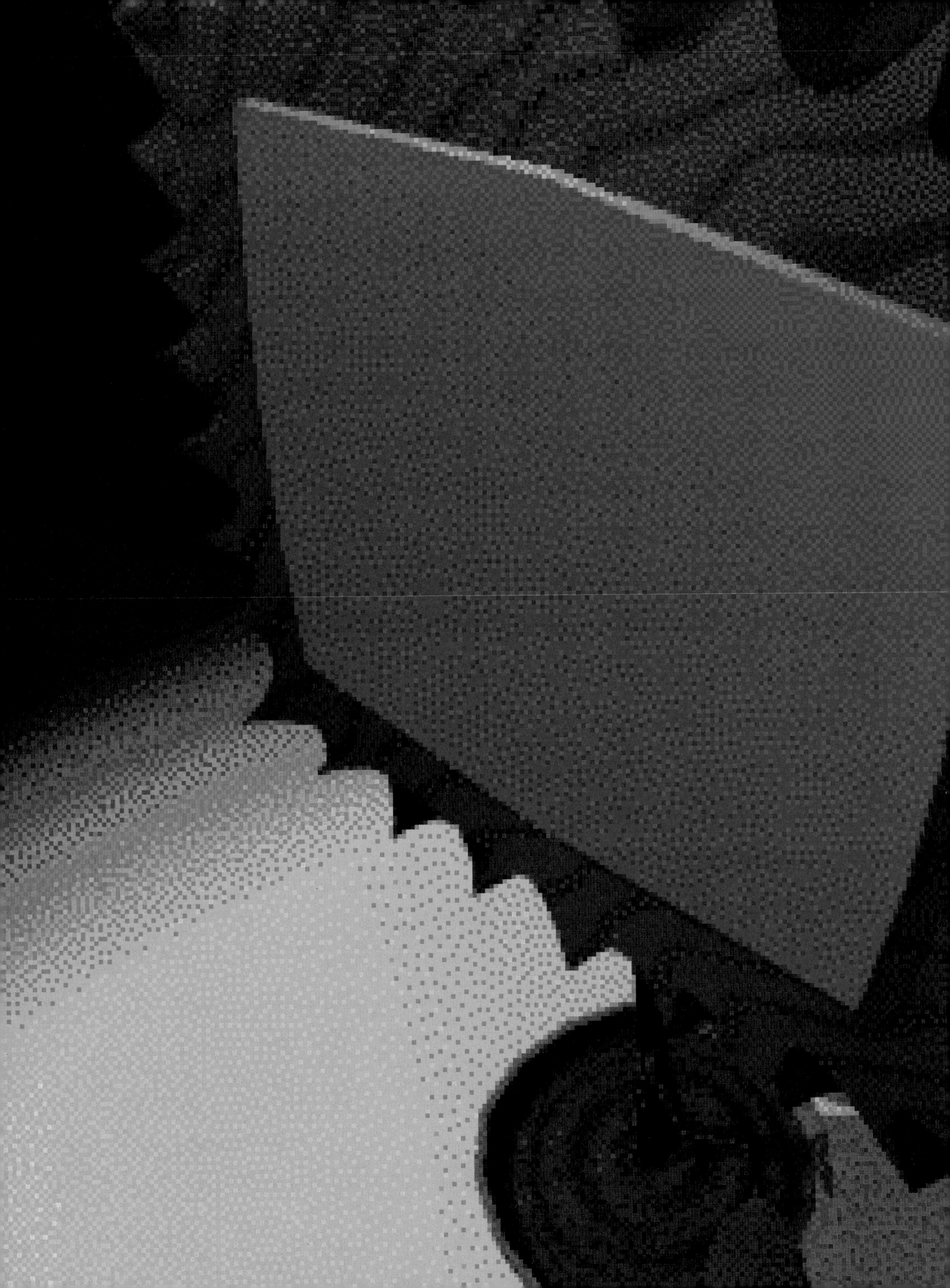

N E W M E D I A

P R O M O T I O N

Some of the most wow-inspiring, kinetic, beautiful, wittiest, and just plain *fun* work being done by New Media designers today is promotional work. ■ No matter the medium in which they work, designers of promotions have similar goals: they want to grab attention, capture hearts, engage minds, influence perceptions, and—when the wind is right—help close a sale. The promotional projects here do all these things and more, for they invite potential customers to scope out the goods in their own fashion, at their own speed, and on their own terms.

OPPOSITE: TANAGRAM, ANTHONY MA AND LANCE RUTTER, ART DIRECTORS (SEE PAGE 51 FOR FURTHER CREDITS)

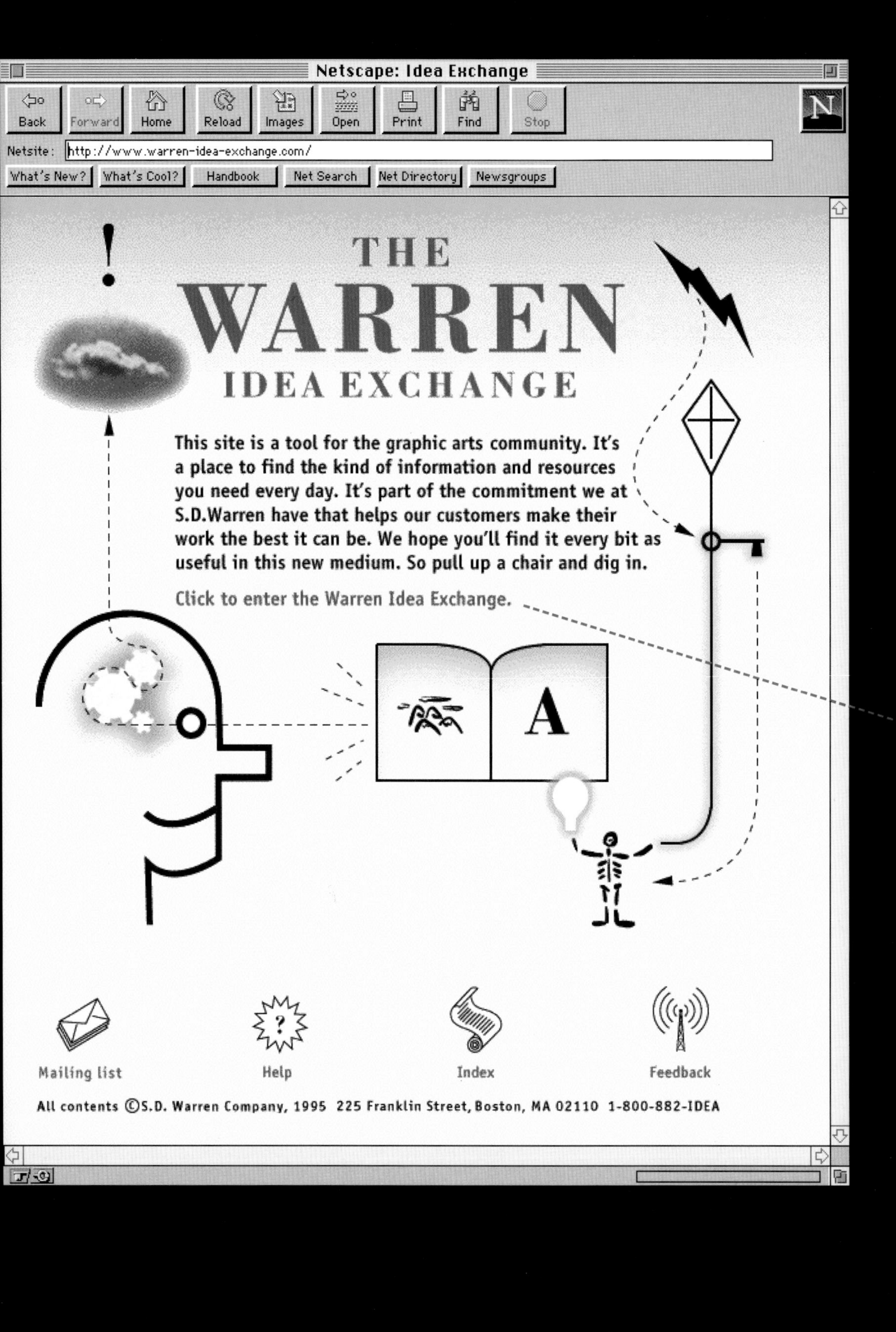

WARREN IDEA EXCHANGE WORLD WIDEWEB SITE

www.warren-idea-exchange.com

CLIENT / PUBLISHER S.D. Warren Company

DESIGN Siegal & Gale, New York, NY. Cheryl Heller, creative director; Paddy O'Plaherty, design director; Andrew Zollie, webmaster; Evan Orensten, Rich Aneser, project managers; Cheryl Heller, Geoff Currier and Jeff Binder, writers; Andrew Zolli, Tom Elia and Kathleen Dolan, programmers; Tony Hahn and Alex Ku, graphic designers; Barnes Tilney, Illustrator; Siegal & Gale, new media production company.

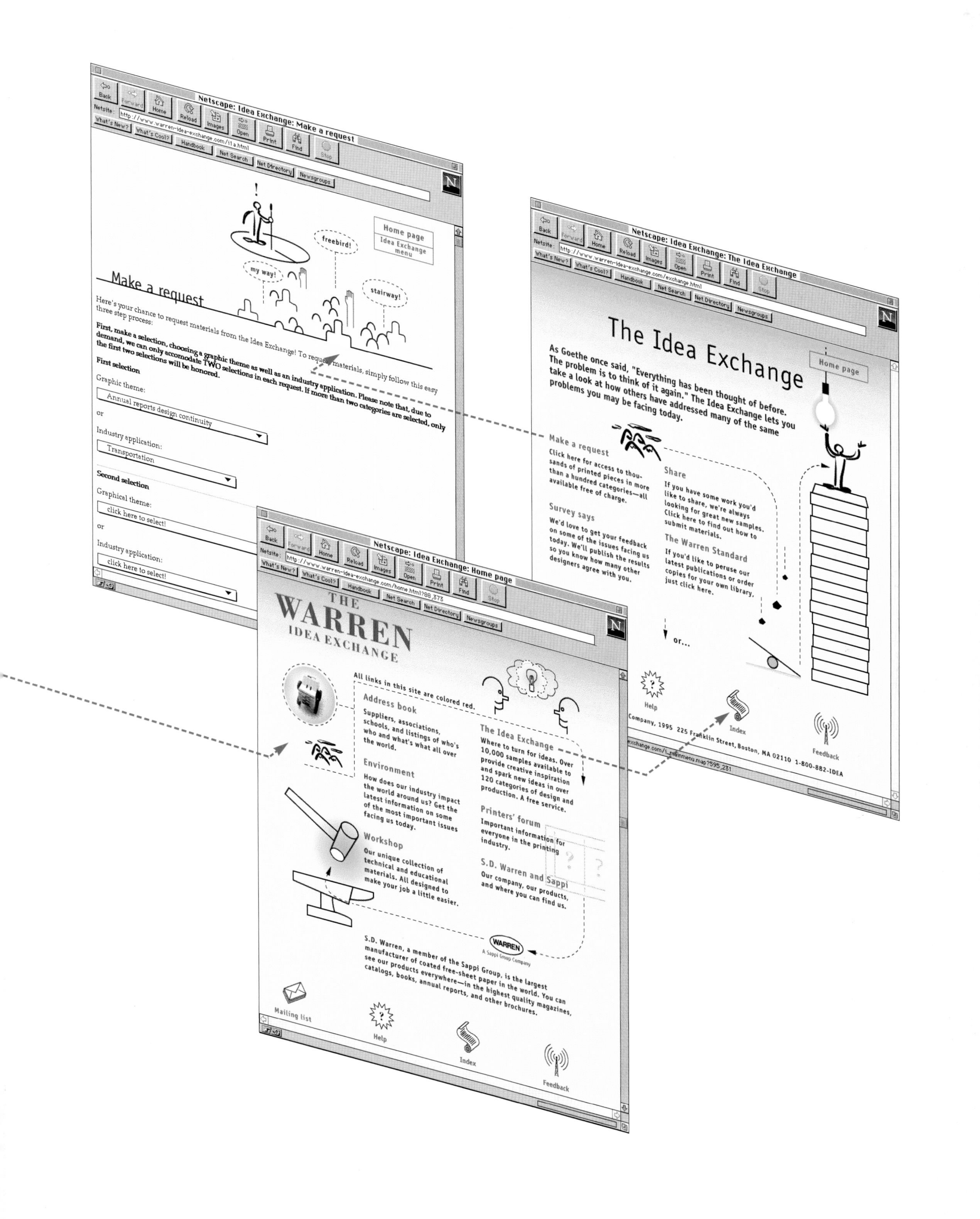

Netscape: Idea Exchange: Make a request
Make a request
Here's your chance to request materials from the Idea Exchange! To request materials, simply follow this easy three step process:
First, make a selection, choosing a graphic theme as well as an industry application. Please note that, due to demand, we can only accomodate TWO selections in each request. If more than two categories are selected, only the first two selections will be honored.
First selection
Graphic theme:
Annual reports design continuity
or
Industry application:
Transportation
Second selection
Graphical theme:
click here to select!
or
Industry application:
click here to select!
Home page
Idea Exchange menu
freebird!
my way!
stairway!
Netscape: Idea Exchange: The Idea Exchange
The Idea Exchange
As Goethe once said, "Everything has been thought of before. The problem is to think of it again." The Idea Exchange lets you take a look at how others have addressed many of the same problems you may be facing today.
Make a request
Click here for access to thousands of printed pieces in more than a hundred categories—all available free of charge.
Survey says
We'd love to get your feedback on some of the issues facing us today. We'll publish the results so you know how many other designers agree with you.
Share
If you have some work you'd like to share, we're always looking for great new samples. Click here to find out how to submit materials.
The Warren Standard
If you'd like to peruse our latest publications or order copies for your own library, just click here.
or...
Home page
Help
Index
Feedback
Company, 1995 225 Franklin Street, Boston, MA 02110 1-800-882-IDEA
Netscape: Idea Exchange: Home page
THE WARREN IDEA EXCHANGE
All links in this site are colored red.
Address book
Suppliers, associations, schools, and listings of who's who and what's what all over the world.
Environment
How does our industry impact the world around us? Get the latest information on some of the most important issues facing us today.
Workshop
Our unique collection of technical and educational materials. All designed to make your job a little easier.
The Idea Exchange
Where to turn for ideas. Over 10,000 samples available to provide creative inspiration and spark new ideas in over 120 categories of design and production. A free service.
Printers' forum
Important information for everyone in the printing industry.
S.D. Warren and Sappi
Our company, our products, and where you can find us.
WARREN
A Sappi Group Company
S.D. Warren, a member of the Sappi Group, is the largest manufacturer of coated free-sheet paper in the world. You can see our products everywhere—in the highest quality magazines, catalogs, books, annual reports, and other brochures.
Mailing list
Help
Index
Feedback

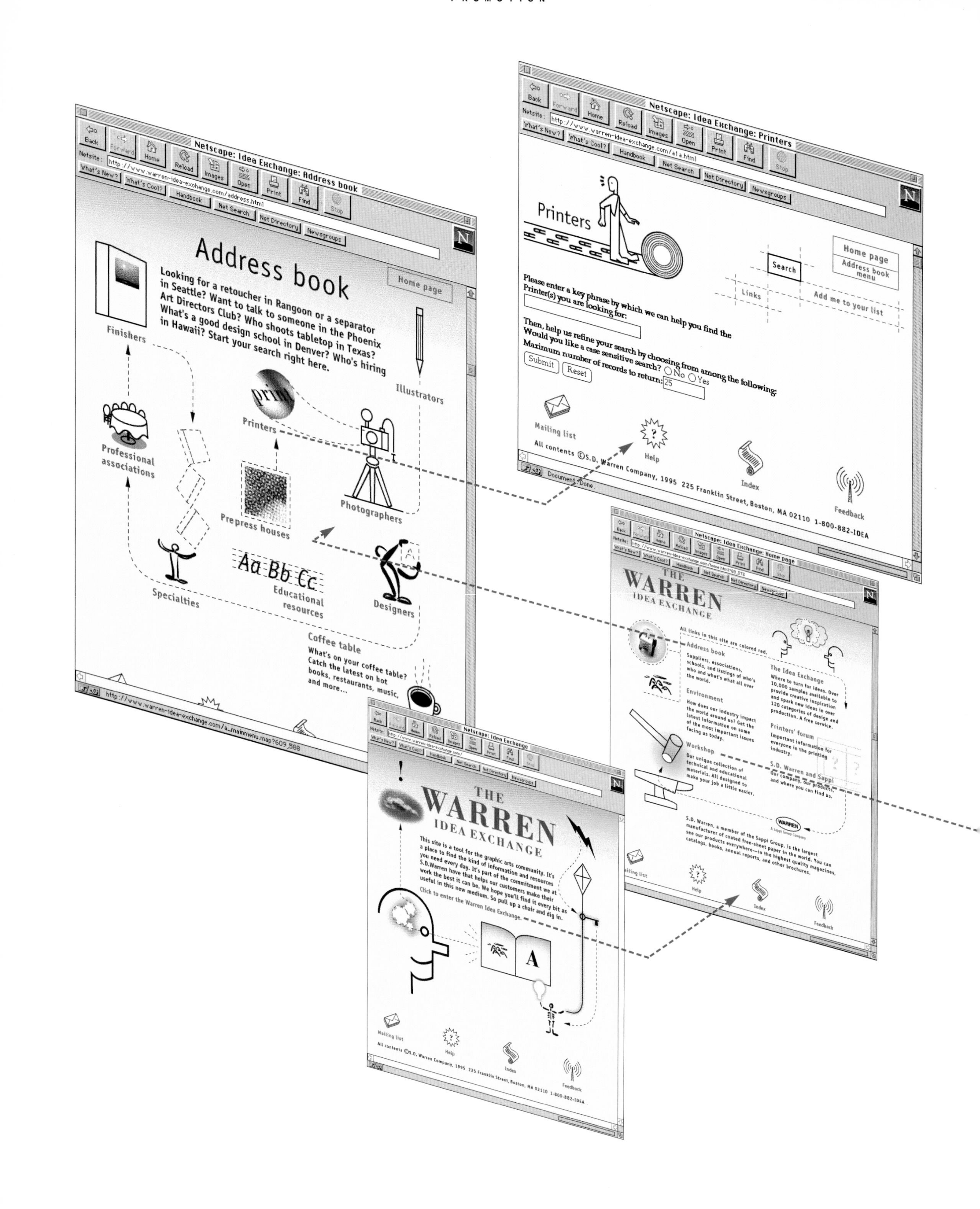
Netscape: Idea Exchange: Address book
http://www.warren-idea-exchange.com/address.html
Address book
Looking for a retoucher in Rangoon or a separator in Seattle? Want to talk to someone in the Phoenix Art Directors Club? Who shoots tabletop in Texas? What's a good design school in Denver? Who's hiring in Hawaii? Start your search right here.
Home page
Finishers
Illustrators
Printers
Professional associations
Photographers
Prepress houses
Specialties
Educational resources
Designers
Coffee table
What's on your coffee table? Catch the latest on hot books, restaurants, music, and more...
Netscape: Idea Exchange: Printers
http://www.warren-idea-exchange.com/a1a.html
Printers
Search
Home page
Address book menu
Links
Add me to your list
Please enter a key phrase by which we can help you find the Printer(s) you are looking for:
Then, help us refine your search by choosing from among the following:
Would you like a case sensitive search? No Yes
Maximum number of records to return: 25
Submit
Reset
Mailing list
Help
Index
Feedback
All contents ©S.D. Warren Company, 1995 225 Franklin Street, Boston, MA 02110 1-800-882-IDEA
Netscape: Idea Exchange: Home page
THE WARREN IDEA EXCHANGE
Netscape: Idea Exchange
THE WARREN IDEA EXCHANGE
This site is a tool for the graphic arts community. It's a place to find the kind of information and resources you need every day. It's part of the commitment we at S.D.Warren have that helps our customers make their work the best it can be. We hope you'll find it every bit as useful in this new medium. So pull up a chair and dig in.
Click to enter the Warren Idea Exchange.

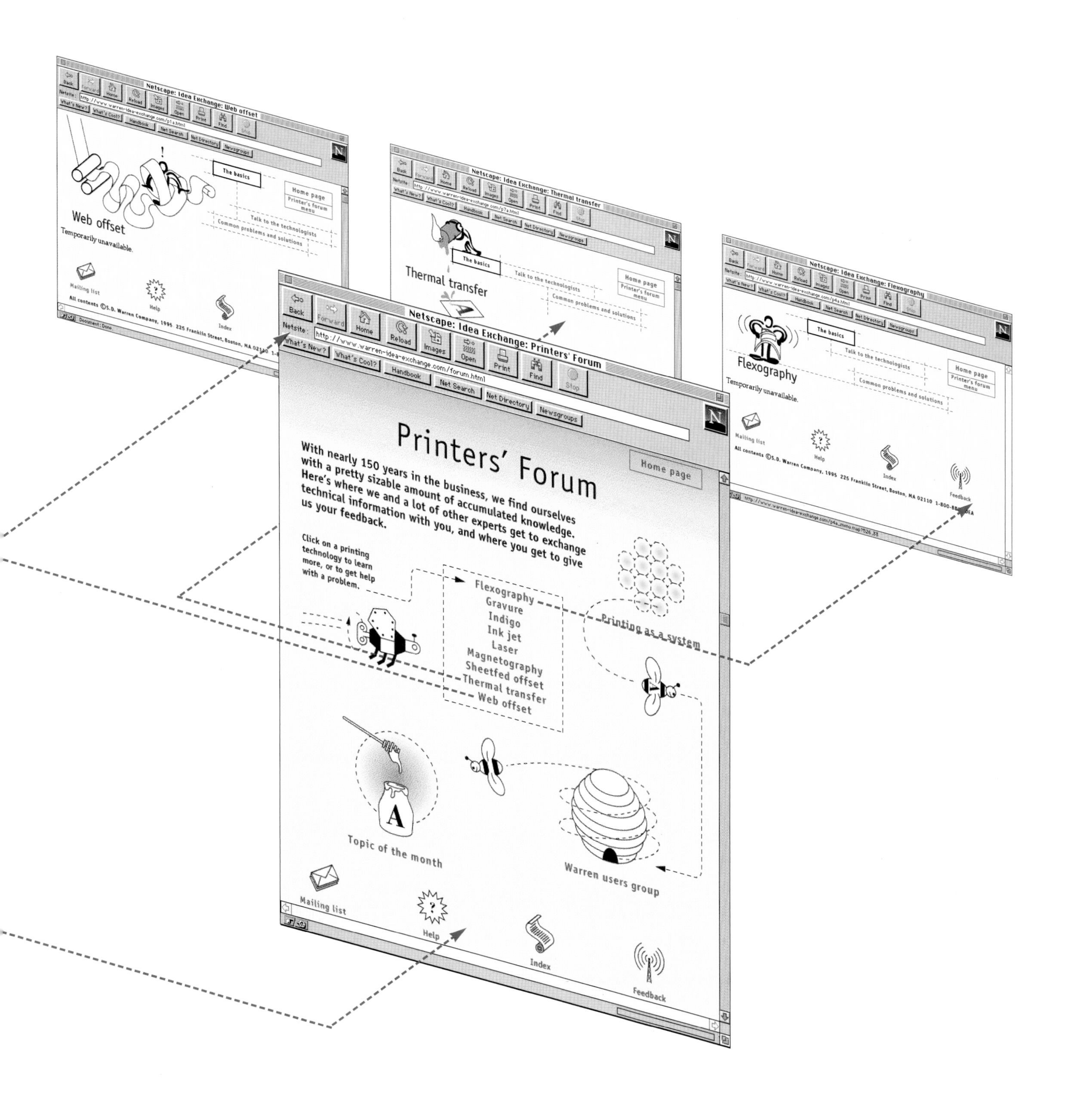

Sporting a clean and clever design, this Web site is a valuable resource. With more than 140 years in the business, Warren has built a site that is chock-full-o-nuts, sharing useful information about everything from how papers are manufactured to job opportunities in distant countries. Visitors are treated to immense amounts of detail about the printing industry, such as tables that specify the number of dots per inch at which images ought to be scanned for prepress work. Visitors navigate by clicking on hot spots that reveal deeper and deeper layers of information; the site is generous, too, providing hot links across the Web to print-related sites.

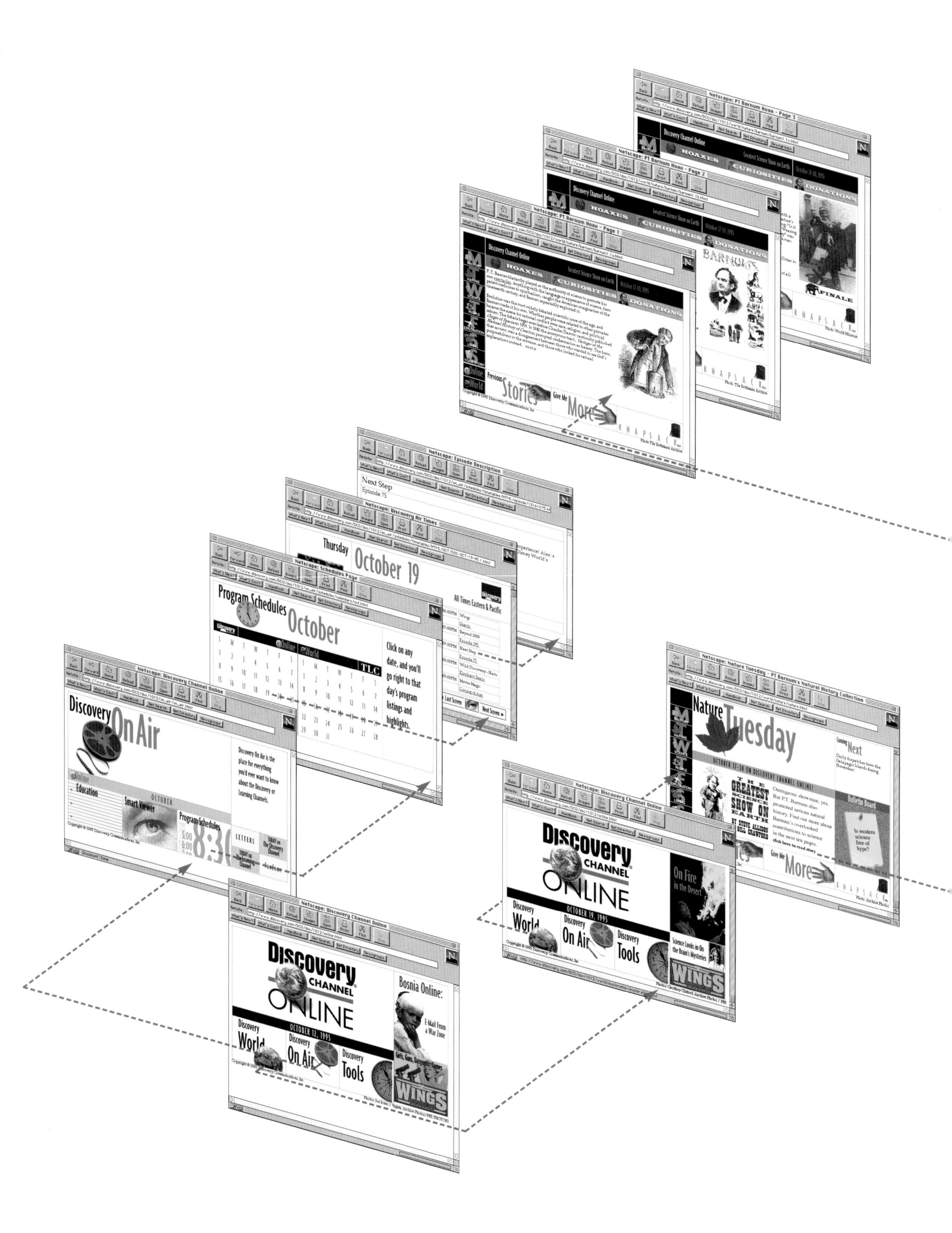
Netscape: PT Barnum Hoax - Page 3
Netscape: PT Barnum Hoax - Page 2
Netscape: PT Barnum Hoax - Page 1
Discovery Channel Online
HOAXES
CURIOSITIES
DONATIONS
Greatest Science Show on Earth
October 17-30, 1995
BARNUM'S
FINALE
KNAPSACK
Photo: World Museum
Photo: The Bettmann Archive
Previous Stories
Give Me More
Netscape: Episode Description
Next Step
Episode 75
Netscape: Discovery Air Times
Thursday
October 19
All Times Eastern & Pacific
Netscape: Schedules Page
Program Schedules
October
TLC
Click on any date, and you'll go right to that day's program listings and highlights.
Netscape: Discovery Channel Online
Discovery On Air
Discovery On Air is the place for everything you'd ever want to know about the Discovery or Learning Channels.
Education
Smart Viewer
Program Schedules
8:30
Netscape: Nature Tuesday - PT Barnum's Natural History Collection
Nature Tuesday
Coming Next
THE GREATEST SCIENCE SHOW ON EARTH
Bulletin Board
Discovery Channel Online
October 19, 1995
Discovery World
Discovery On Air
Discovery Tools
On Fire in the Desert
Science Looks in On the Brain's Mysteries
WINGS
October 17, 1995
Bosnia Online:
E-Mail From a War Zone

This multi-faceted Web site is an evolution of the popular cable channel's themes. Understanding the limitations of on-line requirements, the designers created a well-conceived interface, fitting chunks of information onto a single screen, relieving users of having to scroll. Visitors can navigate through the site by clicking on a showcased subject—P.T. Barnum's circus, for instance—or they can use the Web site's calendar to search out what will be broadcast any day of the month. The banner changes daily, so while on Tuesday visitors might be treated to a brief history of Bosnia—complete with video clips, maps, charts, and text—on Thursday they might visit the site and find themselves headed down to the Galapagos Islands for a swim with sea turtles.

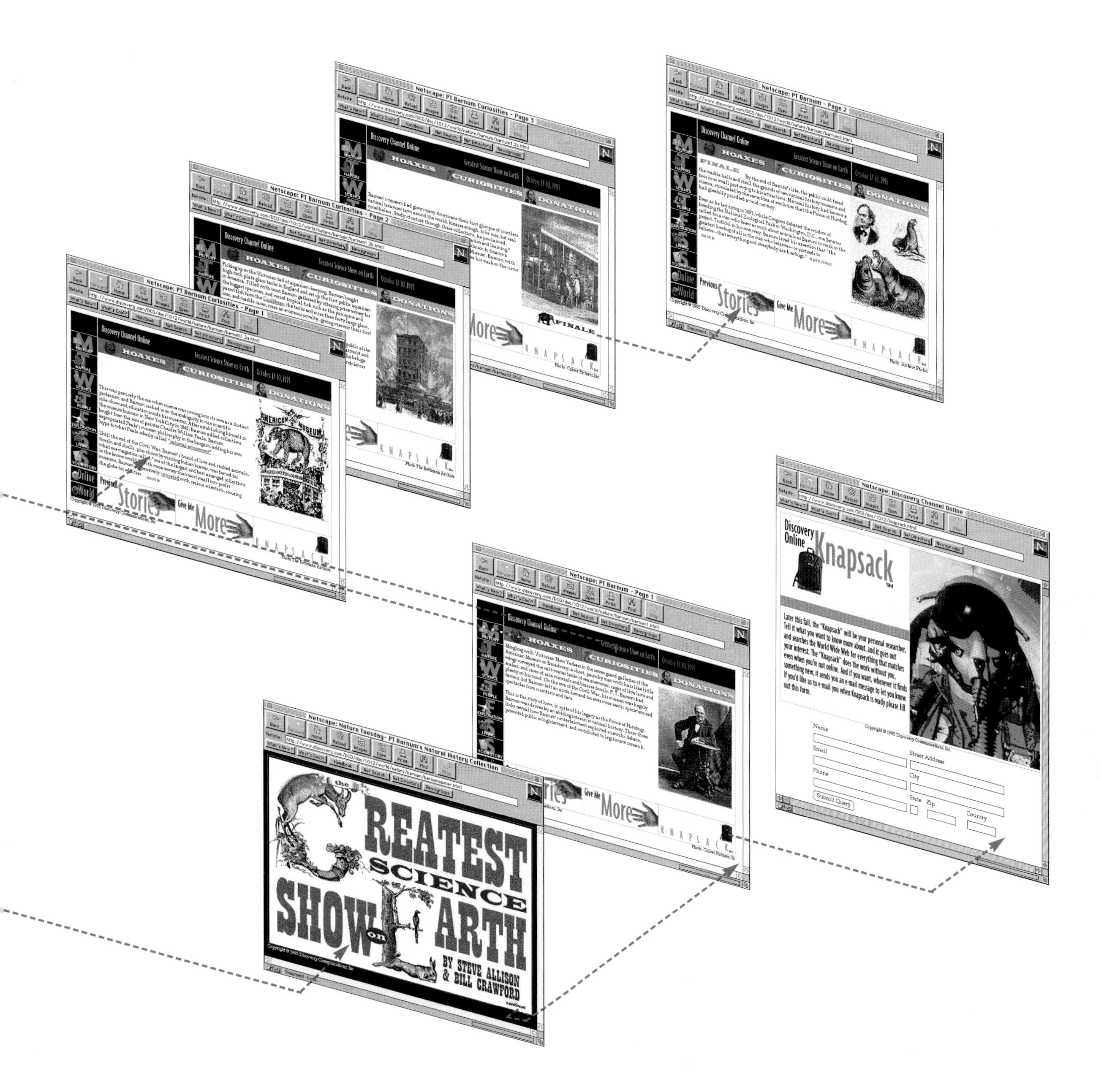

DISCOVERY CHANNEL ONLINE

 www.discovery.com

CLIENT / PUBLISHER Discovery Networks

DESIGN Discovery Communications, Inc., New York NY. John Lyle Sanford, creative director; Saba Ghazi-Amben, Kathryn Poteet, Irwin Chen, Annie Kim and Loreena Persaud, interface designers; Steve Allison and Bill Crawford, writers; Jim Jones and Omar Ahmad, programmers; Constance Miller, managing producer. Jessica Helfand Studio, Jessica Helfand, creative director; Melissa Tardiff, art director; Amnon Dekel, Sue Johnson and Yair Sageev, programmers; Lucy Kneebone, managing producer.

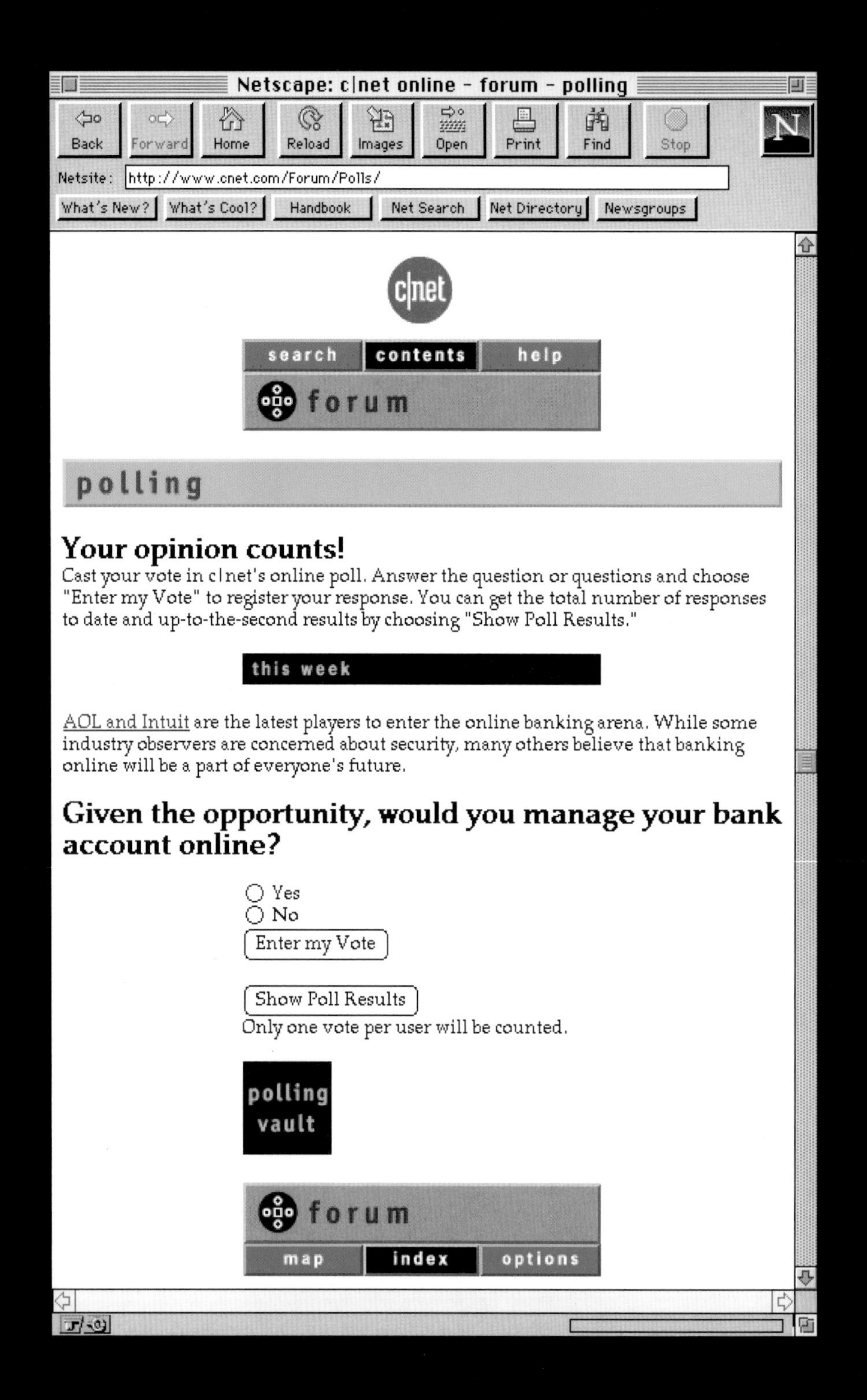

The beauty of this site—which provides a wealth of information about computer technology and the Internet—is how its designers recognized and took advantage of the built-in limitations of web design. For example, currently only three typefaces are available to Web designers, one of them Courier. The folks at c|net seem to have said, "Well, if that's all we've got, we'll make that Courier as big as a barn!" In this way a quantitative change becomes an qualitative one, for the magnification seems almost to transform Courier into a wholly different typeface. ■ A particular bonus of this site is its real-time polling capability, which allows visitors to weigh in on important questions concerning commerce, politics, and culture, and then view up-to-the-minute results of the poll. The site piques interest in the syndicated television program of the same name, just as the program advances the cause of the Web site.

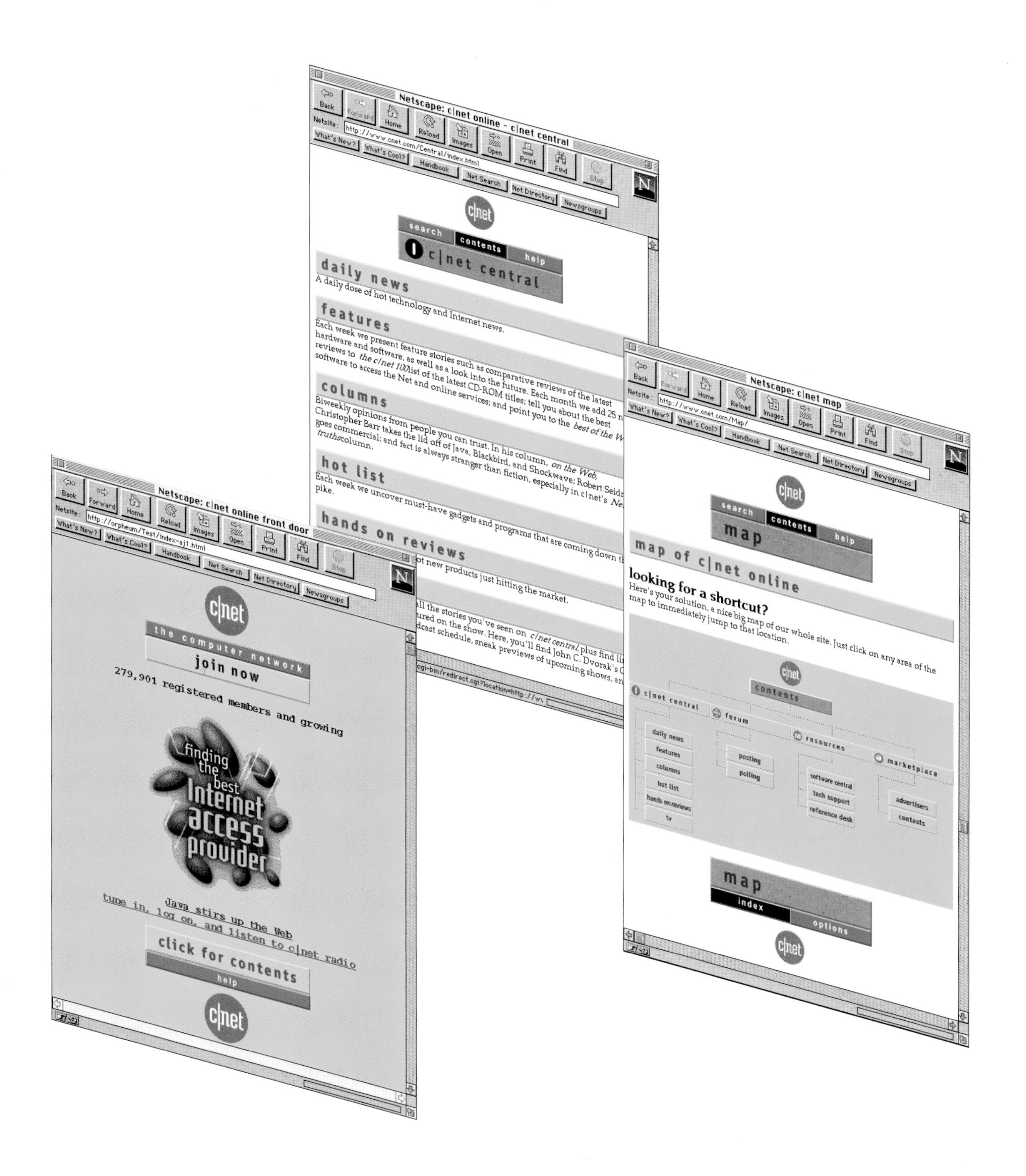

C | NET WORLD WIDE WEB SITE

www.cnet.com

CLIENT / PUBLISHER c|net: the computer network

DESIGN c|net: the computer network, San Francisco, CA. Kevin Wendle, president and executive producer; Fred Sotherland, vice president and creative director; Jonathan Rosenberg, executive vice president, technology; Chris Barr, editor in chief; Andrea Jenkins, art director; Ben Benjamin, Gareth Finucane, Eliza van Gerbig, Helle Abild, Ron Sellars and Oliver Burns, designers.

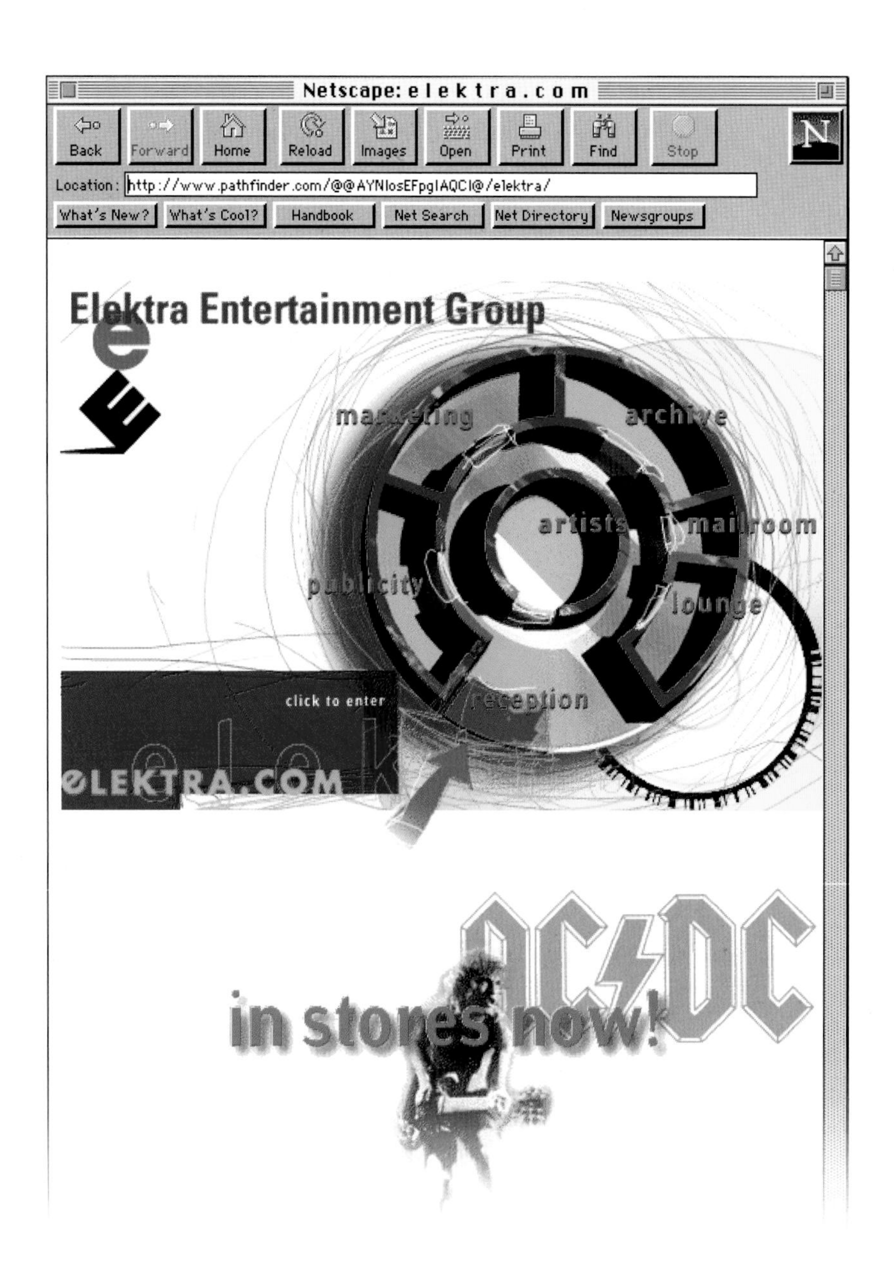

ELEKTRA ENTERTAINMENT WORLD WIDE WEB SITE

CLIENT / PUBLISHER Elektra Entertainment

DESIGN Avalanche Systems, Inc., New York, NY. Peter Seidler, art director; R. Matthew Pacetti, interface designer; Ricardo Tarrega Shayelaw, programmer; R. Matthew Pacetti, graphic designer; Paul Collitan, photographer.

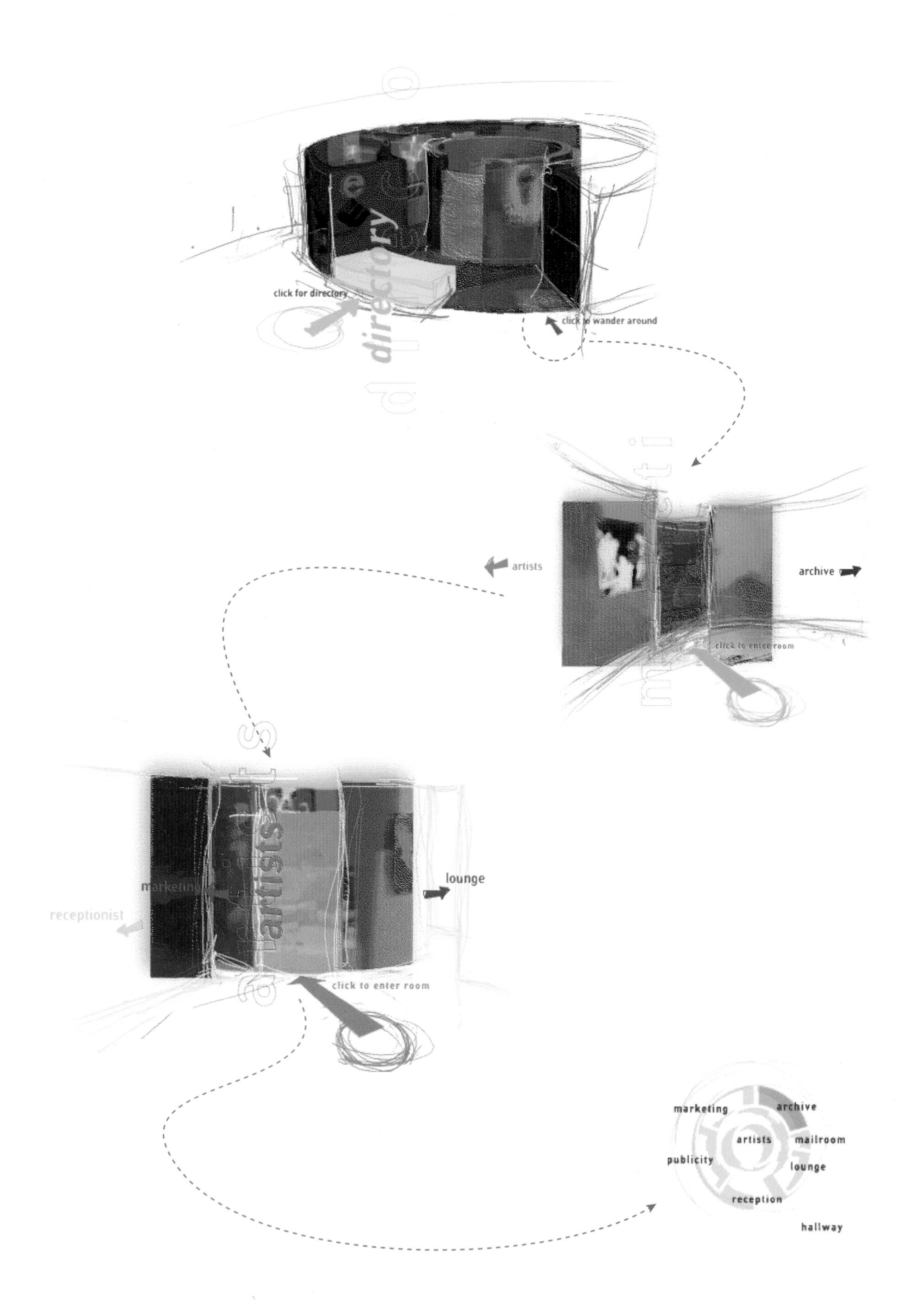

The use of sketches for the navigational construct of this site is impressive. Visitors are met by a virtual receptionist and invited to wander the halls of the maze-like offices to find out more about the company and, naturally, its recording artists. (A cross-section of this maze becomes a navigational tool that lingers in the lower right-hand corner of the screen.) Visitors can slip into the artist's lounge and visit the home pages of singers where they can listen to an interview, watch a music video clip, download a song, or peruse a discography. The look and feel of each home page reflects the attitude of each artist so that visitors will know immediately if they accidentally tripped into the realm of AC/DC on their way to Natalie Merchant.

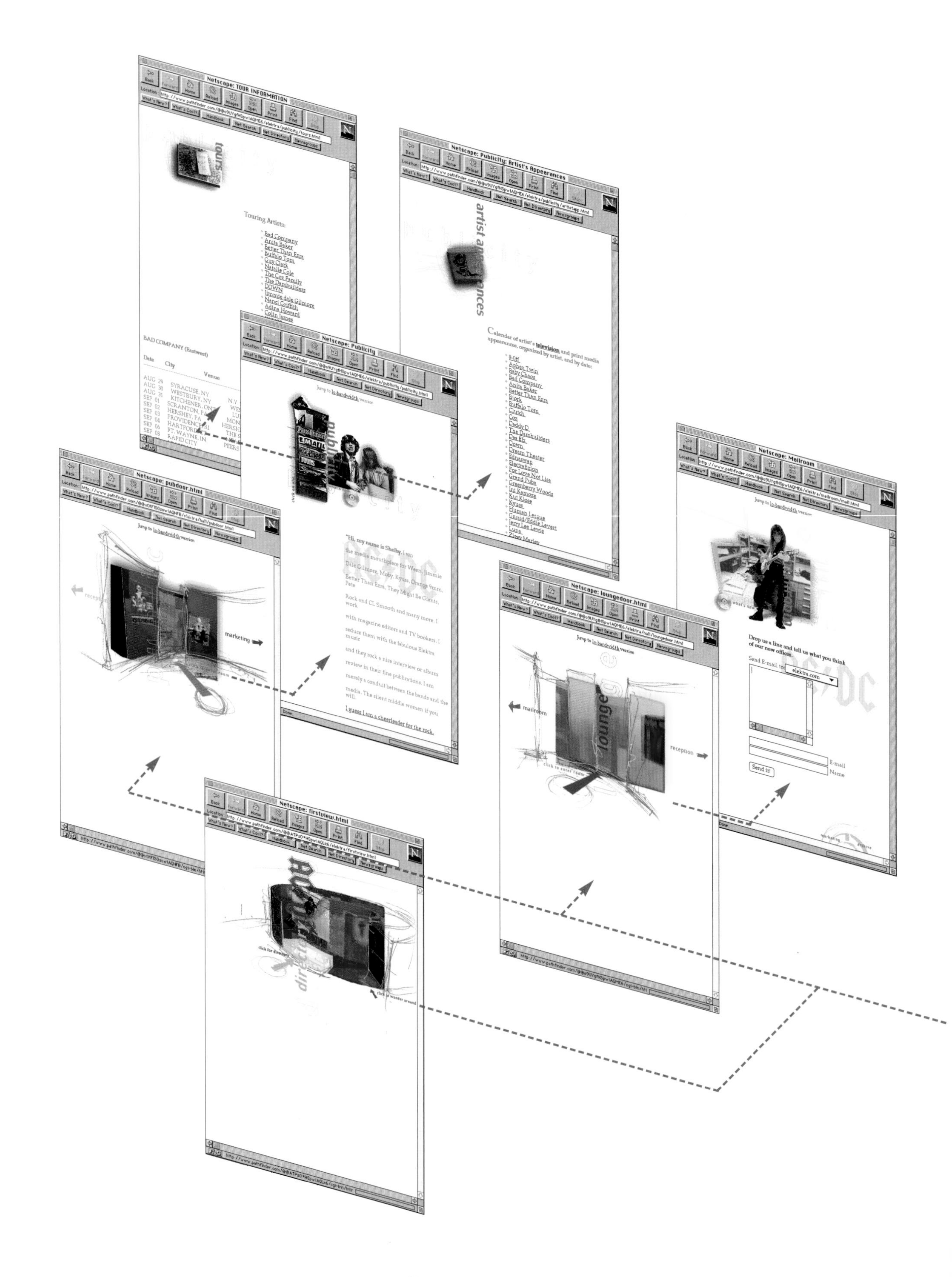

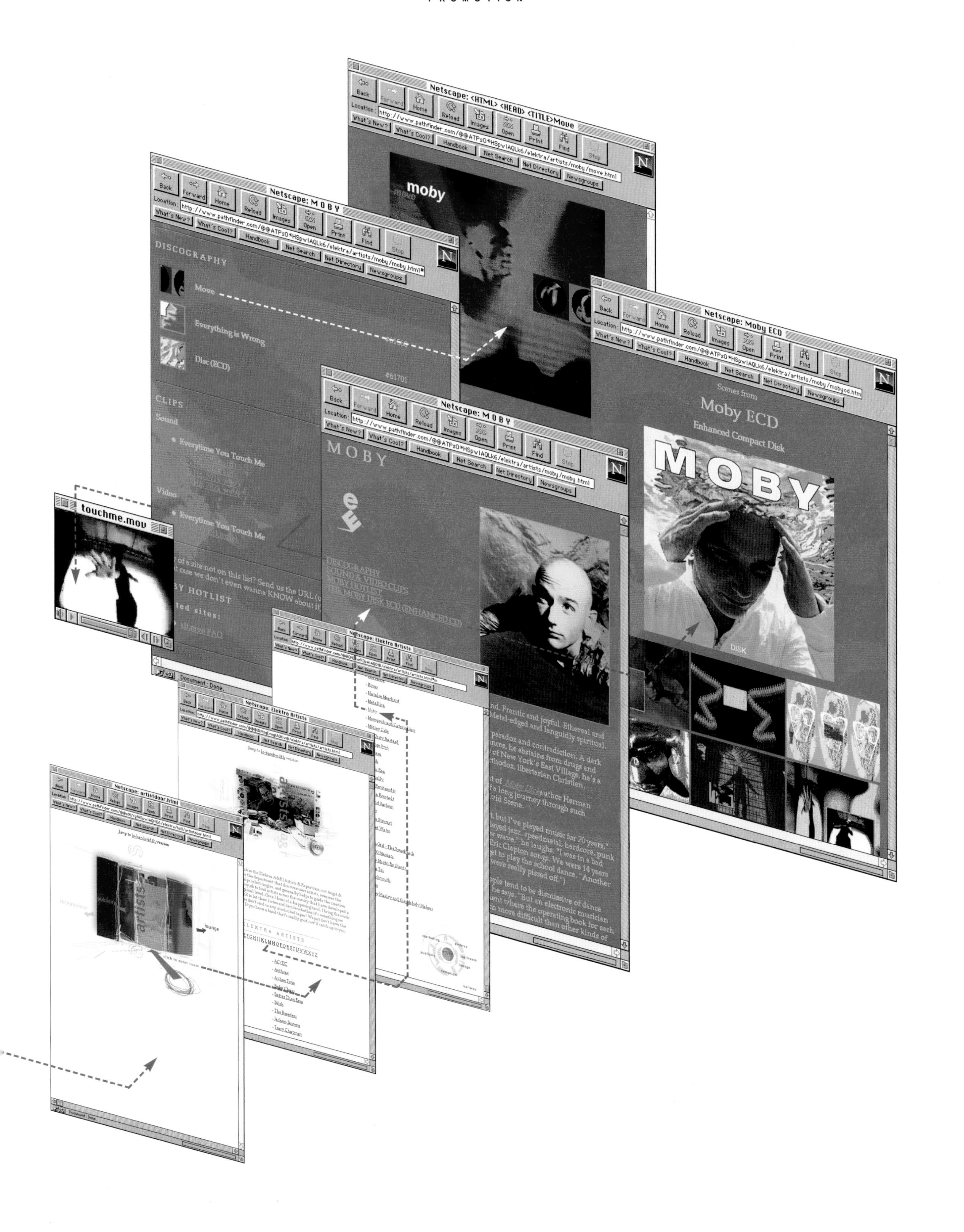
Netscape: <HTML> <HEAD> <TITLE>Move
http://www.pathfinder.com/@@ATPs0*HSpwIAQLk6/elektra/artists/moby/move.html
moby
Netscape: M O B Y
http://www.pathfinder.com/@@ATPs0*HSpwIAQLk6/elektra/artists/moby/moby.html
DISCOGRAPHY
Move
Everything is Wrong
Disc (ECD)
CLIPS
Sound
Everytime You Touch Me
Video
Everytime You Touch Me
touchme.mov
Netscape: Moby ECD
http://www.pathfinder.com/@@ATPs0*HSpwIAQLk6/elektra/artists/moby/mobycd.html
Scenes from
Moby ECD
Enhanced Compact Disk
MOBY
DISK
MOBY
DISCOGRAPHY
SOUND & VIDEO CLIPS
MOBY HOTLIST
THE MOBY DISK ECD (ENHANCED CD)
Netscape: Elektra Artists
Netscape: Elektra Artists
Netscape: artistdoor.html
lounge
click to enter room
Back
Forward
Home
Reload
Images
Open
Print
Find
Stop
Location:
What's New?
What's Cool?
Handbook
Net Search
Net Directory
Newsgroups
Document: Done.

THE SATURN SITE

www.saturncars.com

CLIENT / PUBLISHER Saturn Corporation

DESIGN Hal Riney & Partners Incorporated, San Francisco, CA. Doris Mitsch, creative director, writer, designer and illustrator; Clancy Nolan, producer; Anders Pers, account manager; Brian Jensen, project coordinator. Organic On-Line, Inc., Cindy Kawakami, Matthew Nelson, Bagus Haig, Chris Dolan, Brian Behlendorf and Cliff Skolnik, programmers.

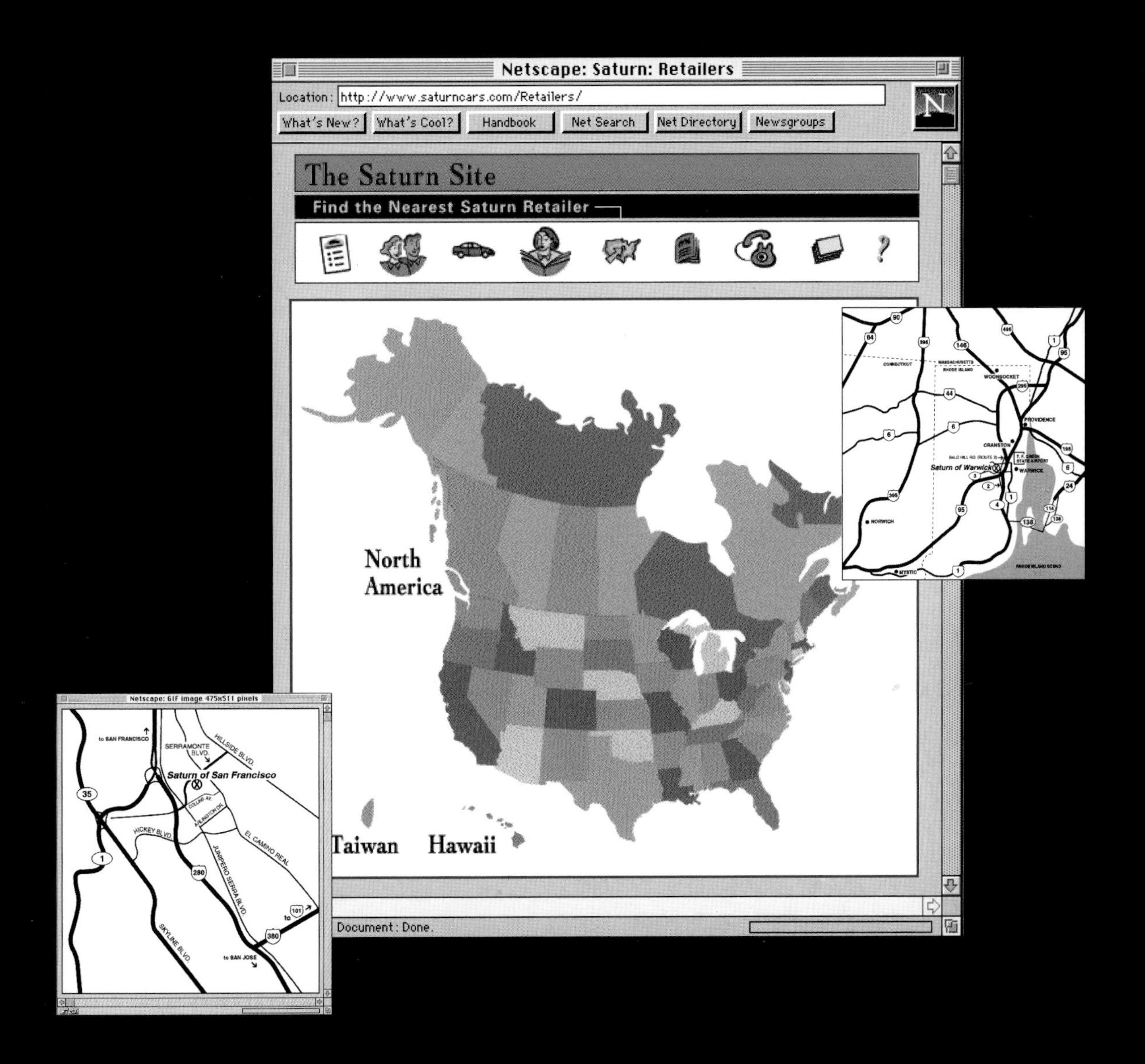

Every company and its subsidiary seem to be on the Web these days, but few sites boast the utility and clarity of Saturn's Web site. Saturn customers are known for an unsightly enthusiasm for their cars and a fanatic loyalty to the company that manufactures, markets, and maintains them. With this site, Saturn provides its far-flung yet chummy customers with a cybernetic clubhouse all their own. Visitors can e-mail one another, pick up valuable maintenance tips, or check out what modifications might be coming down the pike for next year's models. Visitors can also locate the dealers closest to them, and print out a street map to save them from getting lost on the way. The site is thoughtfully designed, particularly in the way that graphics are loaded up to save on transmission time. The general look of the site is clear and uncluttered, and the writing style is relaxed and often witty.

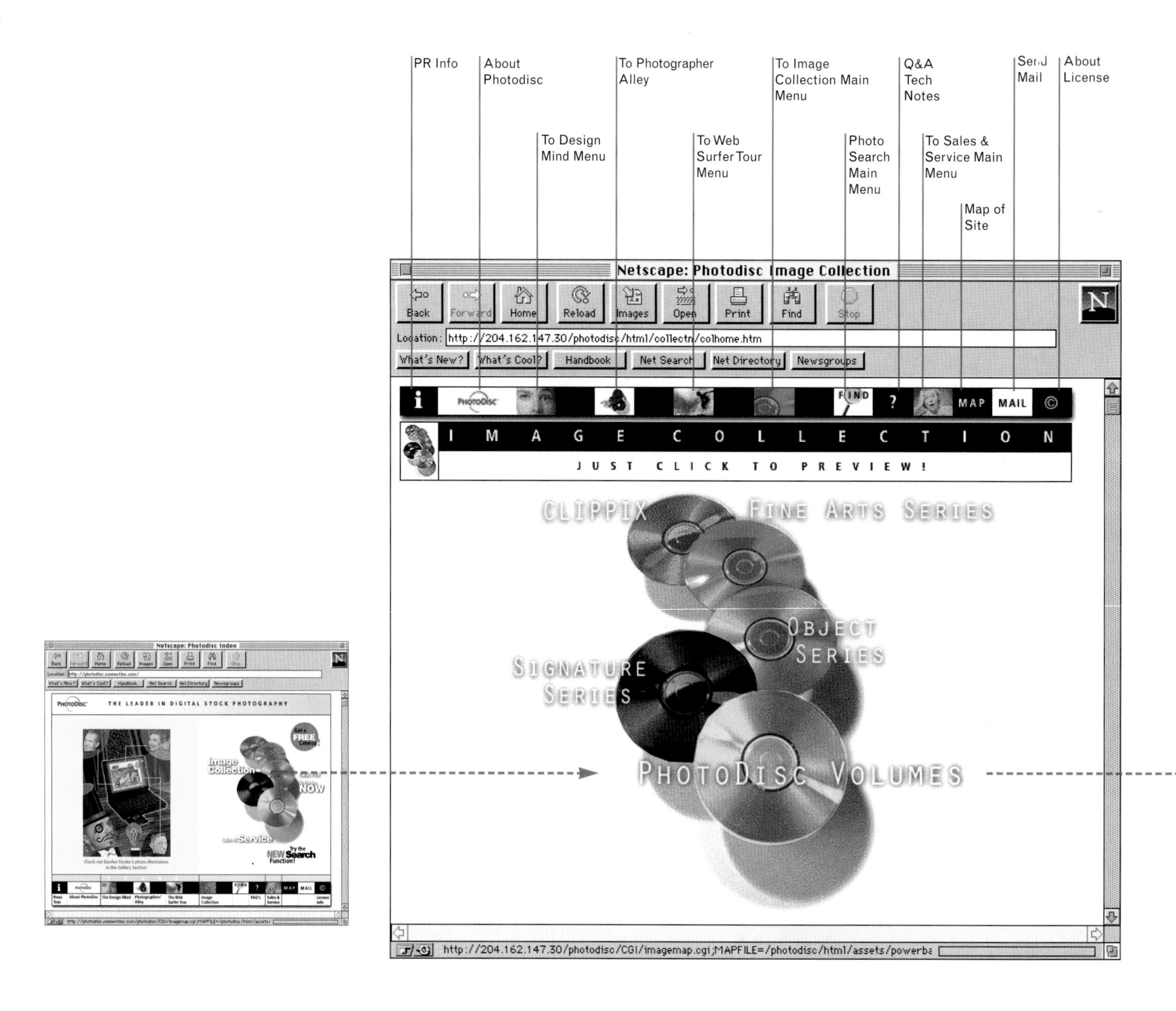

PHOTODISC WORLD WIDE WEB SITE

CLIENT / PUBLISHER Photodisc Inc.

DESIGN Clement Mok designs, Inc., San Francisco, CA. Clement Mok, creative director; Mark Anquoe, HTML programming. PhotoDisc, Inc., Bill Heston and Thaeddaeus Brophy, HTML programming. Connect Inc., Rick Hyde, server connections.

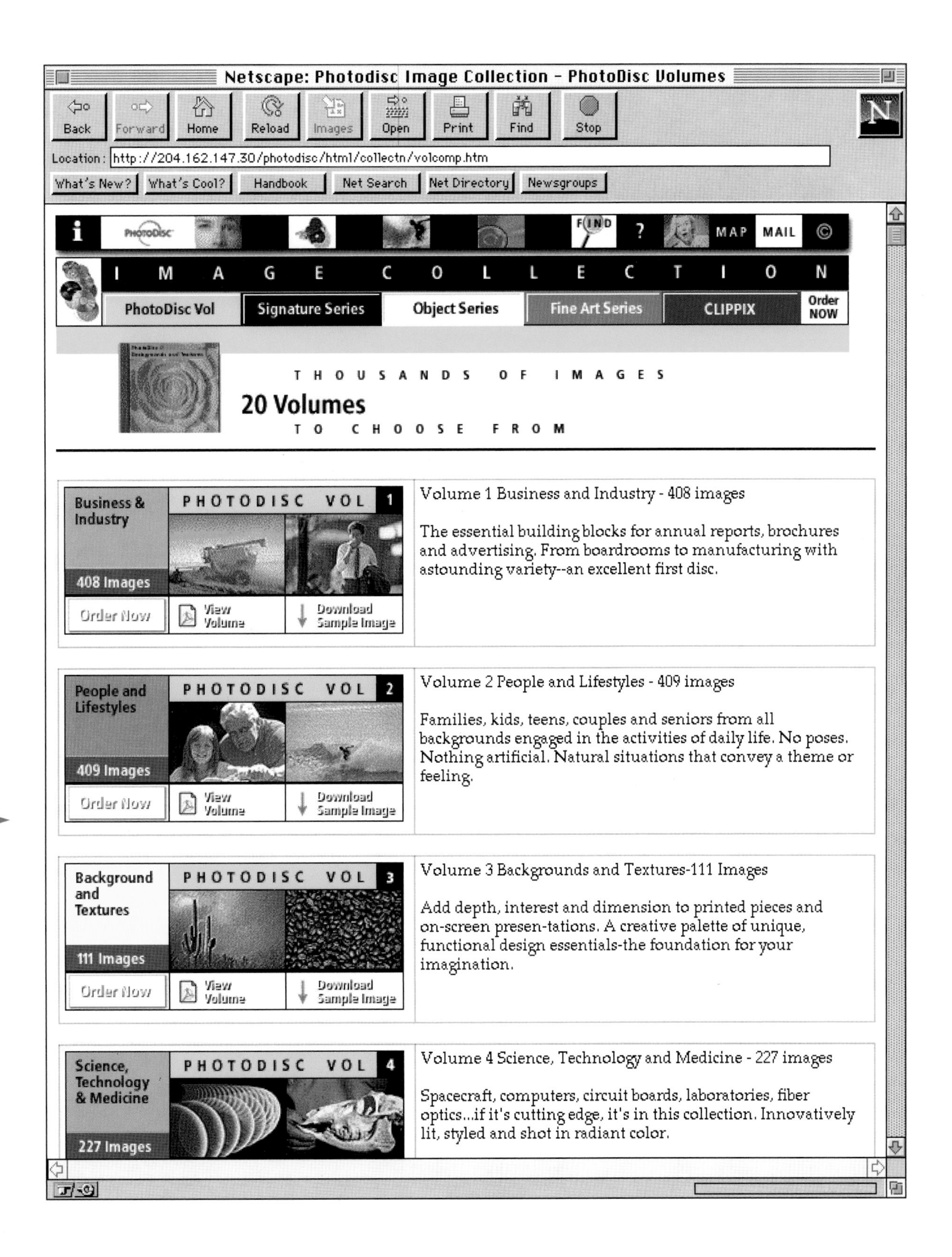

Since Web sites do not allow visitors to open multiple windows simultaneously, navigating them can be a chore, particularly when the site is an on-line catalogue of visual images. The accomplishment of the PhotoDisc Web site is how it allows visitors to access a complex array of images with as few as one—and no more than two—clicks of the mouse. ■ The site's primary navigational construct is a ribbon of images and words that stretches across the top of the page. Clicking on these sends visitors into any area of the site: a designer's forum or a sales menu. When visitors click on the red photo of the CD at the center of the ribbon, they are shown PhotoDisc's Image Collection page, where visitors choose to view images from five categories. The navigational ribbon is visible wherever visitors might wander, and help is always close at hand. ■ The site's interface doubles as its navigational system, so it must be as functional as it is eye-pleasing. It succeeds in this. The interface also manages to reflect the identity and personality of the service—providing photographic images—by using such images as navigational icons.

MERCEDE-BENZ INTERACTIVE

CLIENT / PUBLISHER Mercedes-Benz of North America

DESIGN The Desinory, Inc., Long Beach, CA. Tim Meraz, Rich Conklin, Ulrich Lange, art directors; Ulrich Lange, Chip McCarthy, David Glaze, John Grøtting, interface designers; Christopher Hoffman, writer; John Grotting, Thierry Benichou, programmers; Jann Castor, audio; John Grøtting, Ulrich Lange, animators; COW, new media production company.

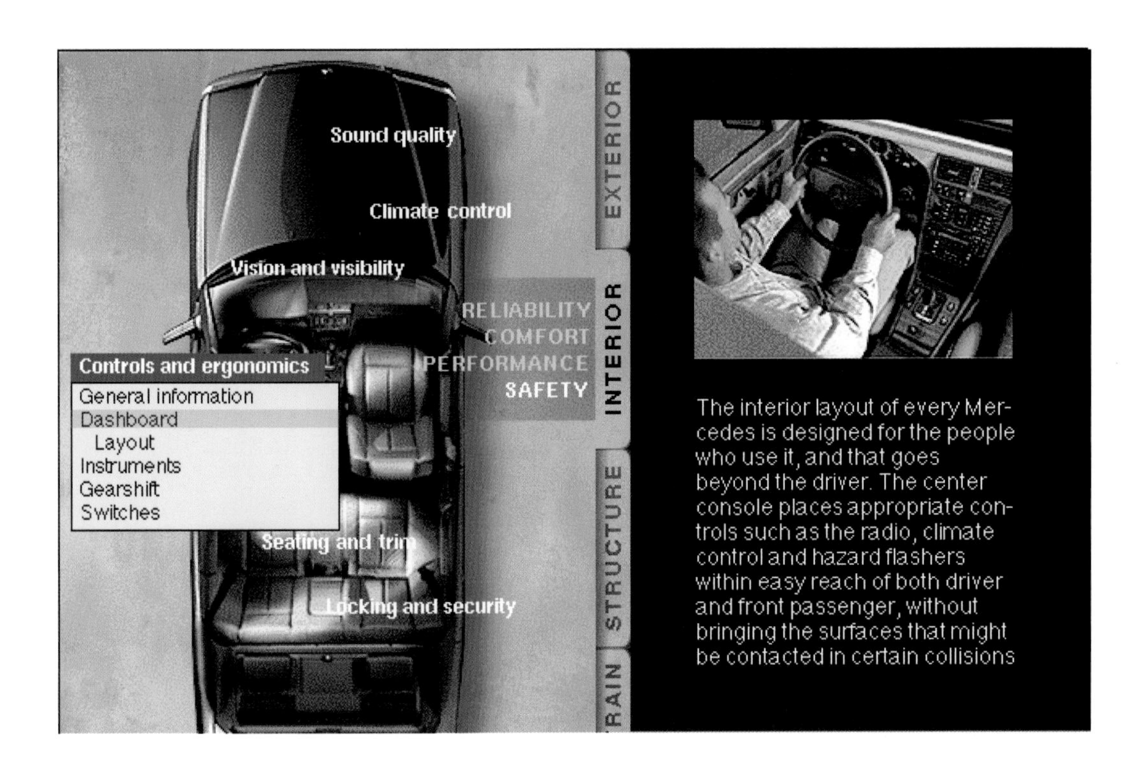

Sleek yet informative, this Mercedez-Benz promotion propels the luxury car brochure into the digital arena with a visual and typographic restraint well-suited to the company's image. Blending the strengths of print-based attributes (photos, text, and lay-out) with sporty, computer-driven navigational features, this electronic brochure's easy-to-read tabs quickly reveal characteristics of the automobile in rich detail, layer by layer, as it explains viewer questions with screen displays that pair sharp images with persuasive text.

THE 1994 IBM INTERACTIVE ANNUAL REPORT

CLIENT / PUBLISHER International Business Machines Corporation

DESIGN Executive Arts Inc., Atlanta, GA. Richard Anwyl, art director; Leif Wells, interface designer; Leif Wells, Paul Parker, Jason Causey and Brian Saunders, programmers; Dave Parrish, video director; John Vogf, digital video director; Matt Rollins and Phil Hamlett, graphic designers; George Lange, photographer (principal); Bill Mayer, illustrator; Alice Lei, audio, music composer and sound effects; Bill Victor, Steve Hallock and Kevin Scholz, animators; James Harris, project manager.

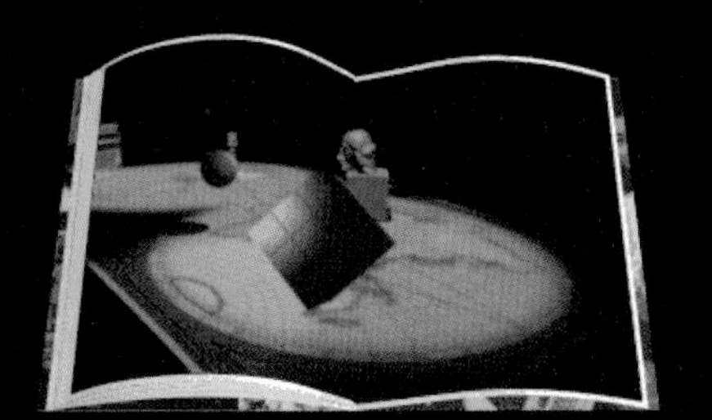

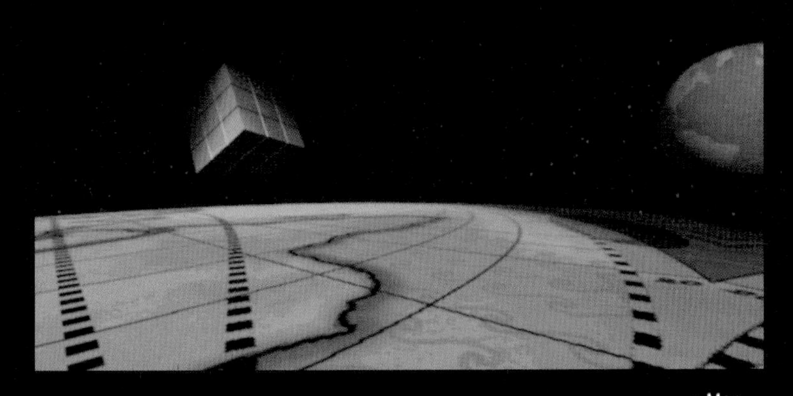

• Map
• Quit

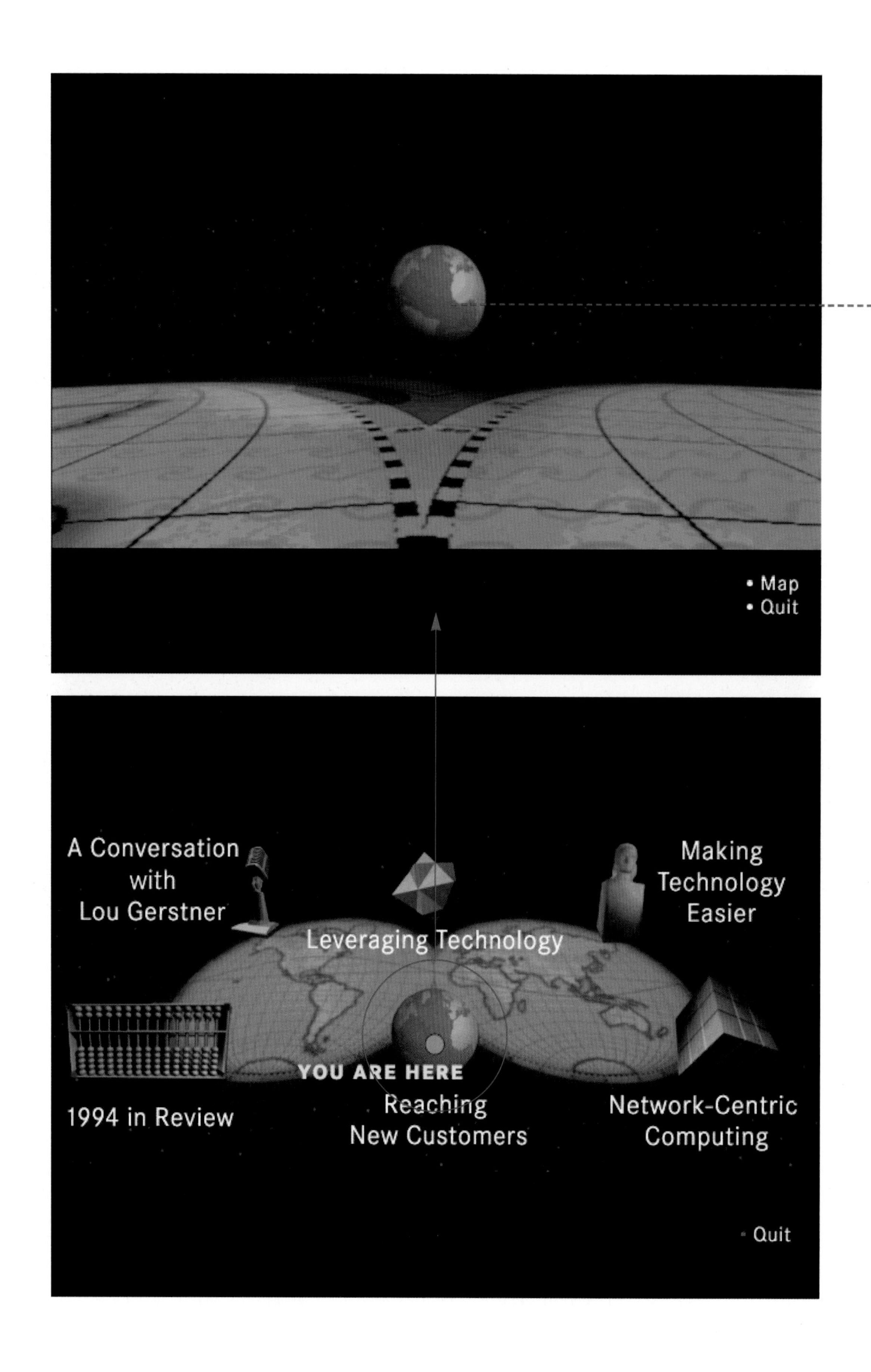

• Map
• Quit
A Conversation with Lou Gerstner
Making Technology Easier
Leveraging Technology
YOU ARE HERE
1994 in Review
Reaching New Customers
Network-Centric Computing
Quit

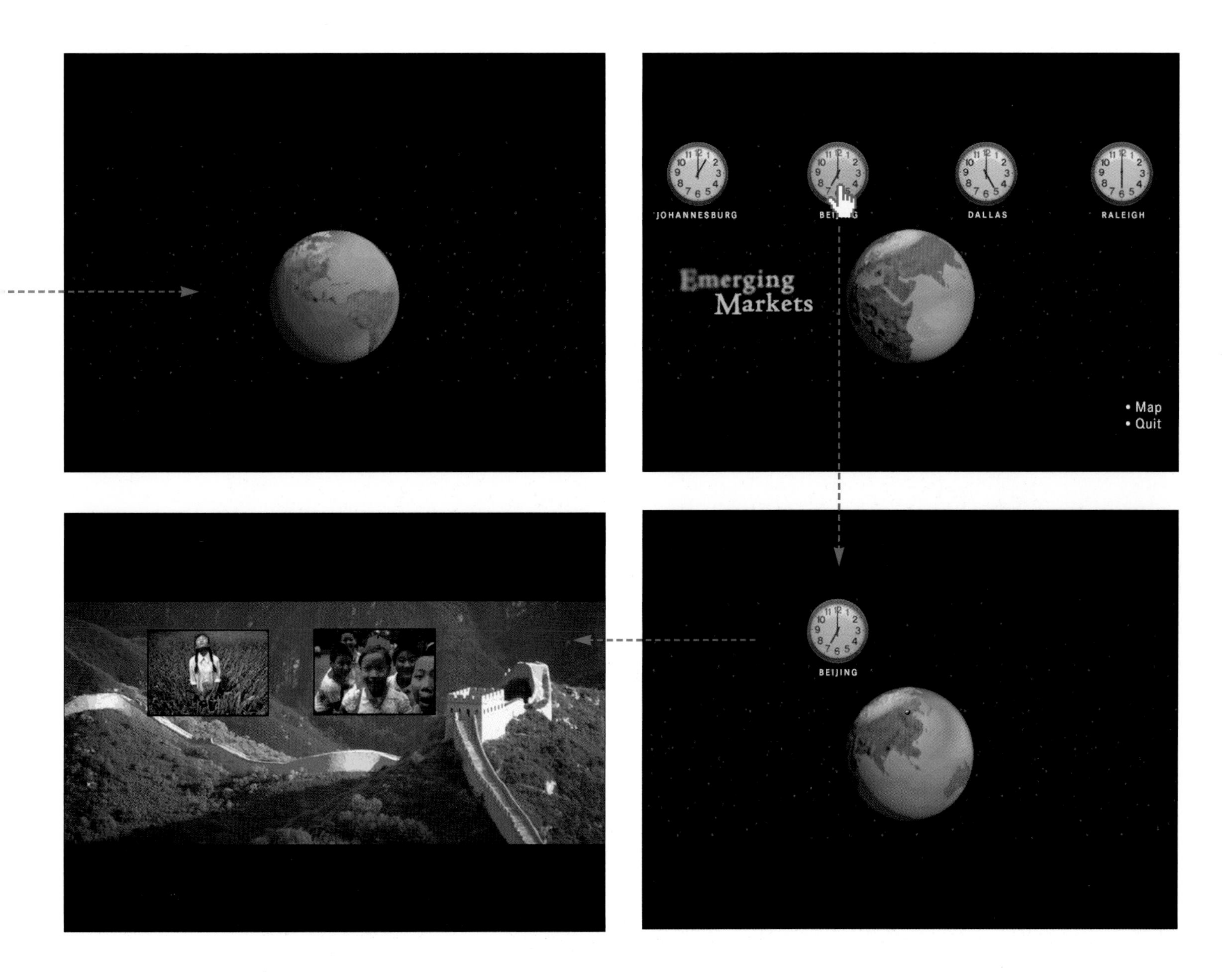

Like thousands of other firms around the world, IBM released a sharp annual report last year to their shareholders. What is unusual is that Big Blue offered two versions: one on paper, and another on CD-ROM. The result is impressive. Shareholders may either dive right into the paper version of the report, which is included on this disk, or explore the interactive multimedia version, which presents shareholders with a landscape that includes a map of the world (with clickable hotspots) and six three-dimensional objects (such as an abacus and a microphone) which represent the six sections of the report. Navigation is simple and powerful, with a hot spot for "Map" and "Quit" always visible in the lower left-hand corner of the screen. Few multimedia packages are accompanied by such explicit voice-over instructions for navigation, apparently in anticipation of use by shareholders unschooled in the chicanery of multimedia designers.

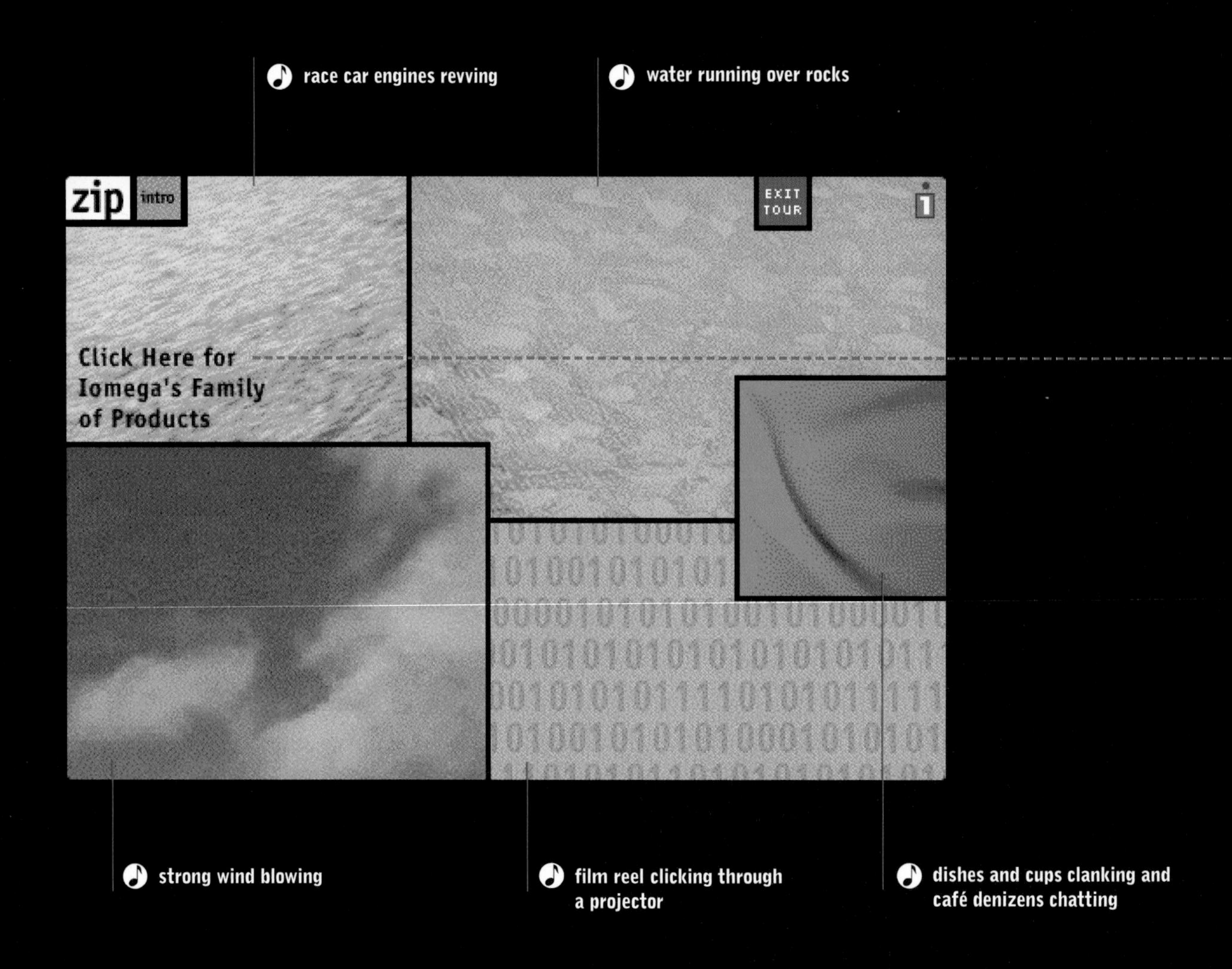

ZIP TOUR

CLIENT / PUBLISHER Iomega Corporation

DESIGN Fitch Inc., Worthington, OH. David Gresham and Chris Pacione, art directors; Chris Pacione and Ed Chung, interface designers; Kate Welker, writer; Chris Pacione and Ed Chung, graphic designers and sound editors. Digital, Patti Anklam, writer.

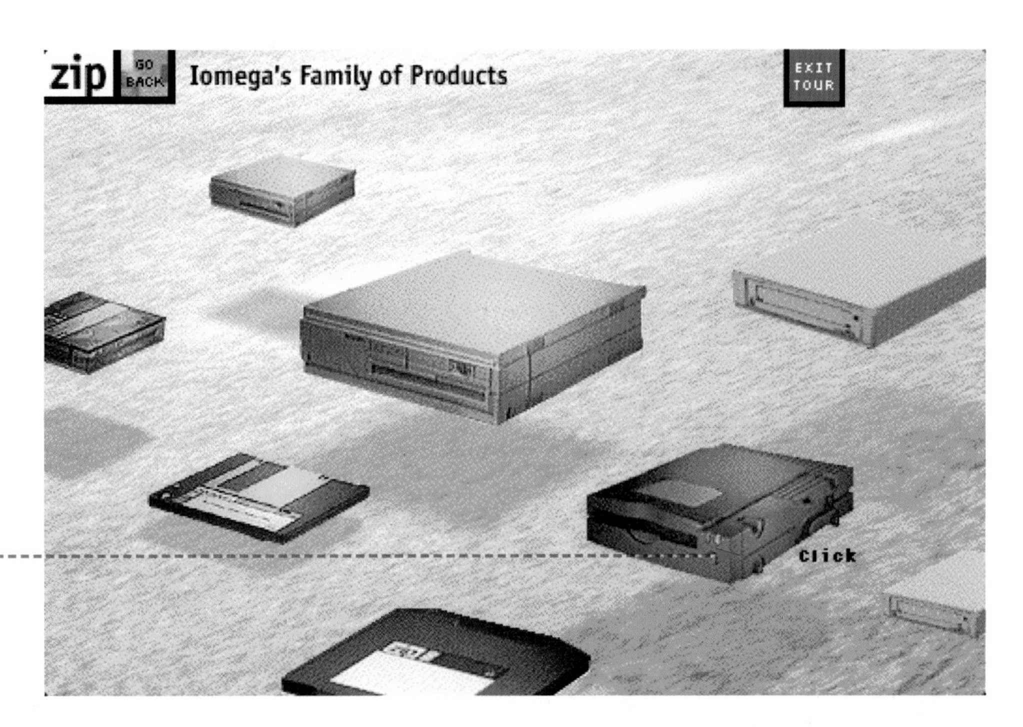

After a zippy narrated slide-show introduction to Zip drives, customers are dumped into one of the most compelling and uncomplicated interfaces around. Passing the cursor over the color-coded boxes activates sounds (race cars whizzing by, water running over rocks), as well as call-outs ("Click Here for Iomega's Family of Products," "Click Here to Order Products.") Clicking on a box sends customers to the specified area. ■ The sound metaphors carry over to the visual design of the subject area, so that the interface box that sounded like race cars yields to an eagle-eye view of Iomega products whizzing by. Passing the cursor over each product changes the color of that product; clicking on it activates a slide show (complete with the *kler-chunk* of the virtual projector advancing) of standard industrial photographs and unadorned marketing text.

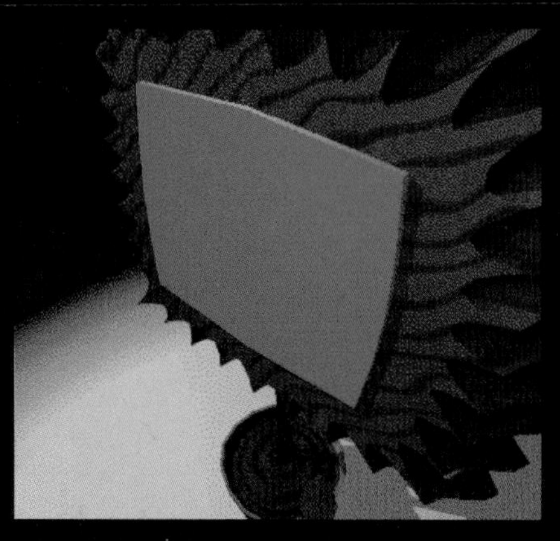

Lush and lively, Tanagram's creativity sprouts biomorphically as a television screen blooms into a wacky digital calling card. The screen is accented with an array of quirky sound effects and advances when one clicks on plump and pulsating pixelated pistils that display photographed samples of the design firm's idiosyncratic aesthetic and exuberant style.

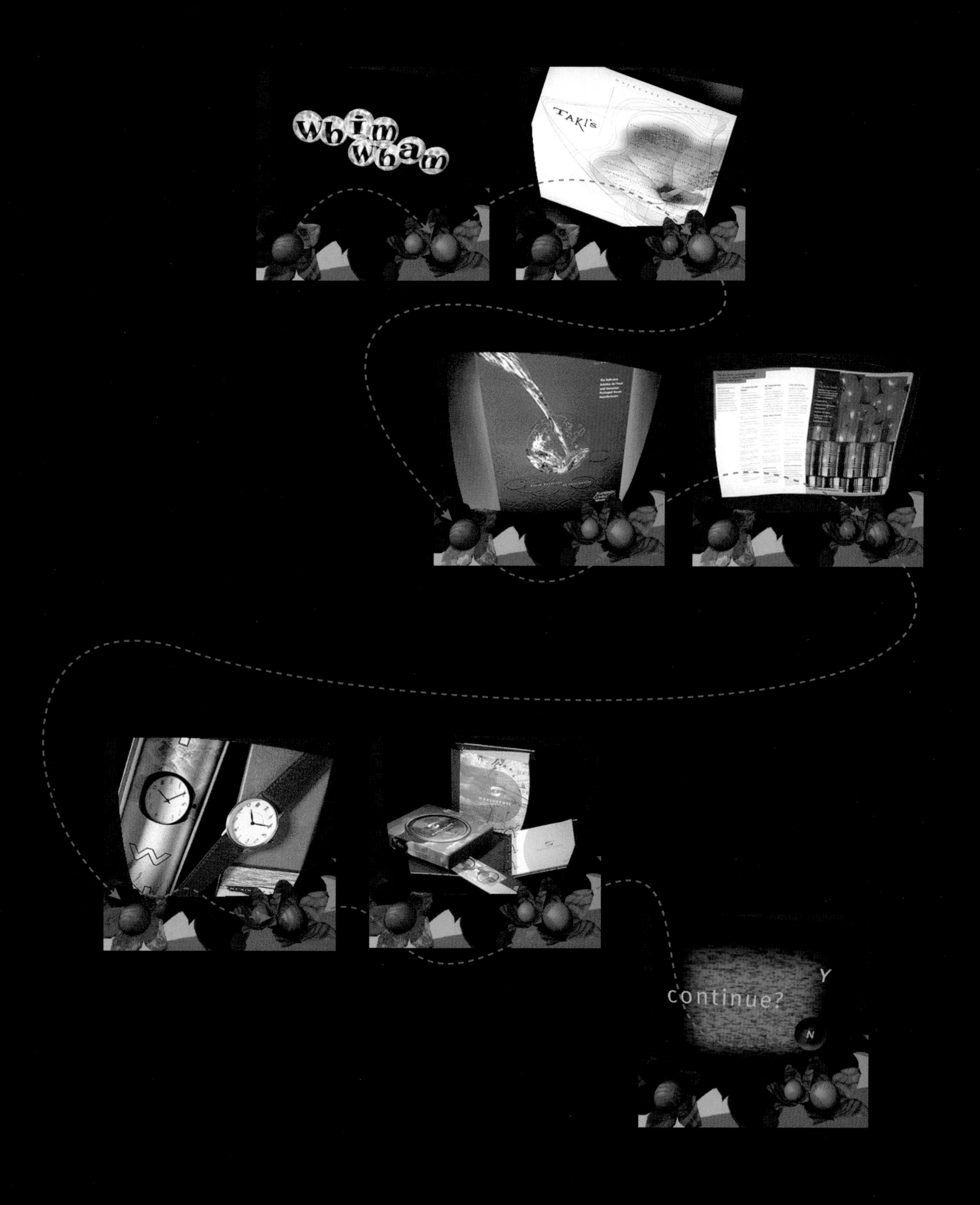

TANAGRAM DIGITAL POSTCARD

CLIENT/PUBLISHER Tanagram

DESIGN Tanagram, Chicago, IL. Anthony Ma, Lance Rutter, Art Directors; Grant Davis, Lance Rutter, interface designers; Grant Davis, programmer; Grant Davis, Lance Rutter, Anthony Ma, Eric Wagner, graphic designers; Eric Wagner, photographer; Grant Davis, Lance Rutter, illustrators; Grant Davis, animator; Eric Wagner, sound editor.

The conventional automobile brochure is nothing to joke about. It is beautiful and boastful, resplendent and sincere, silken to the touch and weighty in the hand. Someone might read it and decide to buy something really, really expensive, so this is serious business. ■ Toyota's electronic brochure launching their Tacoma pickup campaign sports a different attitude. While it has a traditional introductory portion, it includes a valuable "Modern Man's Guide to Life," which potential Tacoma pick-up drivers will want to keep for its immense reference value. This "value-added" offers helpful hints on carving a turkey, shaving with a straight blade razor, detecting forged currency, and landing the plane in case the pilot dies (pictures of gauges provided.) Even more valuable is this CD's publication of the only known set of diagrams detailed enough to illustrate to a man how "to fold a dress shirt."

TOYOTA TACOMA LAUNCH AD

CLIENT/PUBLISHER Toyota Motor Sales U.S.A. Inc.

DESIGN Saatchi & Saatchi DFS/Pacific, Torrance, CA. Dean Van Eimeren, creative director; Alan Segal, art director; Alan Segal and David Tanimoto, interface desginers; Jon Jay and Alan Segal, writers; Arno Harris, programmer and graphic designer; Tim Damon, photographer; Jeff Beverly, audio. Novo Media Group, new media production company.

IF THE PILOT DIES
TIME
FIRST LINES
FOOD
SPORTS
WHAT TO PACK
WHAT TO WEAR
PETS
CRISP SHIRTS
DEODORANT
TOOLS
WOMEN
MONEY
$
HAIR
SHAVING
MODERN MAN'S GUIDE TO LIFE
Far From Everything You Need To Know Brought To You By
TOYOTA

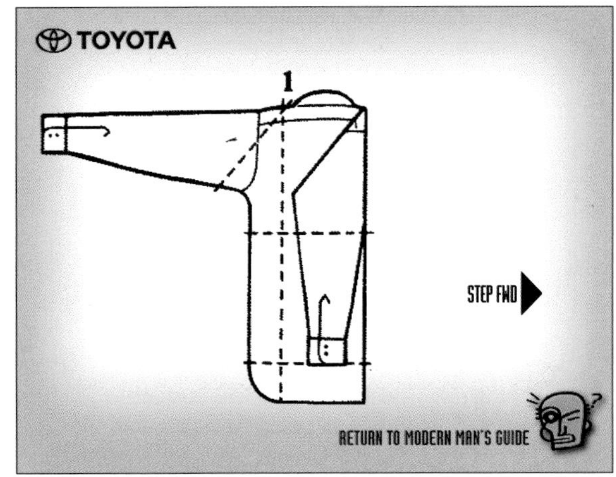

TOYOTA
1
STEP FWD
RETURN TO MODERN MAN'S GUIDE

TOYOTA
LET'S TALK TURKEY...
Carving Position
First move turkey comfortably close and turn it on its side, breast away from carver.
FWD
RETURN TO MODERN MAN'S GUIDE

TOYOTA
SHAVE CAREFULLY!
You may start with light and tentative strokes to test your beard's resistance and your skin's sensitivity, but you should strive to shave yourself with the cold, brilliant boldness of a samurai by imagining yourself making long, clean and sure sweeps with your razor.
STEP REV
STEP FWD
RETURN TO MODERN MAN'S GUIDE

TOYOTA
LET'S TALK TURKEY...
Remove Wing
Next raise wing and cut it off at the second joint. Set wing aside.
REV
FWD
RETURN TO MODERN MAN'S GUIDE

TOYOTA
SHAVE CAREFULLY!
First, you have to have a sharp, hollow-ground razor and a good shaving mug and brush—the best brushes are made of badger fur. Most of all, you need lots and lots of hot water. Every good shave requires successful interplay between your beard's wetness, your razor's keenness and your blade's angle of attack.
STEP FWD
RETURN TO MODERN MAN'S GUIDE

TOYOTA
Compass:
The compass tells you what direction you're headed
Compass
Airspeed Indicator
Attitude Indicator
Altimeter
Vertical Acceleration
Clock
Turn & Slip Indicator
Gyro Heading Indicator
RETURN TO MODERN MAN'S GUIDE

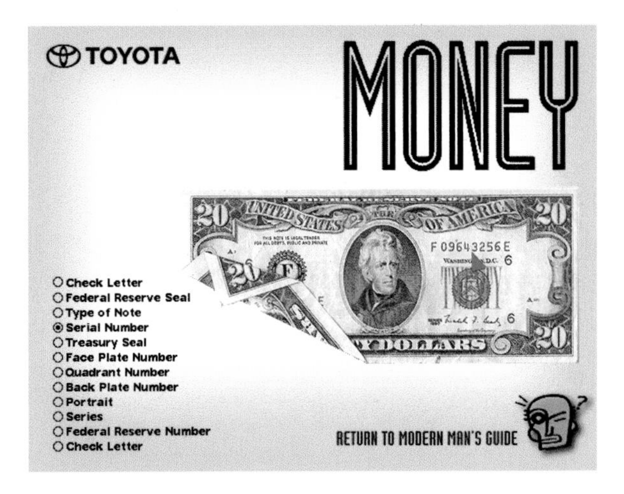

TOYOTA
MONEY
Check Letter
Federal Reserve Seal
Type of Note
Serial Number
Treasury Seal
Face Plate Number
Quadrant Number
Back Plate Number
Portrait
Series
Federal Reserve Number
Check Letter
RETURN TO MODERN MAN'S GUIDE

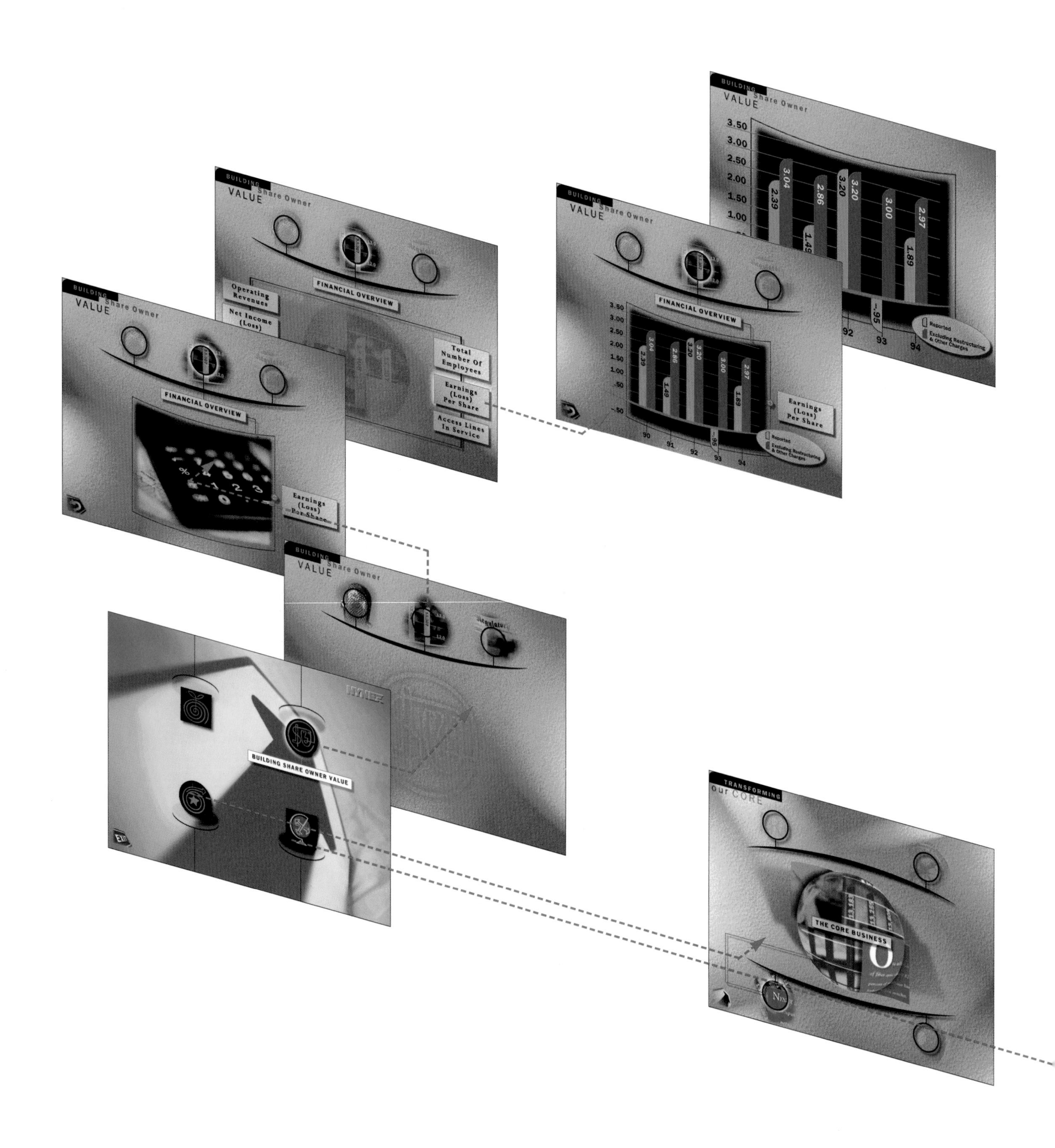

FROM THIS POINT FOWARD 

CLIENT/PUBLISHER NYNEX

DESIGN Magnet Interactive Studios, Washington, DC. Chuck Seelye, art director; Felipe Del Corral and Kathy Manzo, interface designer; Robert Linehan and Rob Wolfford, programmers; Mark James, video director; John Corjeno and Jerry Delk, digital video directors; John McGarity and Jane Levine, photographers; David Kingsley, audio; Marcus Williams, Maurice Davis; Magnet Interactive Studios, new media production company.

Navigating around this promotional CD is the whole point: with an edgy visual style, dynamic rhythms, and deep layering of information, *From This Point Forward* employs a travel metaphor throughout. Users trek around the world of NYNEX's operations by clicking on the stamps of various countries; this action, in turn, spins a cone-shaped globe on its nadir, sending the user (often by way of traffic signs) through multiple layers of information about the company—from marketing fluff to video interviews to financial data—all presented with soothing tones and layouts. Meanwhile, a highly stylized arrow is always present in a corner to help viewers find their way back. Considering NYNEX's position as one of the world's communications giants, they earned the globe-trotting metaphor.

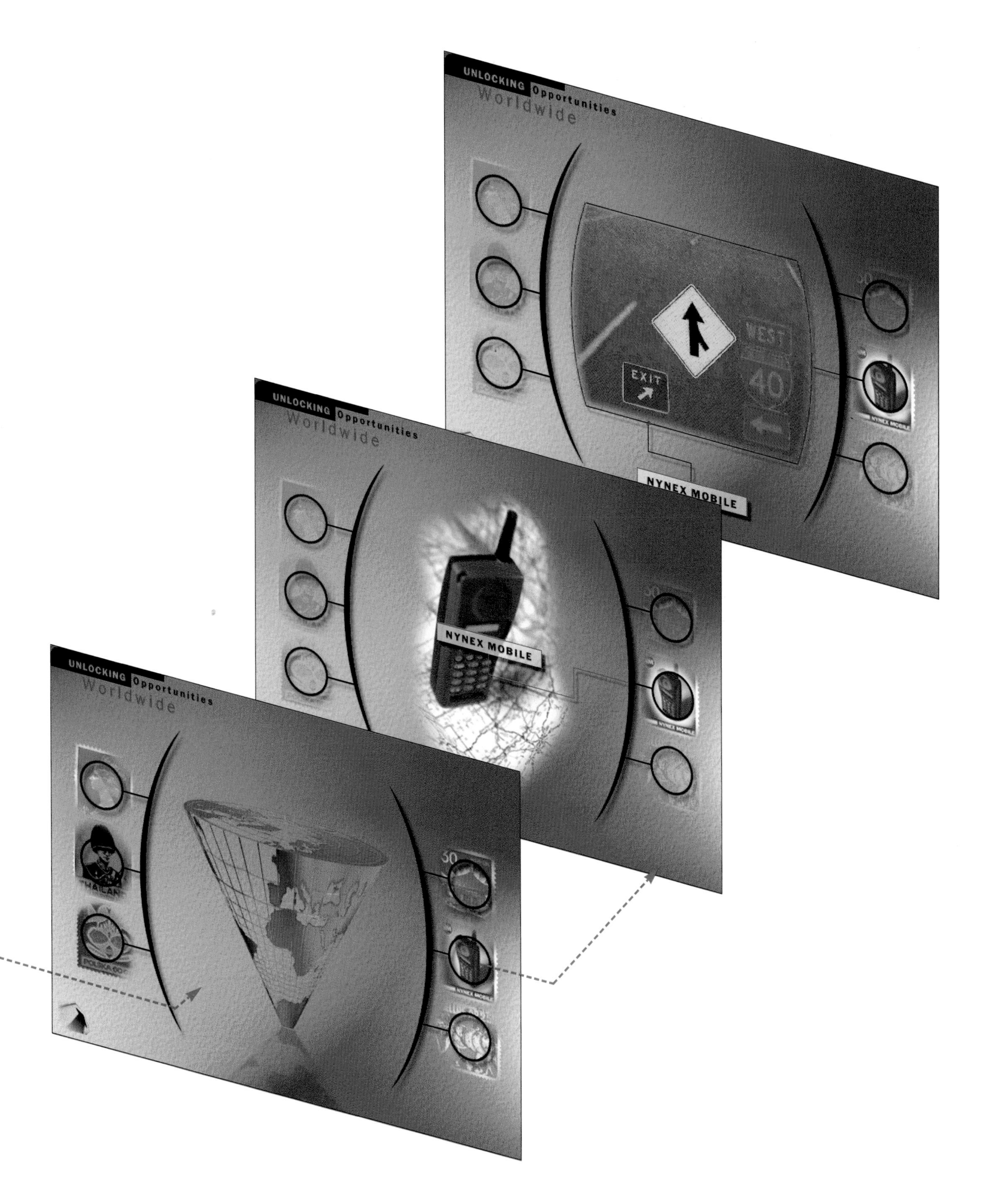

CSA ARCHIVE CD LINE ART SAMPLER 

CLIENT/PUBLISHER CSA Archive

DESIGN Charles S. Anderson Design Co. Minneapolis, MN. Paul Howalt and Charles S. Anderson, art directors; Paul Howalt, interface designer; Renee Valois, writer; Tom Eslinger and Brian Smith, programmers; Joel Templin, packaging. Eager Photo, Darrell Eager, photographer.

Receive this in the mail, and users might be tempted to stamp "RETURN TO SENDER" on it, for this CD-ROM comes in a gunmetal-gray film canister. But open it up, and instead of a reel there is a CD archive of neato '40s-style industrial line art, dingbats, sound clips, and movies—all updated for the '90s market. This is a fully conceived package, from soup to nuts: the hokey, up-beat narration is well-suited to the cheesy newsreel-style footage of the Archive, and coordinates well with the artwork and packaging. Also included in the film canister is a nifty Archive logo pin that users may choose to wear around the house or the office.

CSA
LINE ART
ARCHIVE
CD
SAMPLER
*MOTOR BIKE 50
46
47
48
49
50
ARCHIVE
PLAY
LINE ART
CATALOG
TYPEFACE
MENU
SIZE: 144K
CLICK ON YOUR CSA ARCHIVE ILLUSTRATION TO DOWNLOAD

CSA
DINGBATS
ARCHIVE
CD
SAMPLER
*CLICK ANY KEY q
A COLLECTION OF CSA ARCHIVE
DINGBATS IN TYPEFACE FORMAT
LINE ART
CATALOG
TYPEFACE
MENU
LOWERCASE
CLICK INSIDE THE CIRCLE TO DOWNLOAD THE CSA ARCHIVE DINGBAT TYPEFACE

Archive

Announcing

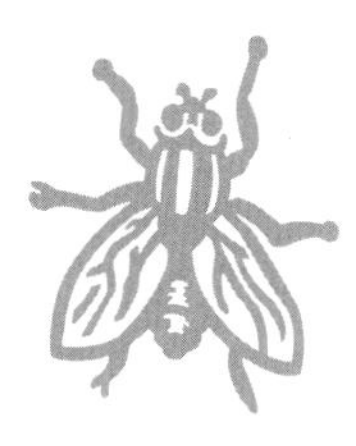

The Best-
Coffee in
town

JOSHUA DISTLER PORTFOLIO

CLIENT / PUBLISHER Joshua Distler Design

DESIGN Joshua Distler Design, Burlingame, CA. Joshua Distler, creative director.

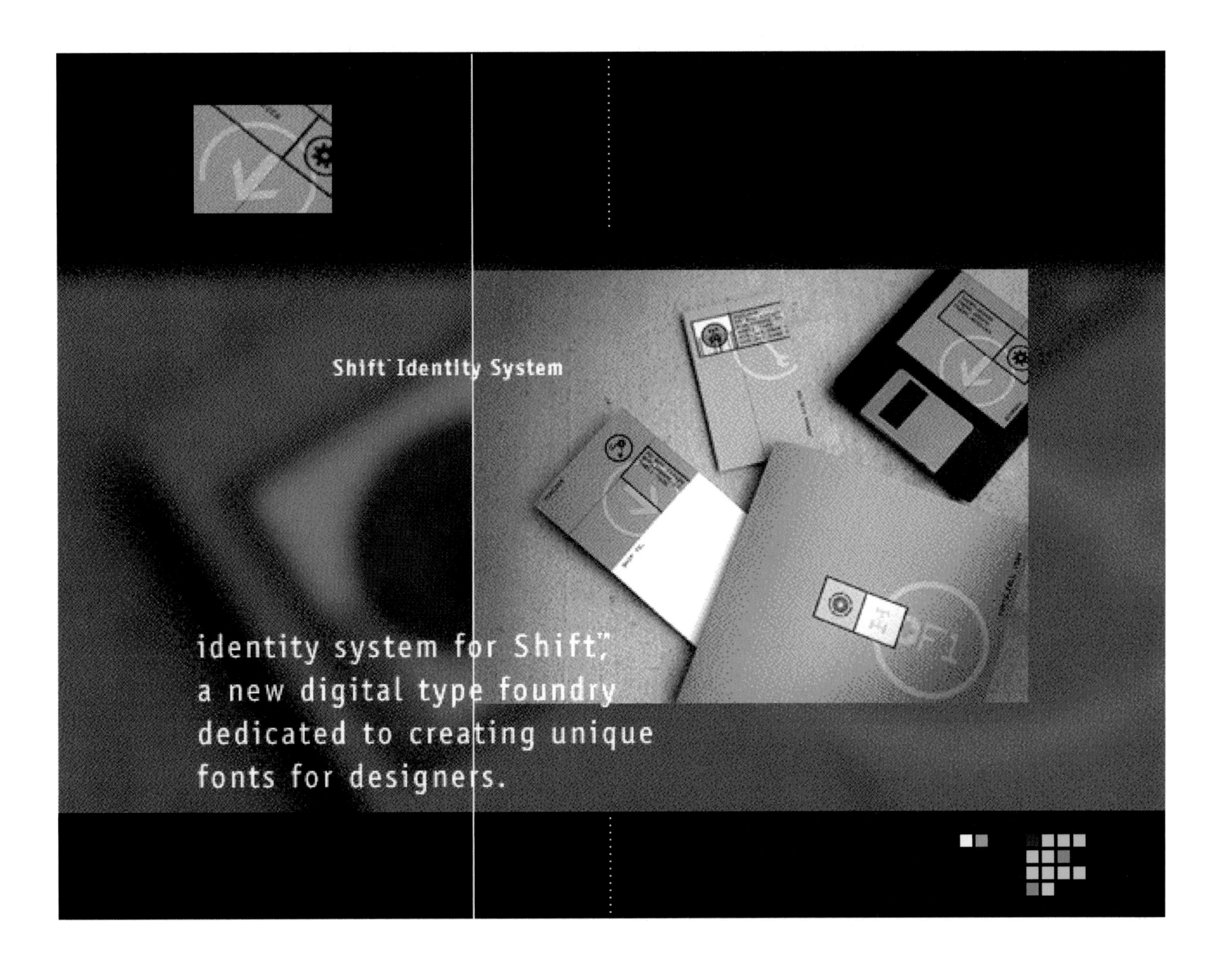

Rhythmic, resourceful and stunningly functional, this electronic self-promotion piece, designed by the creator of the digital font Nucleus, forges a novel approach to on-screen display. The portfolio is accessed by way of a color-coded navigational grid activated one square at a time to reveal minimally captioned artwork and related projects organized in an invisibly-defined hierarchy. As each image gives way to the next, its ghosted duotone lingers on-screen to become the background for its colorful successor, thus yielding a uniquely layered, experiential view of the designer's aesthetic.

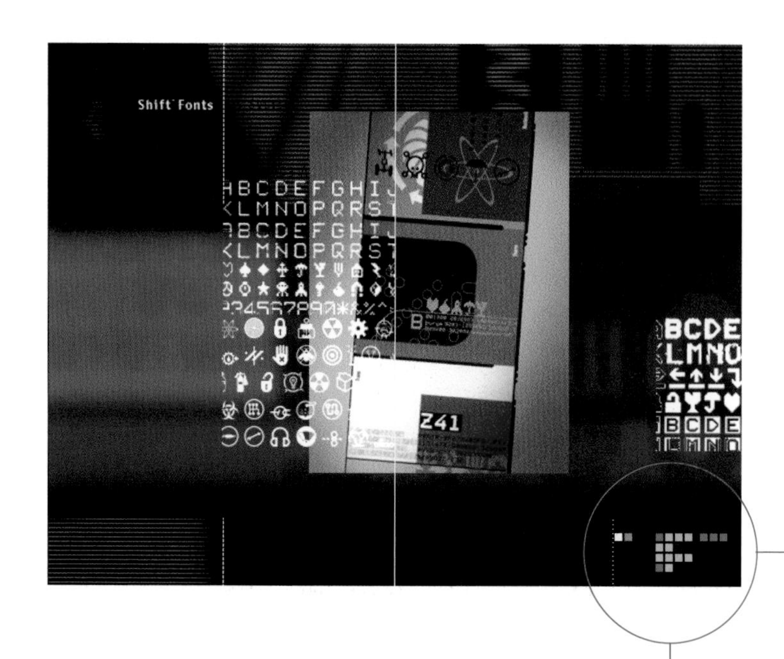
Shift Fonts
Z41

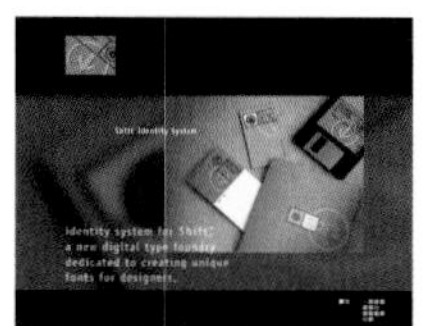

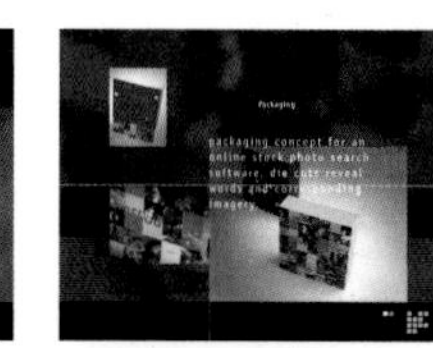

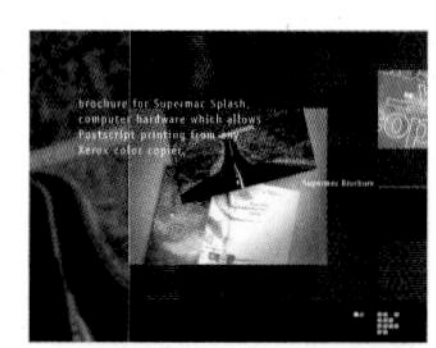

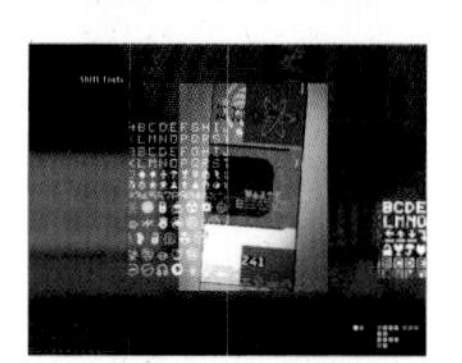

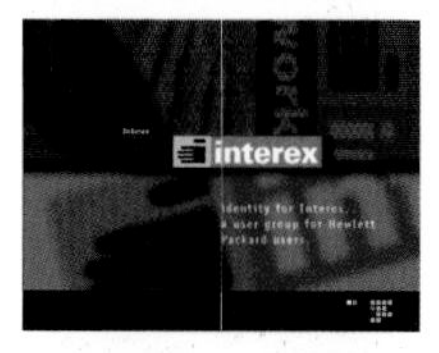

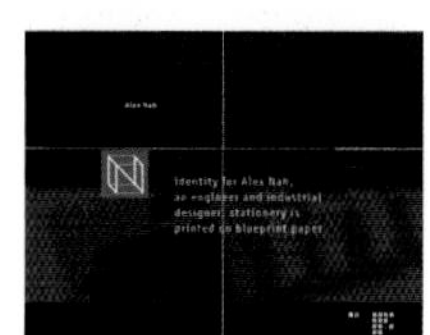

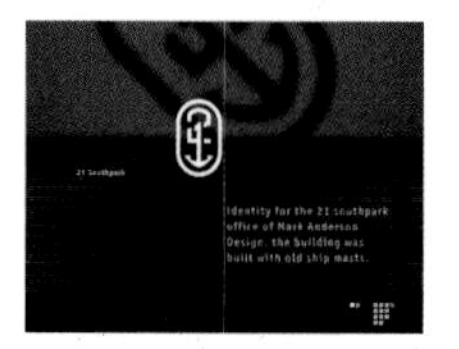

Navigation Controls

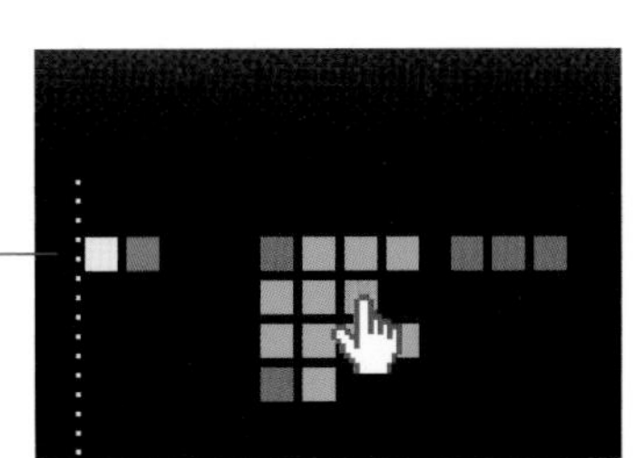

This personal "zine-on-a-floppy" is an effective promotional piece for ZeitGuys, an illustrated font created by Bob Aufuldish and Eric Donelan. The fuzzy aesthetic is accentuated by a palette exclusively comprising black, white, and gray tones. The user passes a cursor over a portion of the woolly gateway image, thereby activating goofy images, enigmatic messages, and crafty designs. This is a tasty little nut to crack.

SELECTED NOTES ZEITGUYS 

CLIENT / PUBLISHER *Zed: The Journal of The Center for Design Studies at Virginia Commonwealth University*

DESIGN Aufuldish & Warinner, San Anselmo, CA. Bob Aufuldish, art director, interface designer, programmer, graphic designer, ZeitGuys designer and audio; Mark Bartlett, writer; David Karam, programmer; Eric Donelan, ZeitGuys designer.

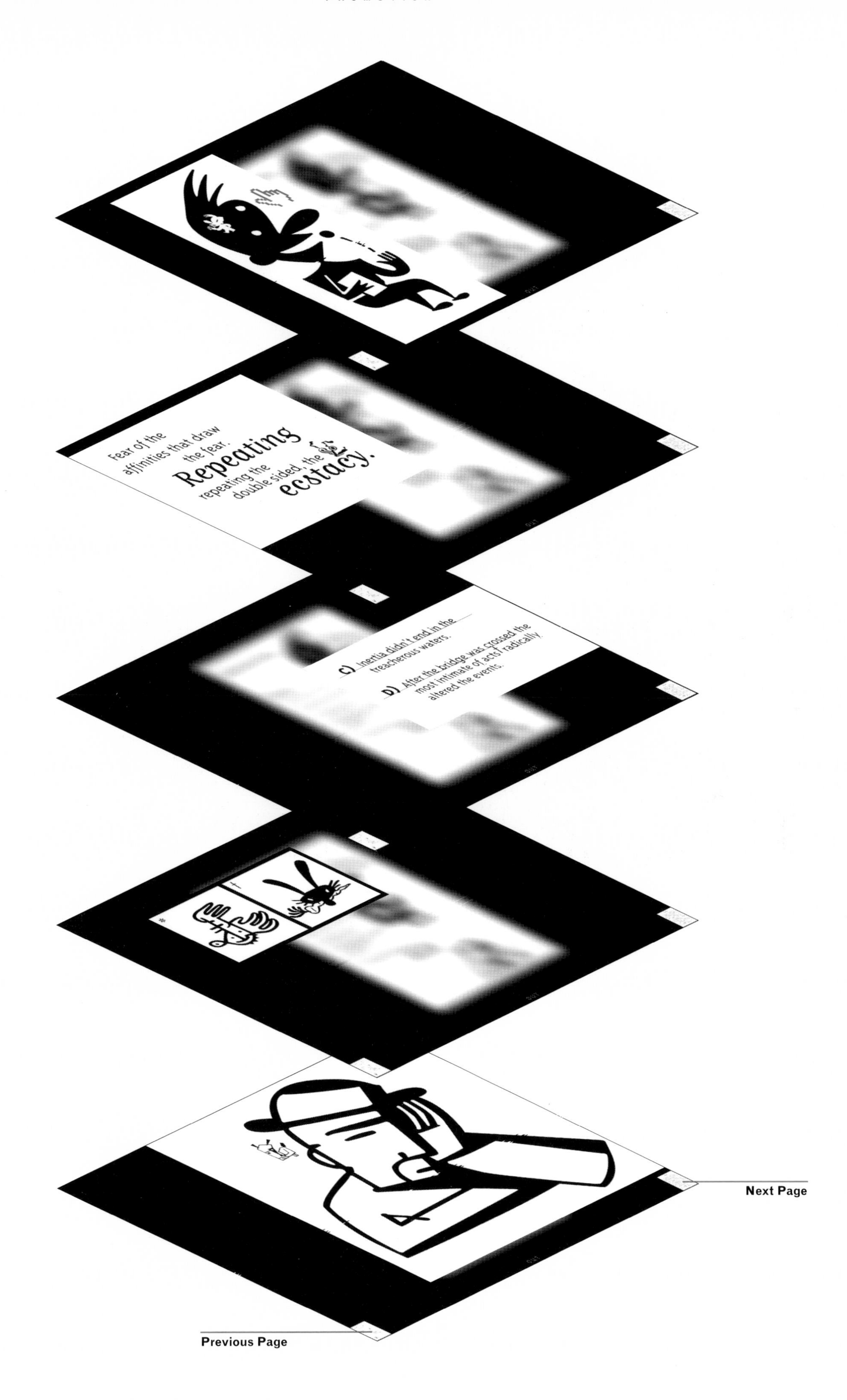
Fear of the
affinities that draw
the fear.
Repeating
repeating the
double sided, the
ecstacy.
C) Inertia didn't end in the
treacherous waters.
D) After the bridge was crossed the
most intimate of acts radically
altered the events.
Next Page
Previous Page

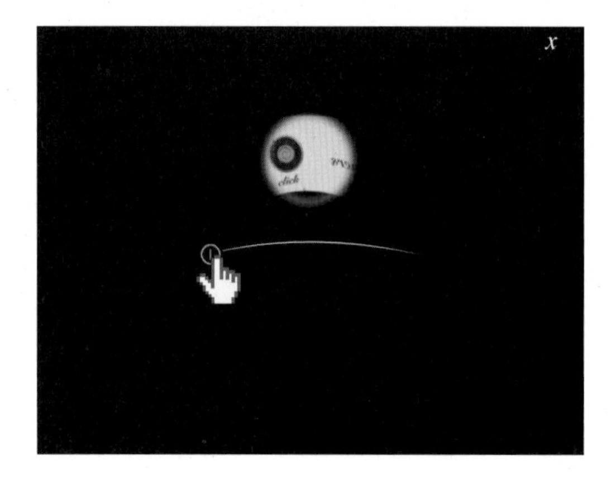

I | O 360 DEMO THING 

CLIENT / PUBLISHER i|o 360 Digital Design

DESIGN i|o 360 Digital Design, New York, NY, Arkadivsz Banasik, Nam Szeto, Dindo Magallanes and Gong Szeto.

x

IN THIS WORLD OF INFORMAT

Surf)ace +

the/medium.com

358

Like most of the creations from the folks at i|o360, this "demo thing" is part poetic prototype/part promotion piece. Downloadable from the company's Web site (http://www.io360.com), the 1.5-MB package allows viewers to drag the cursor across a spare white arc; this offers two clickable hotspots. One invites viewers to click on the word, "Do." Once clicked, the word becomes "UnDo." More clicks advances the word through "DoubleUnDo," "SuperDoubleUndo," and, finally, "Done." A smart nod to Mac users. The other hotspot yields a list of the firm's clients. ■ Once done with wordplay, the demo thing reveals a three-dimensional, navigational device. Slide up and down the Z-axis, and the halo of text atop this geometric staff revolves 360 degrees. Slide down the X- or Y-axis, and a pithy thought for the day scrolls past.

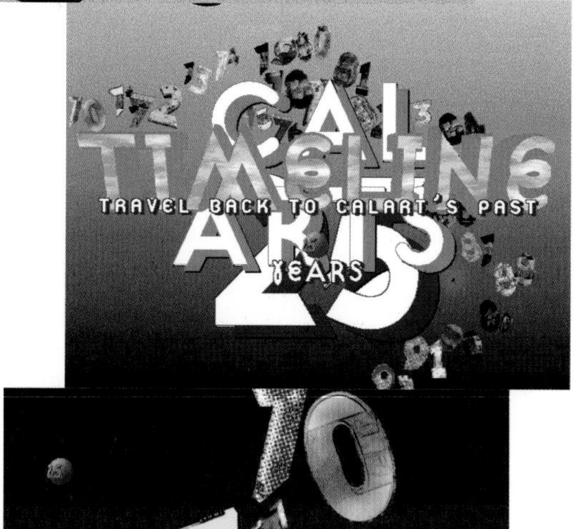
CAL
TIMELINE
TRAVEL BACK TO CALART'S PAST
ARTS
YEARS
25

GET BACK!
GET BACK!

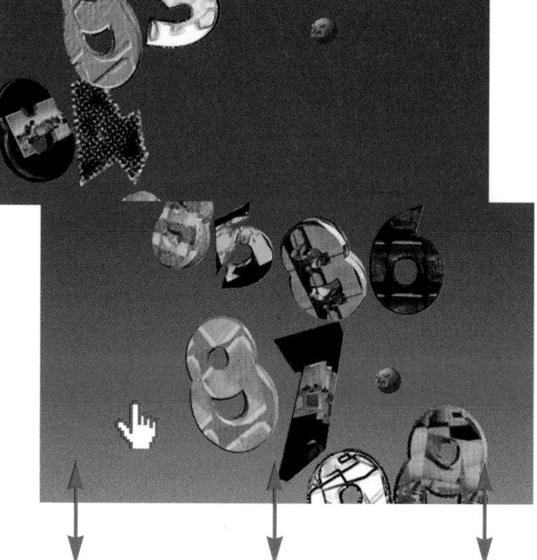

In celebration of its 25th anniversary, this private art school released a CD-ROM that is part art catalogue/ part historical documentary. Viewers can navigate in two ways: scrolling a deluge of years as they fall down the screen, or else scrolling horizontally through a panoramic mural of student and faculty artwork as well as embedded video clips of students discussing the relative merits of the school and art theory.

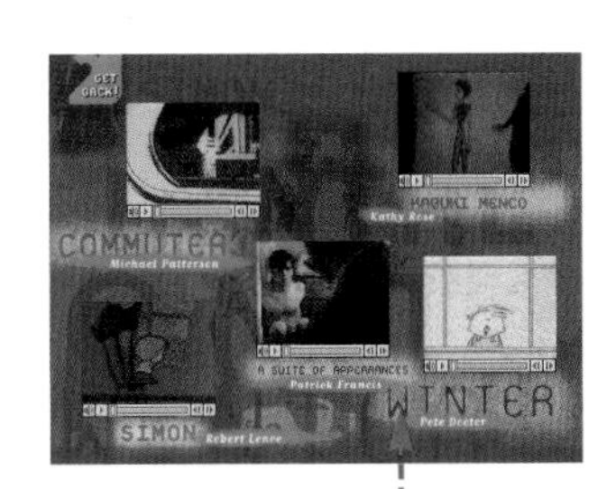

CALARTS 25TH ANNIVERSARY CD-ROM

CLIENT / PUBLISHER California Institute of the Arts

DESIGN Michael Worthington, art director, interface designer, programmer, graphic designer and sound editor; Deborah Littlejohn, interface designer and graphic designer.

ADOBE GRAPHICS SAMPLER

CLIENT / PUBLISHER Adobe Systems, Inc.

DESIGN Jive Turkey Productions, Mountain View, CA. Ethan Diamond, art director, interface designer, programmer; Jonathan Cadoni, art director, interface designer and graphic designer; Peter Chase, writer; Bill Dierssen, Glen Janssens, Paul Lundahl and Auguste Raffael, digital video directors; Andrew Diamond, music composer.

volume 1 A COLLECTIVE IMPROVISATION BY THE ADOBE ALL STAR QUARTET **volume 2** PREMIERE STRAIGHT AHEAD **volume 3** PAGEMAKER COOL **volume 4** PHOTOSHOP SOUL CLINIC **volume 5** ILLUSTRATOR JAM SESSION

the leonhardt group

THE LEONHARDT GROUP

CLIENT / PUBLISHER The Leonhardt Group

DESIGN The Leonhardt Group, Seattle, WA. Brad Wressell, programmer; Jeff Welsh, Jon Cannell and Susan Cummings, graphic designers; Karen Moskowitz, photographer; Philip Glass and Dan Dean, music composers. Bad Animals, audio.

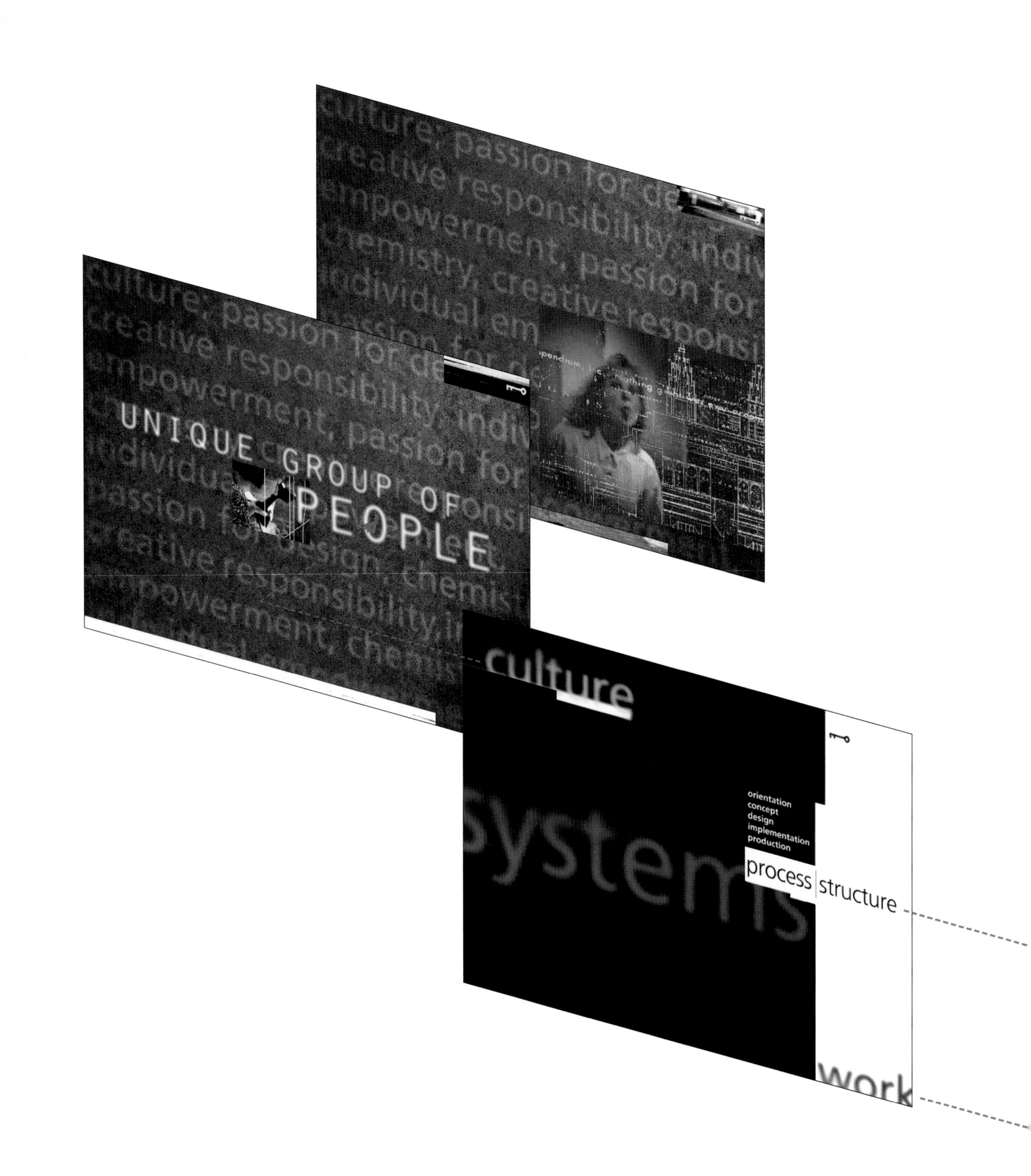
culture; passion for design
creative responsibility, individual
empowerment, passion for
chemistry, creative responsibility
UNIQUE GROUP OF
PEOPLE
culture
systems
orientation
concept
design
implementation
production
process
structure
work

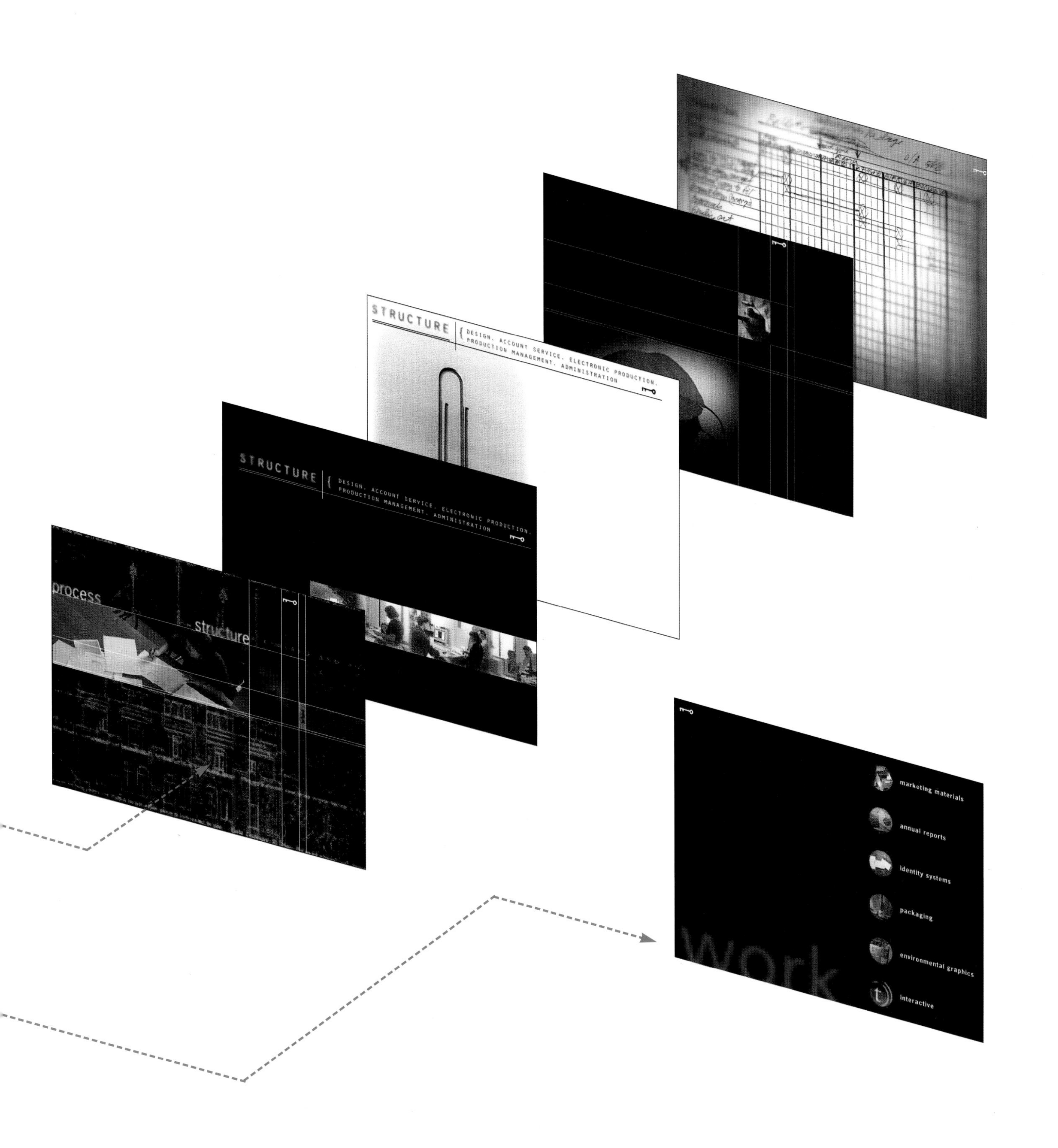
STRUCTURE
DESIGN, ACCOUNT SERVICE, ELECTRONIC PRODUCTION, PRODUCTION MANAGEMENT, ADMINISTRATION
STRUCTURE
DESIGN, ACCOUNT SERVICE, ELECTRONIC PRODUCTION, PRODUCTION MANAGEMENT, ADMINISTRATION
process
structure
marketing materials
annual reports
identity systems
packaging
environmental graphics
interactive
work

Toyota's disk-based brochure has a range of intriguing features, foremost of which are its navigational devices. A picker screen allows viewers to choose from among Toyota models. Once a selection has been made, users can explore options and add-ons by dragging a cursor (which transforms into the shape of the chosen model) beneath buttons that correspond to an option. Clicking the mouse sends users to a new screen where they may (for instance) try different paint jobs; selections change the color of the car accordingly. Another remarkable option is the "walkaround," which allows users to view vehicles from a number of perspectives by dragging the mouse over the image. To keep viewers oriented, an ever-present traffic light at the right edge of the screen offers users the option to stop a presentation (red light), pause (yellow), continue (green), and go back (arrow).

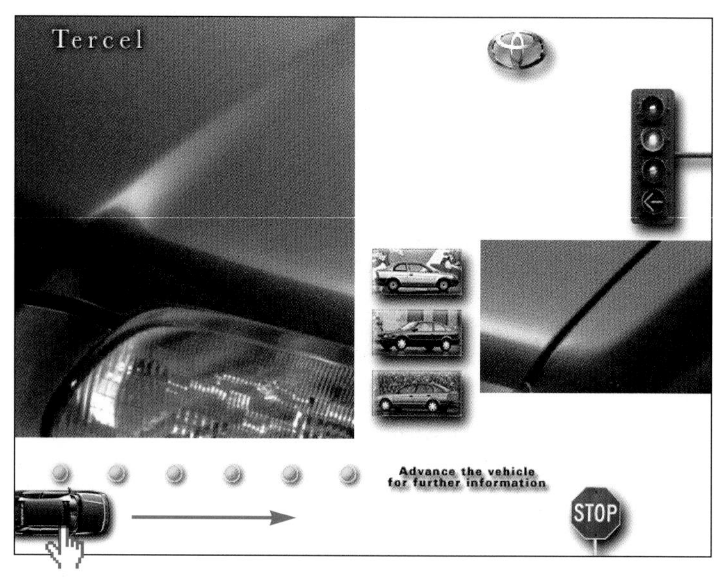

TOYOTA INTERACTIVE

CLIENT / PUBLISHER Toyota Motor Sales U.S.A. Inc.

DESIGN Saatchi & Saatchi, Torrance, CA. Dean VanEimeren, creative director; David Tanimoto, art director, interface designer and graphic designer; Greg Koorhan, interface designer; Allen McMullen, writer; Greg Koorhan and Scott Gustlin, programmers; Jeff Beverly, video director and audio; Brad Gill and Terry Medwig, graphic designers; Kevin Hulsey, illustrator; many, photographers. DNA Productions, Doug Lenier and Andy Howe, music composers. Exits to Elsewhere, new media production company.

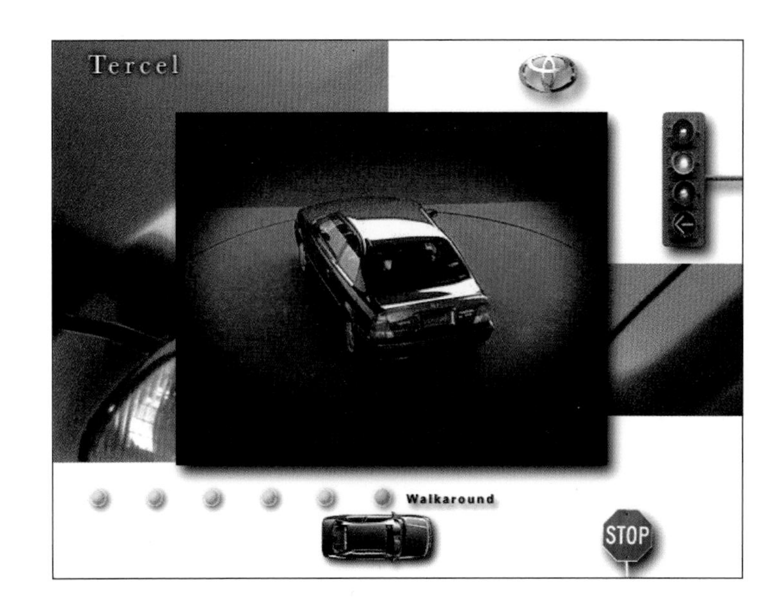
Tercel
Walkaround
STOP

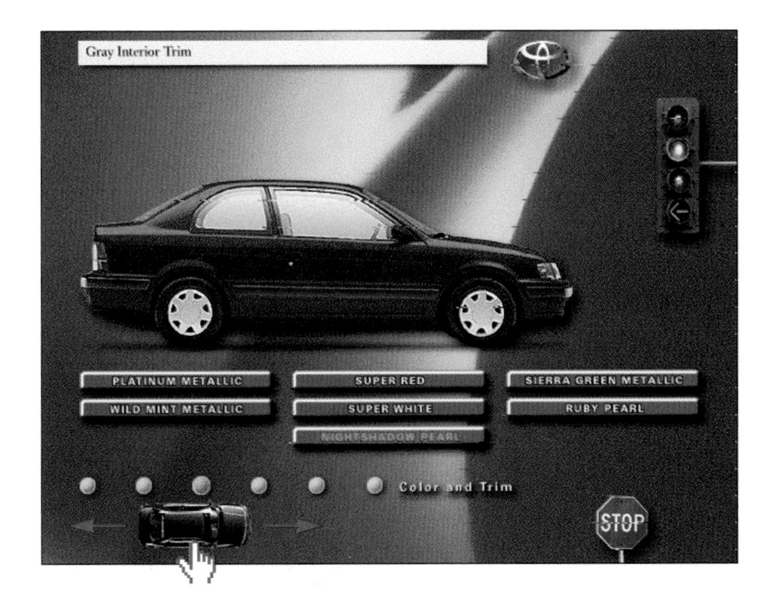
Gray Interior Trim
PLATINUM METALLIC
SUPER RED
SIERRA GREEN METALLIC
WILD MINT METALLIC
SUPER WHITE
RUBY PEARL
NIGHTSHADOW PEARL
Color and Trim
STOP

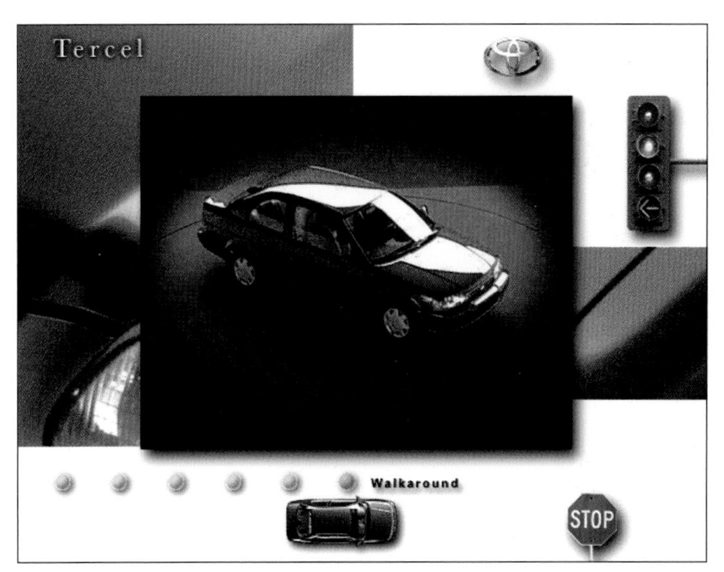
Tercel
Walkaround
STOP

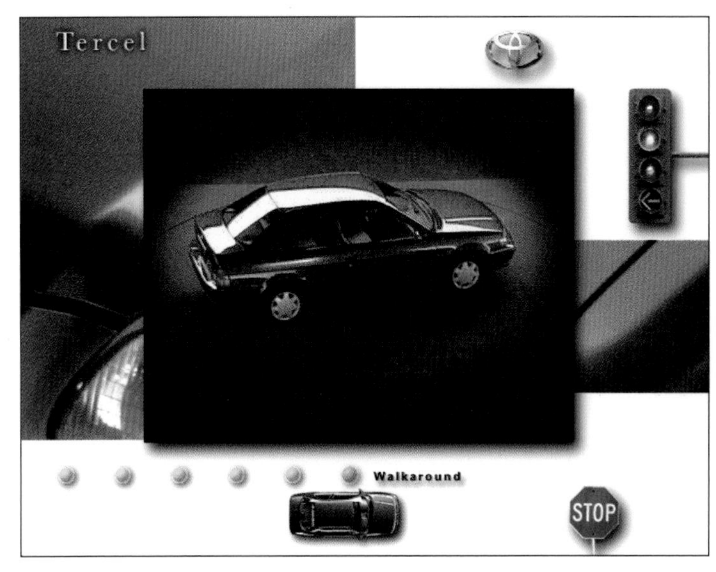
Tercel
Walkaround
STOP

"Got a light?"

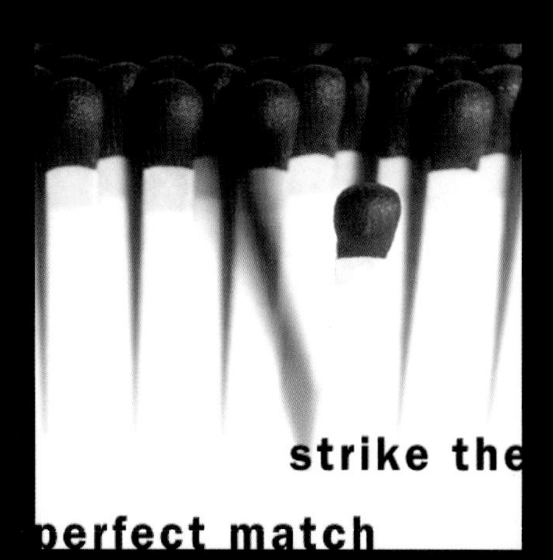

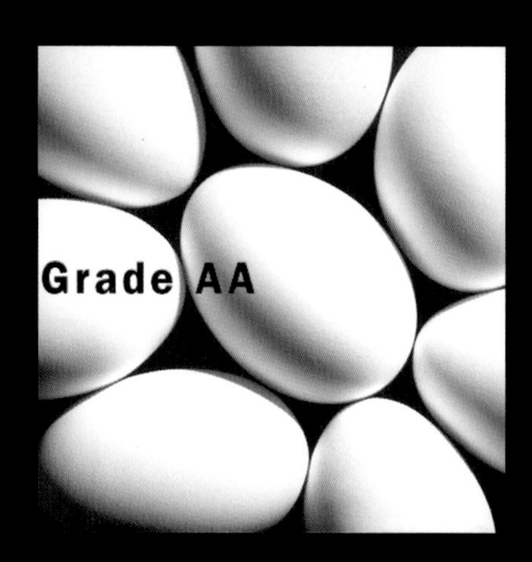

J.W. Fry

he makes it

over easy.

Elegant and playful, this self-promotion for the photographer J.W. Fry blends attractive images with clever copy. The opening sequence begins with the sound of a match igniting; photographic images of matches, stovetop burners, and flames dissolved into one another. The closing sequence plays with images—and a few brief words on the subject—of chicken eggs, and winds up with an animated photograph of a photograph of an egg "frying" in a skillet, complete with sizzle. Sandwiched between these sequences are a couple of dozen examples of Fry's fine photographic work.

J.W. FRY PHOTOGRAPHY 

CLIENT / PUBLISHER J.W. Fry Photography

DESIGN Yamamoto Moss, Minneapolis, MN. Jeff Schweigert, art director, interface designer and graphic designer; Chris Cortilet, art director and graphic designer; Scott Franson, interface designer and programmer; Amie Valentine, writer; Karen Bleadon, programmer; J.W. Fry, photographer.

NucleusOne™

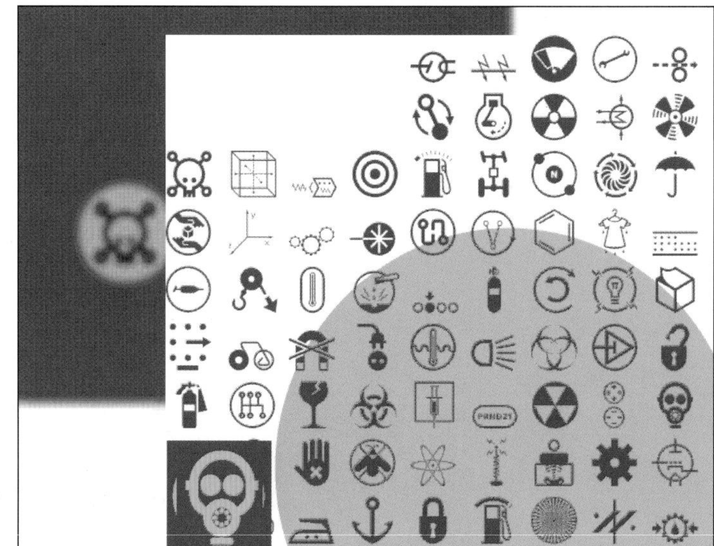
PRND21

This interactive guide to the NucleusOne foundry of picture fonts is a blast to dabble around in. The navigation prompts of this demo are driven by visual icons that wink and blink at viewers. When the interface is clicked, characters are sent flipping, twirling, spinning, and gyrating. Users may then dig deeper to find an array of 73 industrial symbols and icons, all gymnastic in their own right.

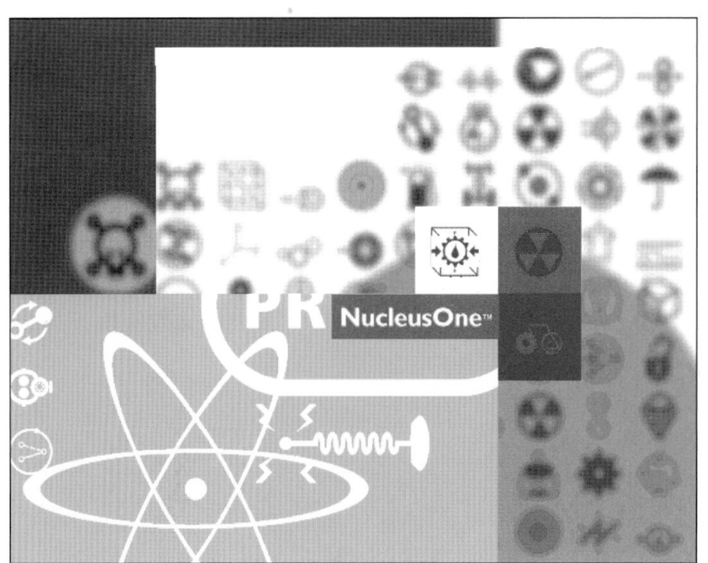

NUCLEUSONE FONT GUIDE

CLIENT / PUBLISHER NucleusOne

DESIGN NucleusOne, Burlingame CA. Joshua Distler, creative director.

This clean and clever chestnut fits on a floppy and wastes no time getting to the point. Viewers move the cursor over one of the four objects to enliven them: snowy static falls across the television screen, the eye blinks and spins, the circle within the square falls apart and reconstructs, the egg within the diamond revolves. Clicking on any of these objects sends users into areas of this interactive portfolio of May & Company's design and promotion work. The egg within the diamond, for instance, yields a highly compressed video of a 30-second television spot.

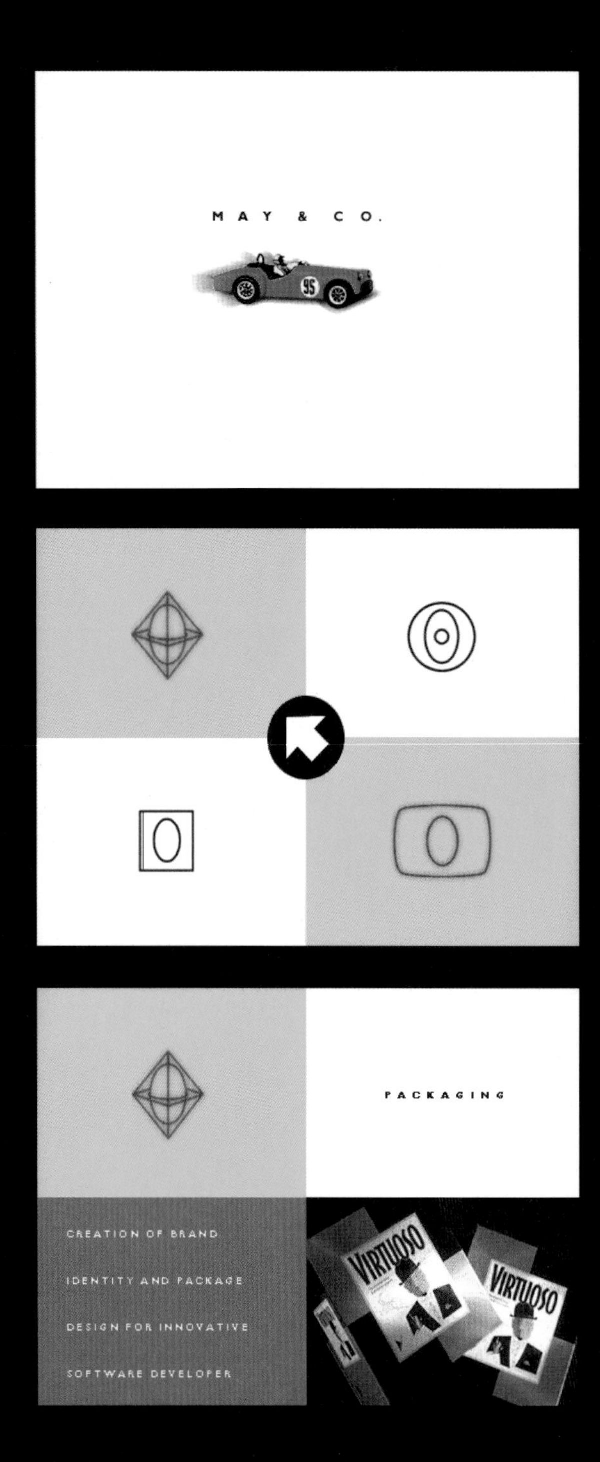

MAY & COMPANY PORTFOLIO

CLIENT/PUBLISHER May & Co.

DESIGN May & Co., Dallas, TX. Douglas May, art director, interface designer and graphic designer; Heather Ezell, interface designer, graphic designer, illustrator and animator; David Fowler, writer; David Hannah, programmer, audio and sound editor; Gordon Willis Jr., video director; Dick Patrick, photographer; Bruce Falconer,

NEW MEDIA

TITLES

The sheer diversity of New Media titles is staggering. Here is a dramatically morphing collage of sight and sound, over there is a compelling journey to a finely wrought ancient city, clever exercises teach us how to see, a muck-raking documentary describes the dawn of the Atomic Age, a trippy trip passes through a ghostly maze, the construction and operation of a wooden warship is described in detail, and an unparalleled collection of art is opened up for an intimate tour, just to name a few. ■ Whatever their content, these titles educate and entertain. So dig deep. While the visual element of these projects was typically at the heart of the designers' intentions, these projects also deserve distinction for their underlying interactive and navigational structures—the nervous system and the blood flow of these creations.

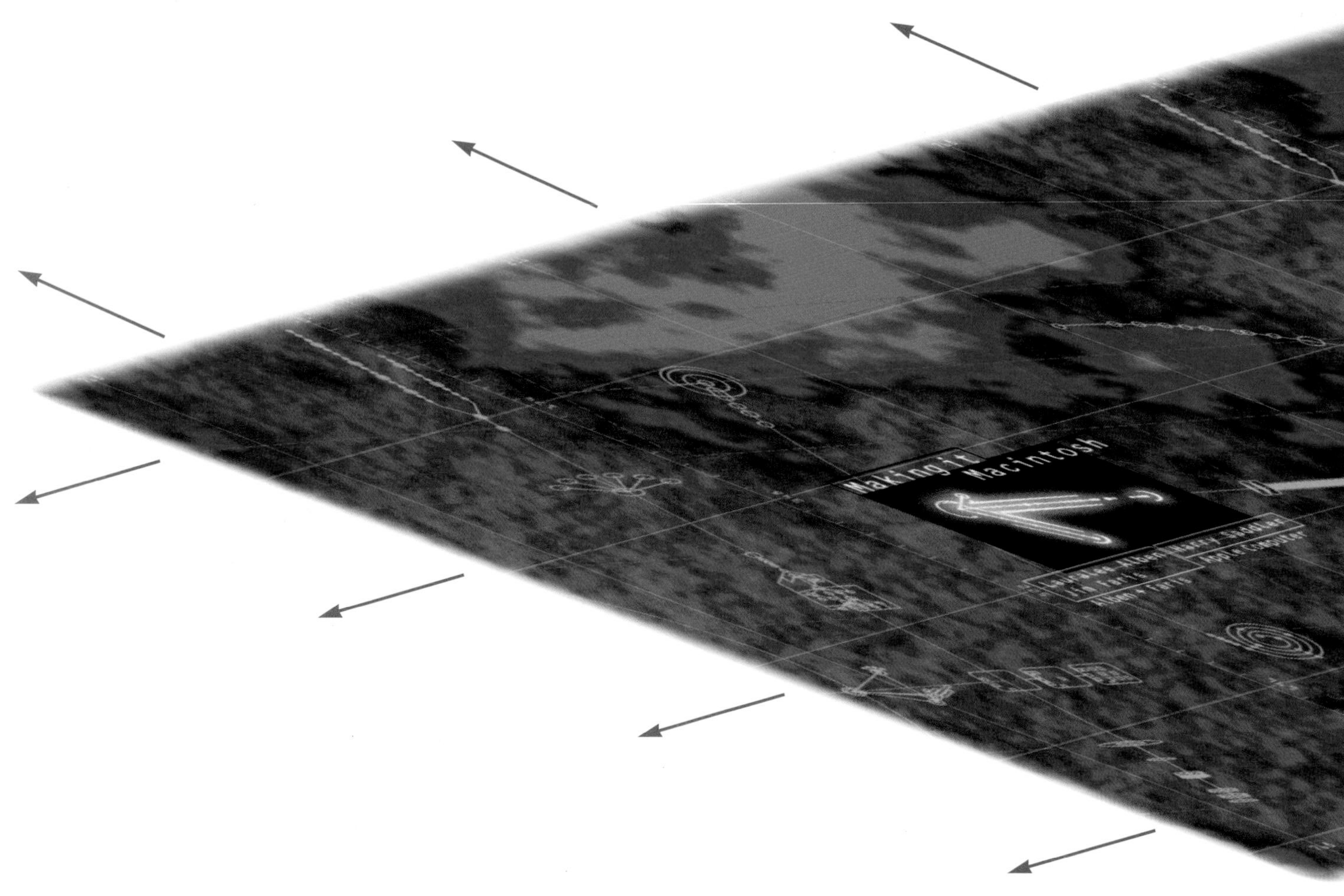

INTERACT—ACD JOURNAL

CLIENT / PUBLISHER American Center for Design

DESIGN IDEO, San Francisco, CA. Peter Spreenberg, art director; Peter Spreenberg, interface designer; Peter Spreenberg, programming; Peter Spreenberg, graphic designer; Gordon Kurtenbach, music composer; IDEO, new media production company.

This interactive CD design journal is the sister of the version published on paper. Among the remarkable elements of *Interact—ACD Journal* is the navigation method: moving the cursor to the far edge of the screen (up or down/right or left/diagonal) sends the journal scrolling in a virtual loop; users can fail to realize this is happening until they begin recognizing objects they have seen before. The cursor activates hot spots, which bring various design projects to the fore: experimental animations, slideshows, interactive exercises, and musings on the art and craft of design.

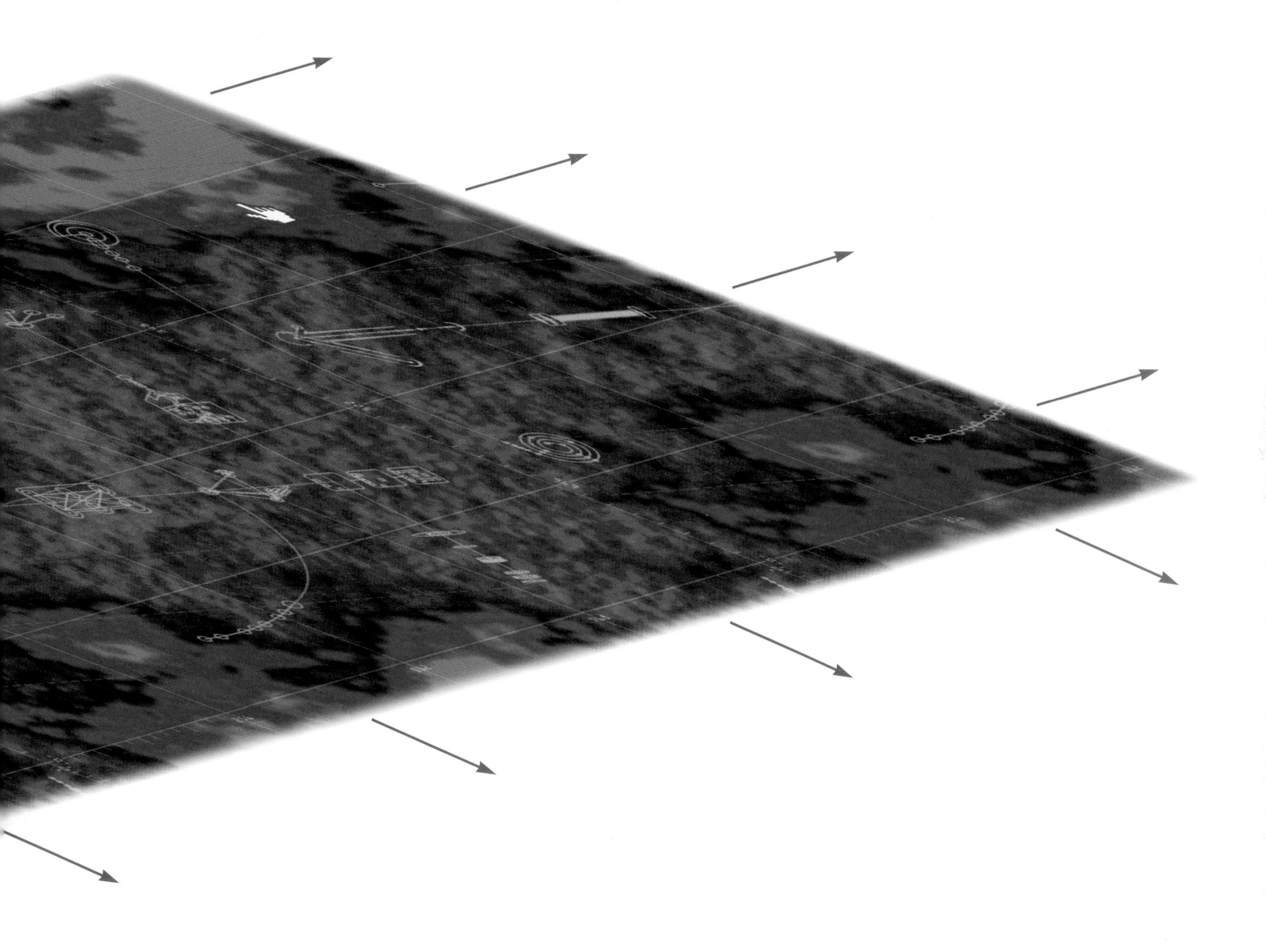

Billed as the "greatest private collection of impressionist and post-impressionist paintings," the Barnes Collection is indeed impressive. *A Passion for Art* leads viewers on a tour of the collection assembled around the turn of the century by the Pennsylvanian industrialist, philanthropist, and patron of the arts, Dr. Albert Barnes. The chief interface is a floor plan of a virtual museum, which invites viewers to click on one of 22 galleries to view paintings.

A PASSION FOR ART

CLIENT / PUBLISHER Corbis Publishing

DESIGN Corbis Publishing, Bellevue, WA. Curtis G. Wong, creative director and producer; Pei-Lin Nee, interface designer and art director; Karyn Esielonis, Mary Tavener Holmes, Chiyo Ishikawa, Carol Ivory, Suzanne Kotz, Susan L'Engle, Heather McPherson, Hal Opperman, Christopher Riopelle, Peter Selz, Martha Smith, Janis Tomlinson and Carol Troyen, writers; James C. Gallant, developer; Pei-Lin Nee and Cecil Juanarena, graphic designers; Dennis Brack, Nicholas King, Edward Owen, Tess Steinkolk and Gradon Wood, photographers; Ella Brackett, Eileen H. Monti and Curtis Wong, sound editors; Patrick O'Donnell and Bill Radcliffe, additional programmers; Lorna Price, editor; Lisa Anderson, segment editor; Ted Evans and Vince Peddle, segment production; Eileen H. Monti, assistant producer; Eileen H. Monti, Macintosh Version Producer; Jennifer Tobin, Macintosh Version Developer.

PAINTINGS
Paul Gauguin 1848-1903
Haere pape, Inv. #109
1892, oil on canvas, 36 x 26 1/2 in.
About This Painting
Portfolios
Biographies
Paintings

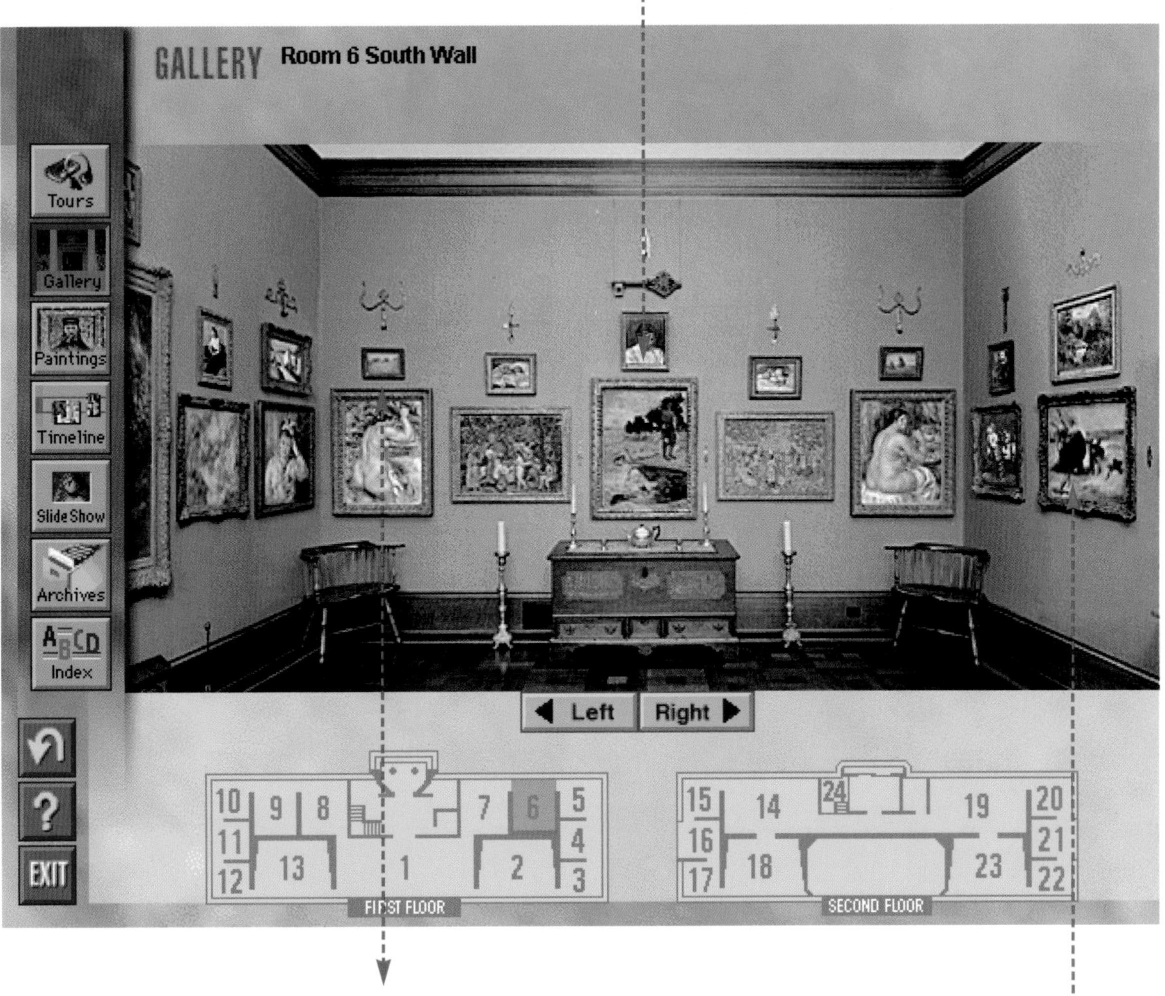
GALLERY
Room 6 South Wall
Tours
Gallery
Paintings
Timeline
Slide Show
Archives
Index
EXIT
Left
Right
FIRST FLOOR
SECOND FLOOR

PAINTINGS
Georges Seurat 1859-91
Harbor of Grandcamp, Inv. #1185
1885, oil on wood panel
About This Painting
Portfolios
Biographies
Paintings

PAINTINGS
Edouard Manet 1832-83
Tarring the Boat, Inv. #166
1873, oil on canvas, 19 1/4 x 23 5/8 in.
About This Painting
Portfolios
Biographies
Paintings

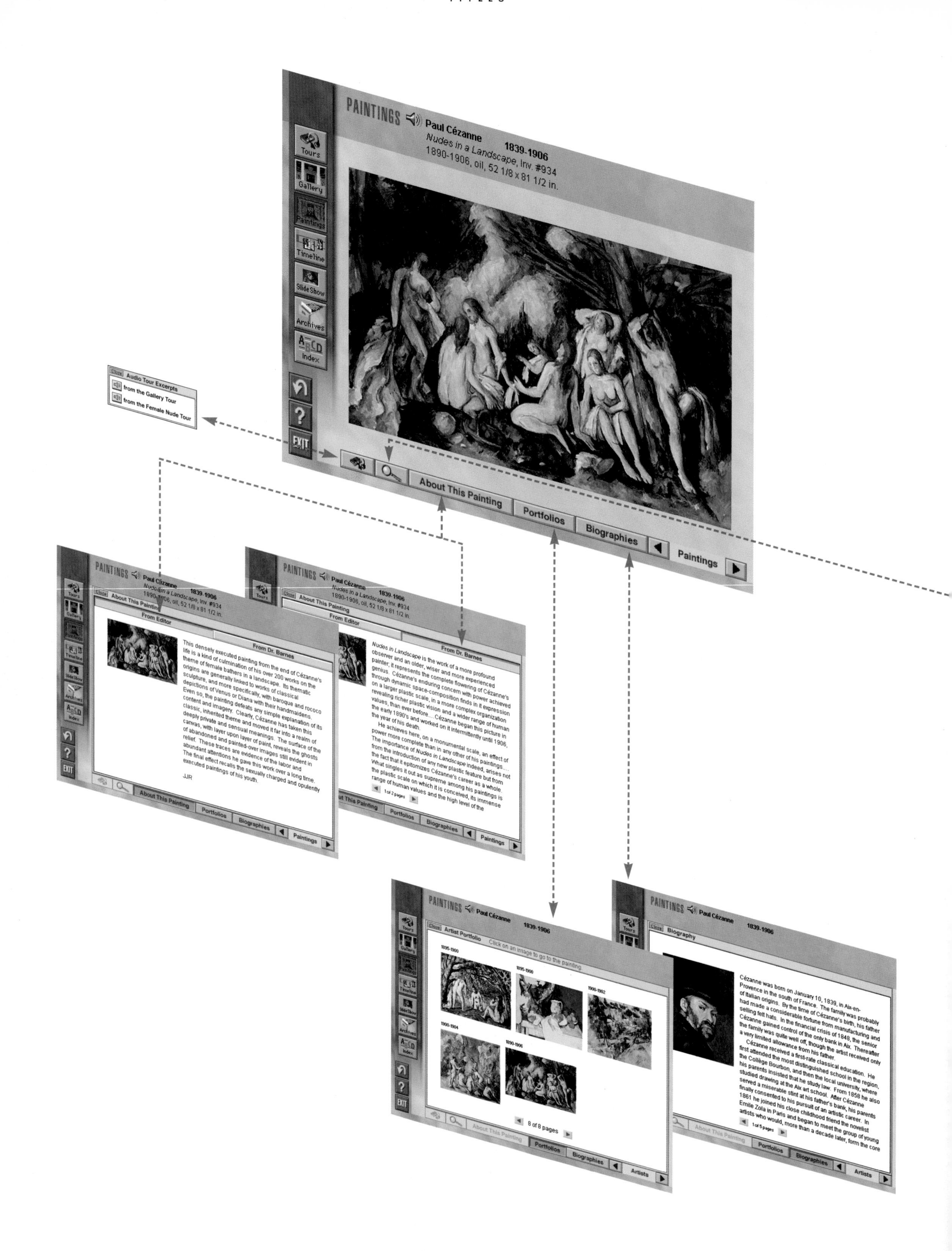
PAINTINGS
Paul Cézanne
1839-1906
Nudes in a Landscape, Inv. #934
1890-1906, oil, 52 1/8 x 81 1/2 in.
Tours
Gallery
Paintings
Timeline
Slide Show
Archives
Index
EXIT
About This Painting
Portfolios
Biographies
Paintings
Audio Tour Excerpts
from the Gallery Tour
from the Female Nude Tour
From Editor
From Dr. Barnes
Artist Portfolio
Click on an image to go to the painting
8 of 8 pages
Biography
Artists

Paintings are rendered in stunning detail: as the screen fills with a reproduction of Cezanne's *Nudes in a Landscape* viewers may choose to zoom in on a particular portion of the painting and scroll horizontally or vertically to scrutinize fine points; a "super zoom" feature is a nice touch, bringing the texture of the paintings to life, revealing even the direction and shape of brush strokes. Viewers may read commentary on the painters and their other work, and then cobble together their own slide show with a handy built-in function.

GALLERY Room 2 North Wall
Tours
Gallery
Paintings
Timeline
Slide Show
Archives
Index
EXIT
Left
Right
FIRST FLOOR
SECOND FLOOR

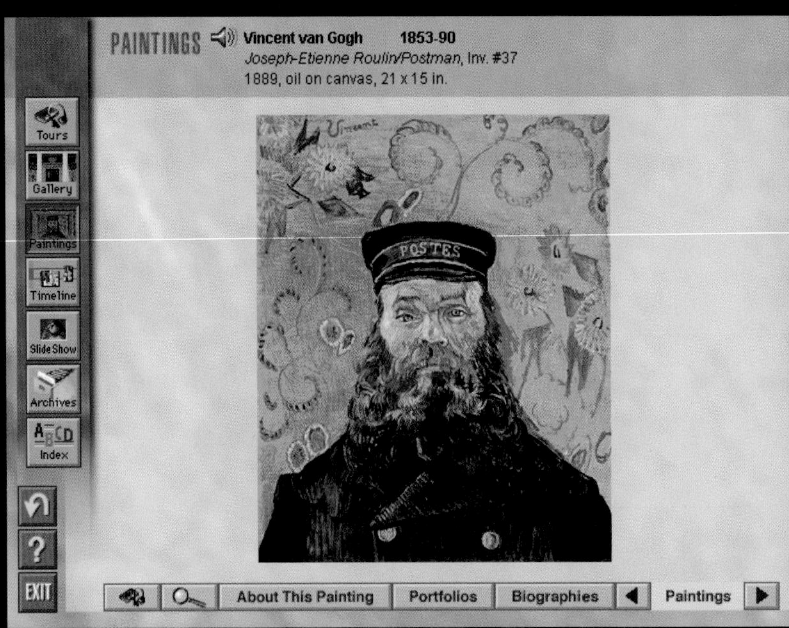
PAINTINGS
Vincent van Gogh 1853-90
Joseph-Etienne Roulin/Postman, Inv. #37
1889, oil on canvas, 21 x 15 in.
POSTES
Tours
Gallery
Paintings
Timeline
Slide Show
Archives
Index
EXIT
About This Painting
Portfolios
Biographies
Paintings

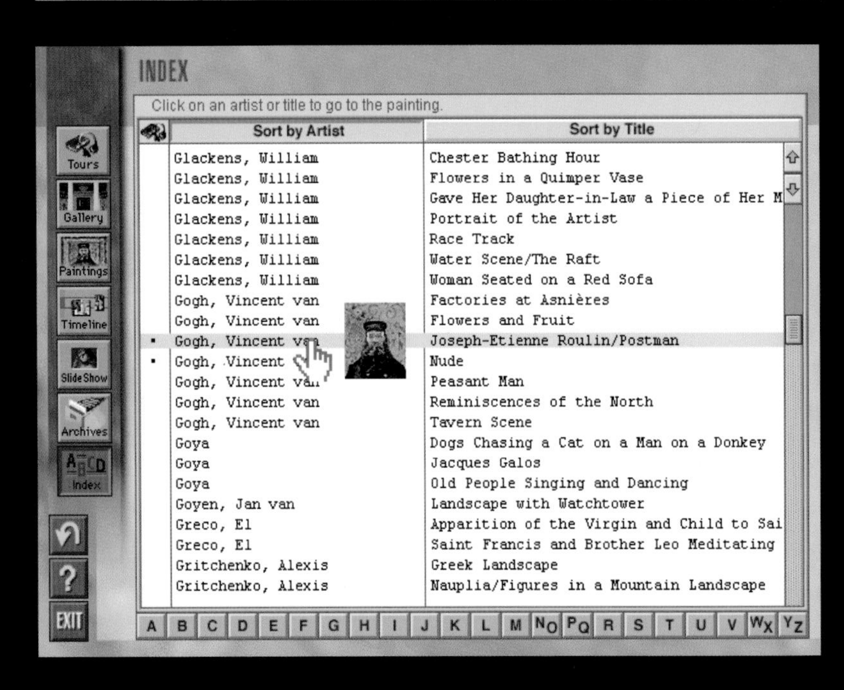
INDEX
Click on an artist or title to go to the painting.
Sort by Artist
Sort by Title
Glackens, William Chester Bathing Hour
Glackens, William Flowers in a Quimper Vase
Glackens, William Gave Her Daughter-in-Law a Piece of Her M
Glackens, William Portrait of the Artist
Glackens, William Race Track
Glackens, William Water Scene/The Raft
Glackens, William Woman Seated on a Red Sofa
Gogh, Vincent van Factories at Asnières
Gogh, Vincent van Flowers and Fruit
Gogh, Vincent van Joseph-Etienne Roulin/Postman
Nude
Peasant Man
Gogh, Vincent van Reminiscences of the North
Gogh, Vincent van Tavern Scene
Goya Dogs Chasing a Cat on a Man on a Donkey
Goya Jacques Galos
Goya Old People Singing and Dancing
Goyen, Jan van Landscape with Watchtower
Greco, El Apparition of the Virgin and Child to Sai
Greco, El Saint Francis and Brother Leo Meditating
Gritchenko, Alexis Greek Landscape
Gritchenko, Alexis Nauplia/Figures in a Mountain Landscape
Tours
Gallery
Paintings
Timeline
Slide Show
Archives
Index
EXIT
A B C D E F G H I J K L M NO PQ R S T U V WX YZ

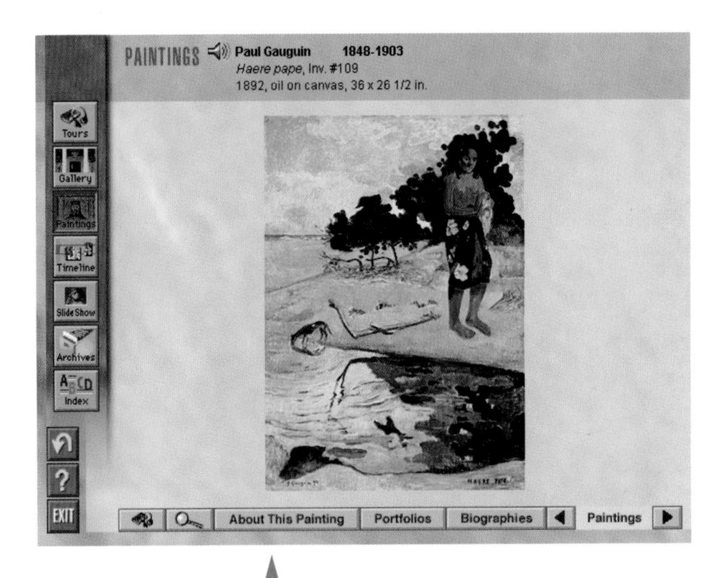

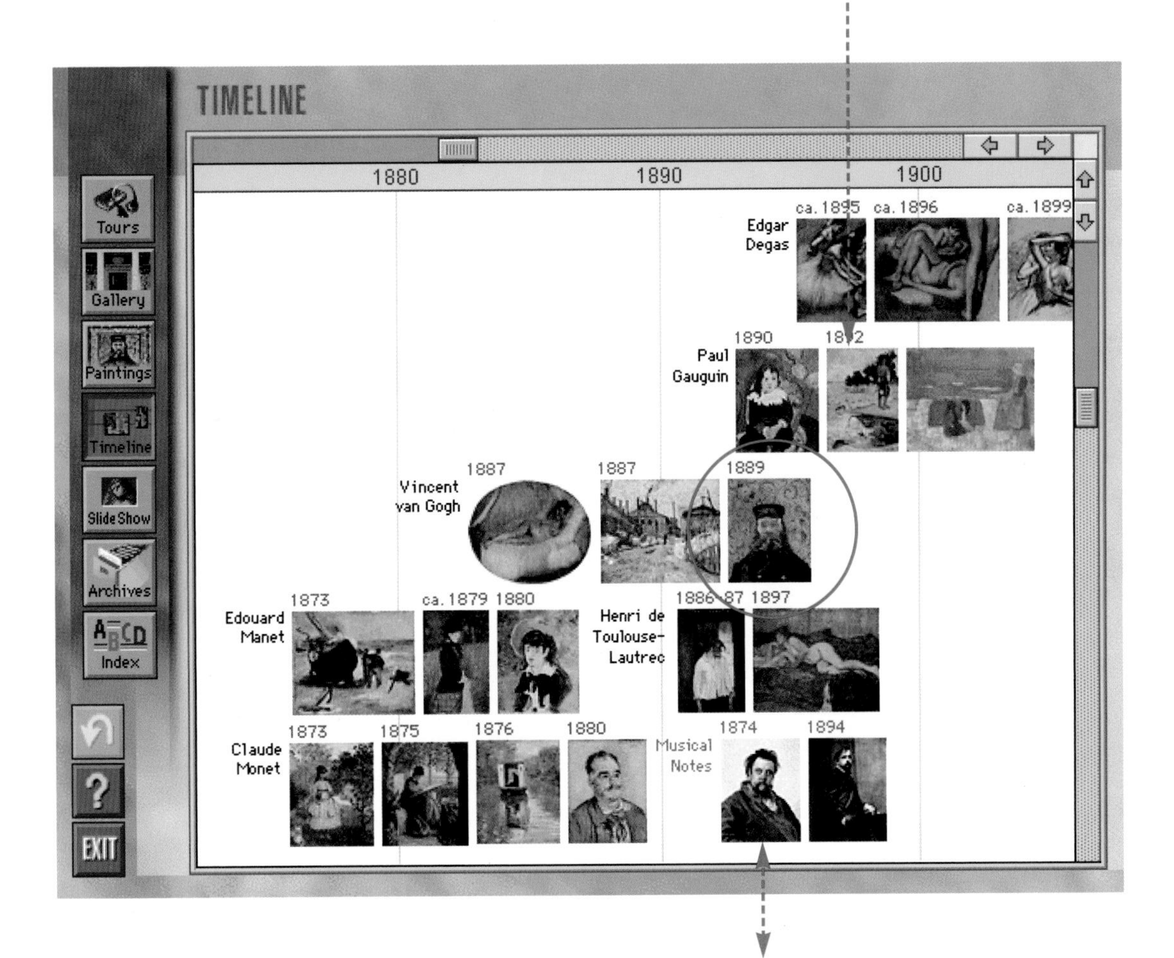

Viewers can take advantage of a visually rich timeline which places each painting and artist within the context of history to document artistic developments. An alphabetical/visual index is included as the cursor scrolls, a miniaturization of each painting pops up to the side of the titles; clicking on this image will fill the screen with an enlarged rendering of the painting.

Close **1874: *Pictures at an Exhibition* by Mussorgsky**

In the 1874 piano composition *Pictures at an Exhibition*, Russian composer Modest Mussorgsky attempted to musically represent an exhibition of 10 paintings by deceased Russian artist Victor Hartmann; this same work was later orchestrated by Ravel. An early musical talent, Mussorgsky spent several years in the army before developing his progressive, experimental style. Mussorgsky, one of the "Mighty handful" of prominent Russian composers, has enjoyed renewed popularity in the 20th century.

The Day After Trinity is an immense storehouse of information about the building of the first atomic bomb and how the life of its architect, Robert Oppenheimer, came unraveled. The beauty of this title is how elegantly its elements are interwoven, and the ease with which users can gain access to this repository. ■ The disk is brimming with valuable material: it includes the complete 88-minute documentary film of the same name (in compressed video); real-time commentary delivered by the film's director, a documentary scholar, and a cultural critic; declassified files of the Manhattan Project from the FBI and the scientific community; a gallery of nearly 100 photographs, complete working transcripts and biographical notes on everyone who appears in the film; and a pop-up glossary of technical terms. ■ Viewers can easily pause, reverse, or advance the video (the frame of which can be expanded to 13 inches). They can view supplementary documents and film commentary directly pertinent to the portion of the film they are watching by clicking on the ever present control bars that demurely hug the bottom and right margins of the frame. Choosing a picture from the gallery of still photographs launches viewers into areas of the film, commentary, or supplemental information. Viewers can search for information with a built-in "Find" function, as well as make annotations at any time in a virtual notebook.

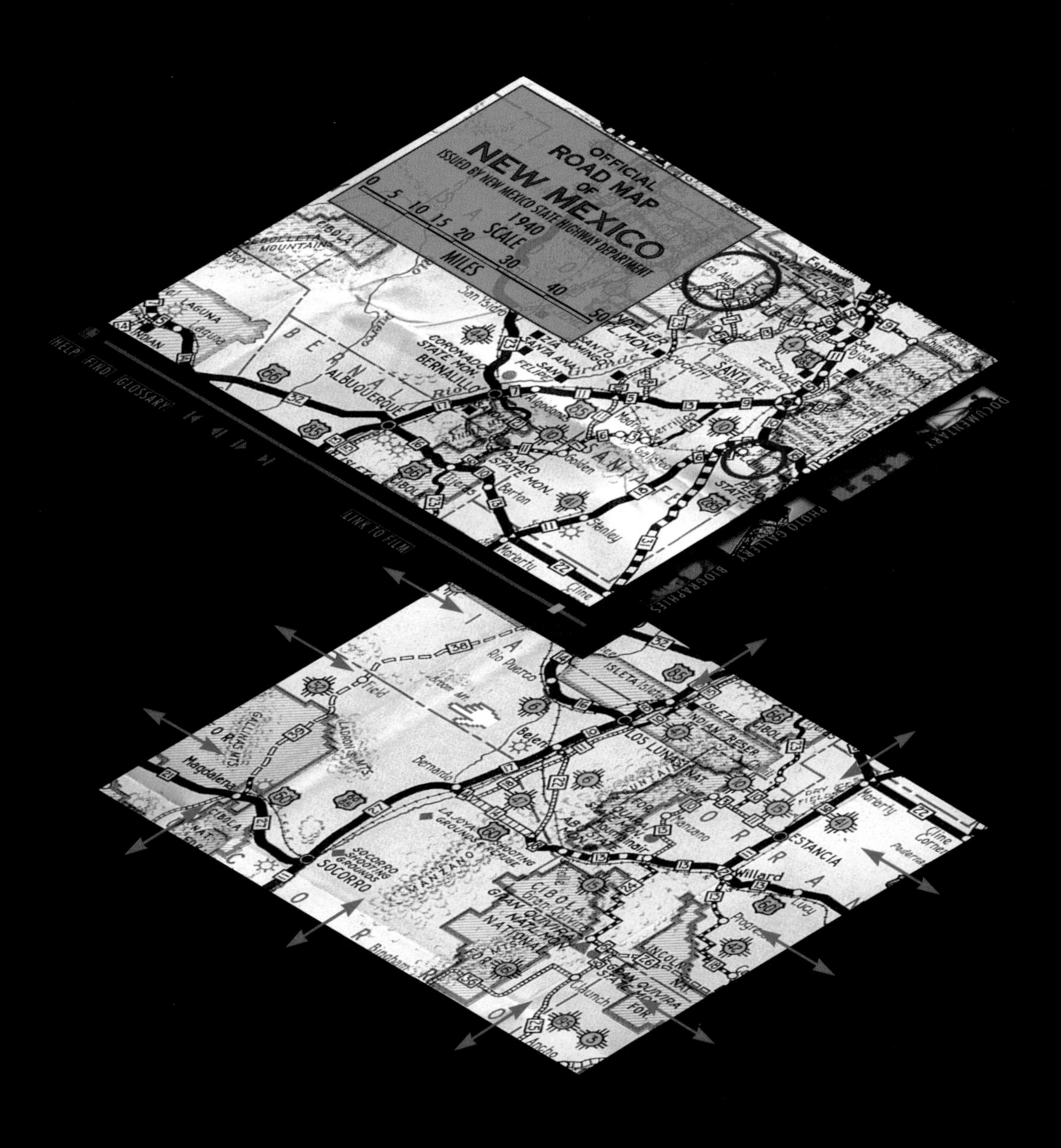

THE DAY AFTER TRINITY

CLIENT/PUBLISHER The Voyager Company

DESIGN The Voyager Company, New York, NY. Jane Gorrell, creative director; Jane Gorrell, Paul Schrynemakers and Colin Holgate, interface designers; Colin Holgate, progammer; Paul Schrynemakers, graphic designer; Paul Supkof, sound editor; Jackie Kain, series director/producer; Jon Else, director of original film.

THE MULTIMEDIA CARTOON STUDIO 

CLIENT / PUBLISHER Vanguard Media

DESIGN Vanguard Media, New York, NY. Byron Preiss, executive producer; Tim Nolan, producer; Michael Pinto, director; Brian Cirulnick, associate director; Rich Sanders and Ikar Kozak, programming; Michael Pinto, interface and graphic design. The Cartoon Bank, cartoon content. Byron Preiss Multimedia Company, publisher.

This easy-to-use productivity application allows users to create their own cartoons from a palette of stock character types, facial expressions, body positions, props, scenes, etc. The cartoonists themselves decide how the characters will interact, and then write original copy for the speech and thought balloons. Fun, flexible, and quick, *Cartoon Studio* is designed for the children's software market, though its colorful interface has been spotted on the computer monitors of grown men and women with day jobs as well.

Instead of a bedlam of cybernetic marvels, *Robert Mapplethorpe—An Overview* simply offers viewers an astonishing catalogue of one of the century's great artists, all at the click of a mouse. ■ This fully curated desk-top exhibit leads the viewer over the late photographer's career through gateways—calla lillies or black male nudes, let's say—allowing viewers to study photographs, read commentary or biographic information, or watch compressed videos of Mapplethorpe's colleagues. In the end, technical alchemy cannot always win the day; the smart money will always be on a grand vision and a fierce spirit.

ROBERT MAPPLETHORPE—AN OVERVIEW

CLIENT/PUBLISHER Digital Collections, Inc.

DESIGN Digital Collections, Inc., Alameda, CA. Eric Kotila, art director; Eric Kotila and Donald Farnsworth, interface designer; Eric Kotila, writer; Donald Farnsworth, programming; Robb Lazarus and Jay Johnson, digital video director; Eric Kotila and Donald Farnsworth, graphic designers; Robert Mapplethorpe, photographer; Donald Farnsworth, Mike Bemesderfer, Erik Ian Walker and Bob Lindner, audio; Erik Ian Walker, music composer; Erik Ian Walker, Donald Farnsworth and Mike Bemesderfer, sound editors; Mac McCall, Peter Cury, Eric Kotila, Jonas Marson, Susanna Richards, Jacline Deridder, Frances Killam, Endoree Luke, Sally Hamaji, Marilyn da Silva, Stephane Krieshok, Margitta Dietrick and Alex Henning, imaging; Mac McCall and Peter Cury, production assistance. Nigel Finch BBC/Arena Productions, video director. Digital Collections, Inc., new media production company. In association with The Estate of Robert Mapplethorpe.

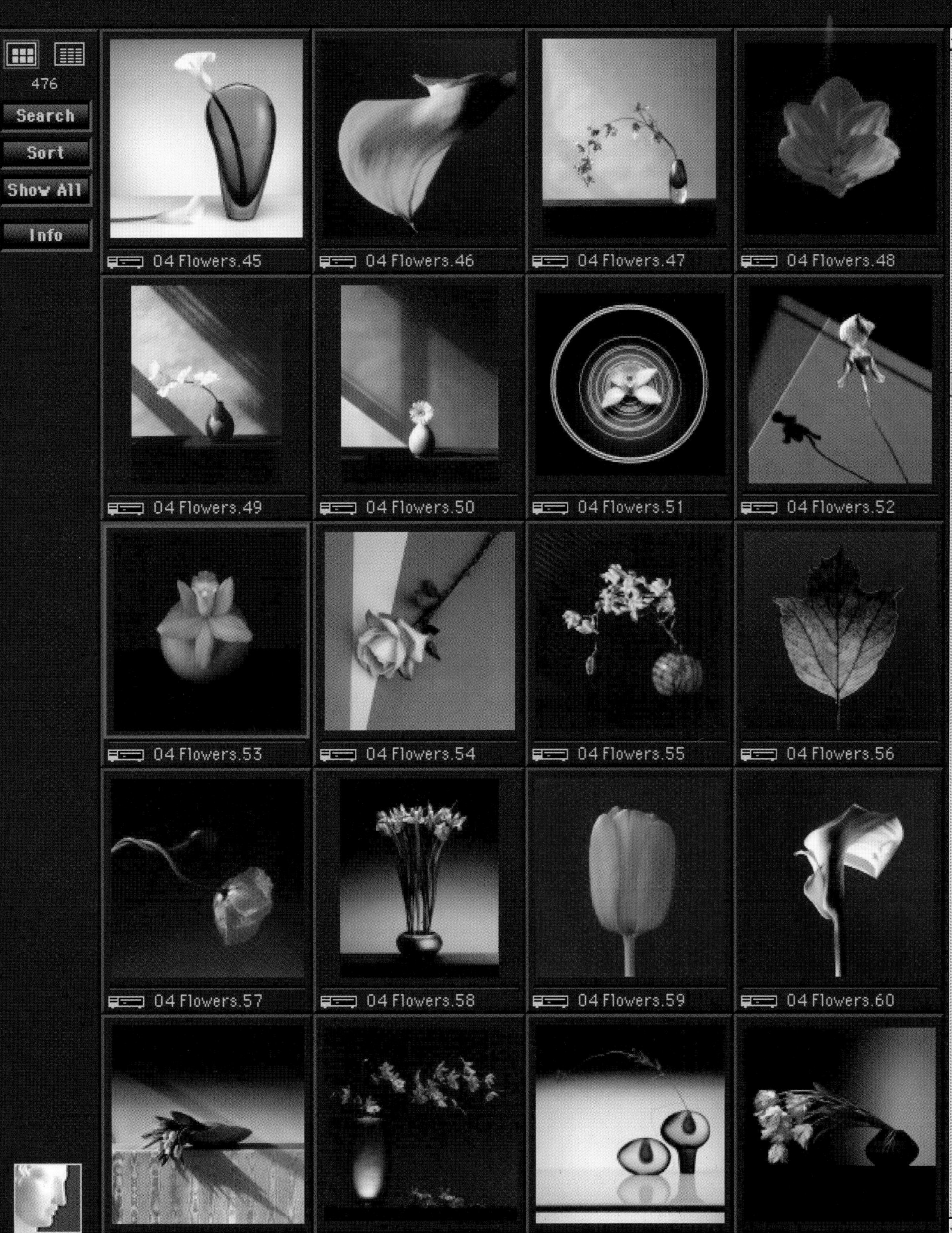
ImageAXS-CD™: Photo Gallery
476
Search
Sort
Show All
Info
04 Flowers.45
04 Flowers.46
04 Flowers.47
04 Flowers.48
04 Flowers.49
04 Flowers.50
04 Flowers.51
04 Flowers.52
04 Flowers.53
04 Flowers.54
04 Flowers.55
04 Flowers.56
04 Flowers.57
04 Flowers.58
04 Flowers.59
04 Flowers.60
04 Flowers.61
04 Flowers.62
04 Flowers.63
04 Flowers.64
Multimedia

Robert Mapplethorpe

hat's why I
alking about
uch because
if you say too
loose too
ne mystery."

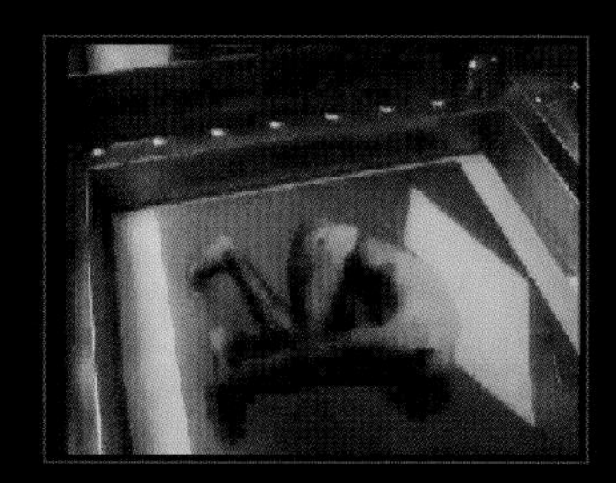

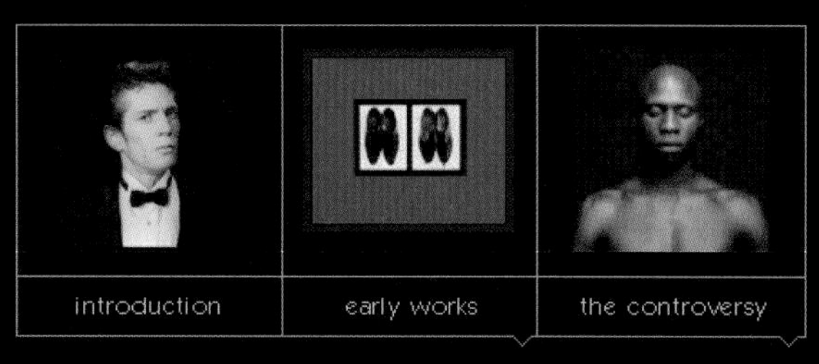

table of contents

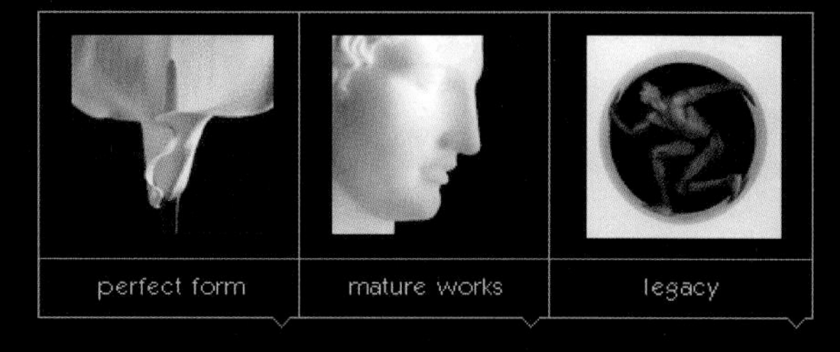

pplethorpe's
n art of per-
izing exquis-
nts and
ting them

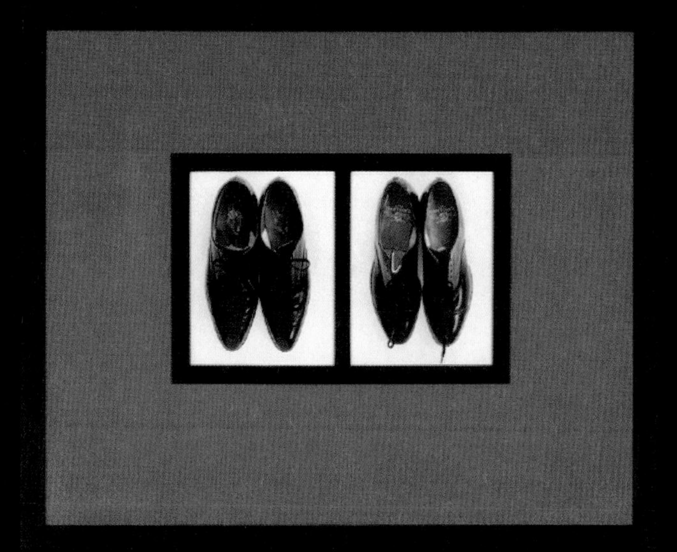

"A reluctant photographer, Robert Mapplethorpe first shot Polaroids for his collage material."

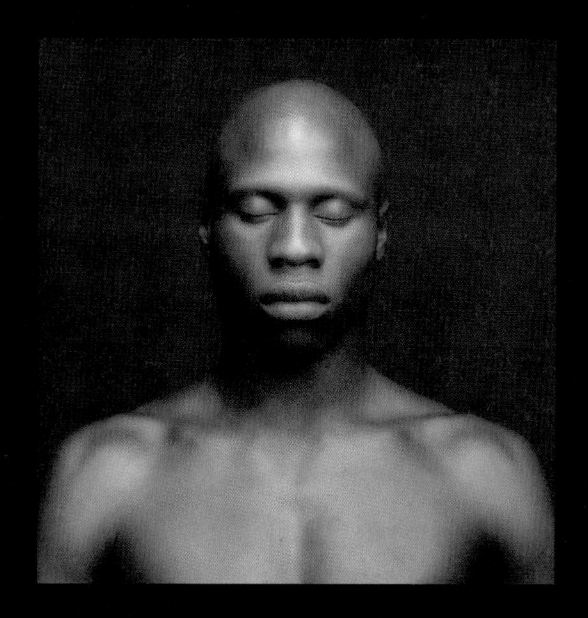

"Almost singlehandedly Robert Mapplethorpe brought high art images of the African American male to the top the public conciousness"

"His flowers are photographs at the peak, hinting at the fragility that underlies perfection."

ORCHID
1987

GADGET

CLIENT / PUBLISHER Synergy Interactive Corporation

DESIGN Synergy Interactive Corporation, San Francisco, CA. Haruhiko Shono, art director; Haruhiko Shono, interface designer; Hirokazu Nabekura, writer; Haruhiko Shono, programmer; Haruhiko Shono, digital video director; Isao Konaka, graphic designer; Haruhiko Shono, illustrator; Koji Ueno, music composer; Haruhiko Shono, sound editor; Masanori Awata, executive producer; Eri Osada, assistant producer.

This train for East End

Gadget deposits players into something resembling a Franz Kafka story directed by Fritz Lange, and ported to their computer by the makers of *Myst*—only it is the player who is pitched about by the whims of nature and cruelties of humanity. From the makers of *Alice, Gadget* is set in a Central European city, some time in the 1930s. Dramatic and eerie, *Gadget* sets players on a mission: track down Horselover, a scientist who can help players avert annihilation threatened by a comet hurtling toward Earth. Production values are extraordinarily high, from the witty 3-D computer graphics to the cinematic techniques such as widely arcing dolly shots and long-range zooms. With this title, the creators of *Gadget* have contrived a fully realized world view.

Grand Central Railway

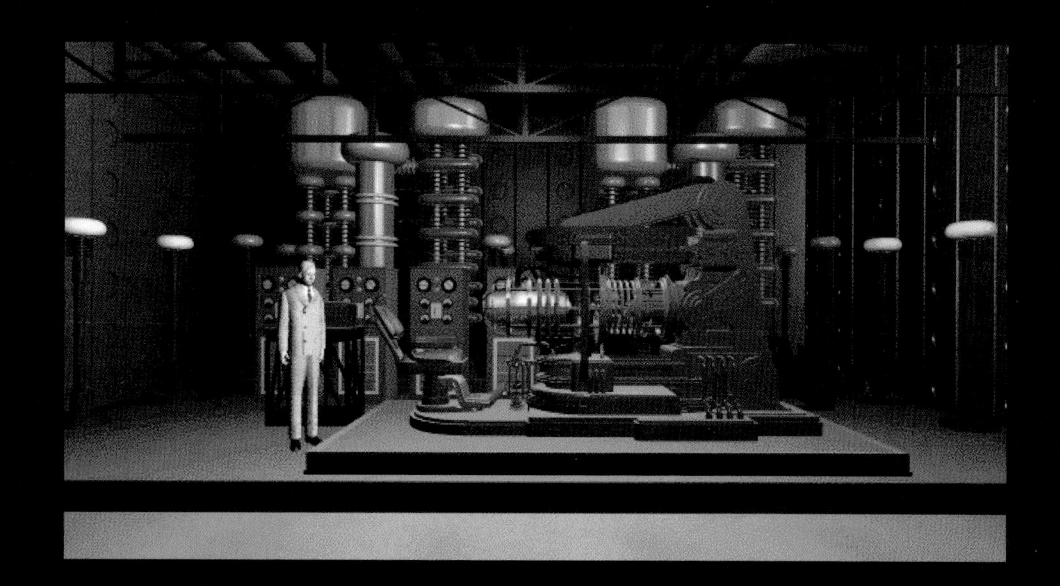

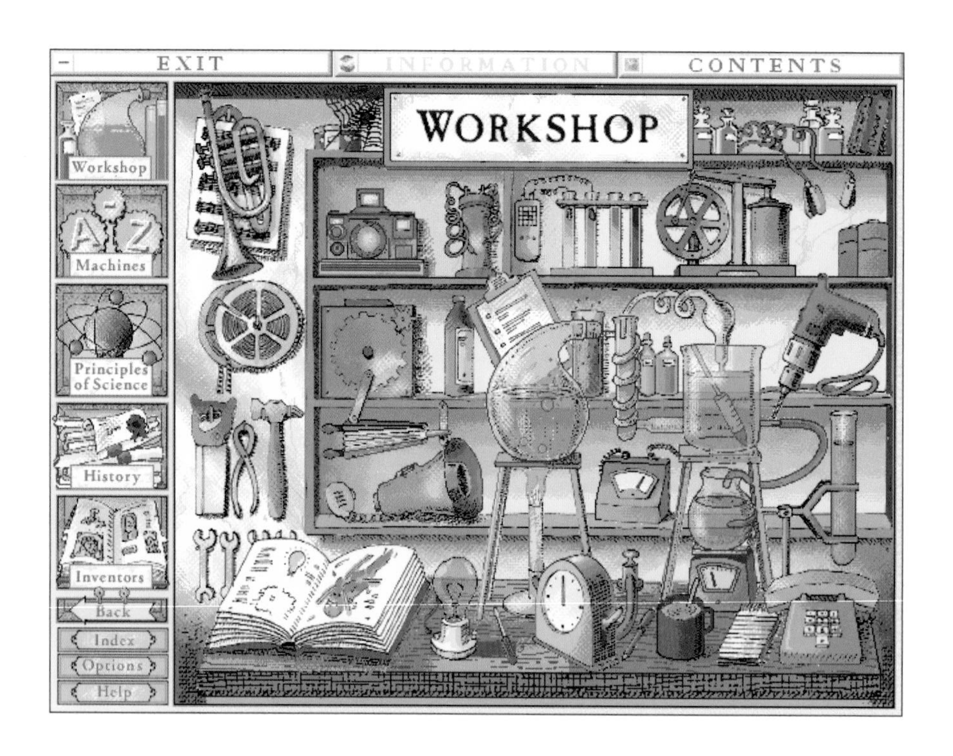

THE WAY THINGS WORK

CLIENT / PUBLISHER Dorling Kindersley Multimedia

DESIGN Dorling Kindersley Multimedia, London, Great Britain. David Game, editorial lead; Tony Foo, design lead; Helen Dowling, Sarah Larter and Tony Pearson, editorial; Sarah Cavan, Alison Donovan and Andy Walker, design; Matt O'Brian, Russel Harding, Eugene Jordan, Sarah Nunan and Iain Pusey, digital animation and imaging; Alan Green, Sarah Keogh and Tony Walters, cel animation; Mick Barrett, David Fathers and Derek Worrell, illustation, Sid Wells and Ian Hawkridge, audio; Roy Margolis and Graham Westlake, software development; Tom Forge, senior technical lead; Clifford Rosney, managing editor; Susie Breen, managing art editor; Jack Challoner BSC (HONS) ARCS, PGGE; Katie Evans BA (CANTAB) and David Glover PhD, Richard Platt BA, writers; Bob Clayton, Tim Crone PhD, Jeff Harding, and Robin Loerch, voice talent. Based on the book by David Macaulay.

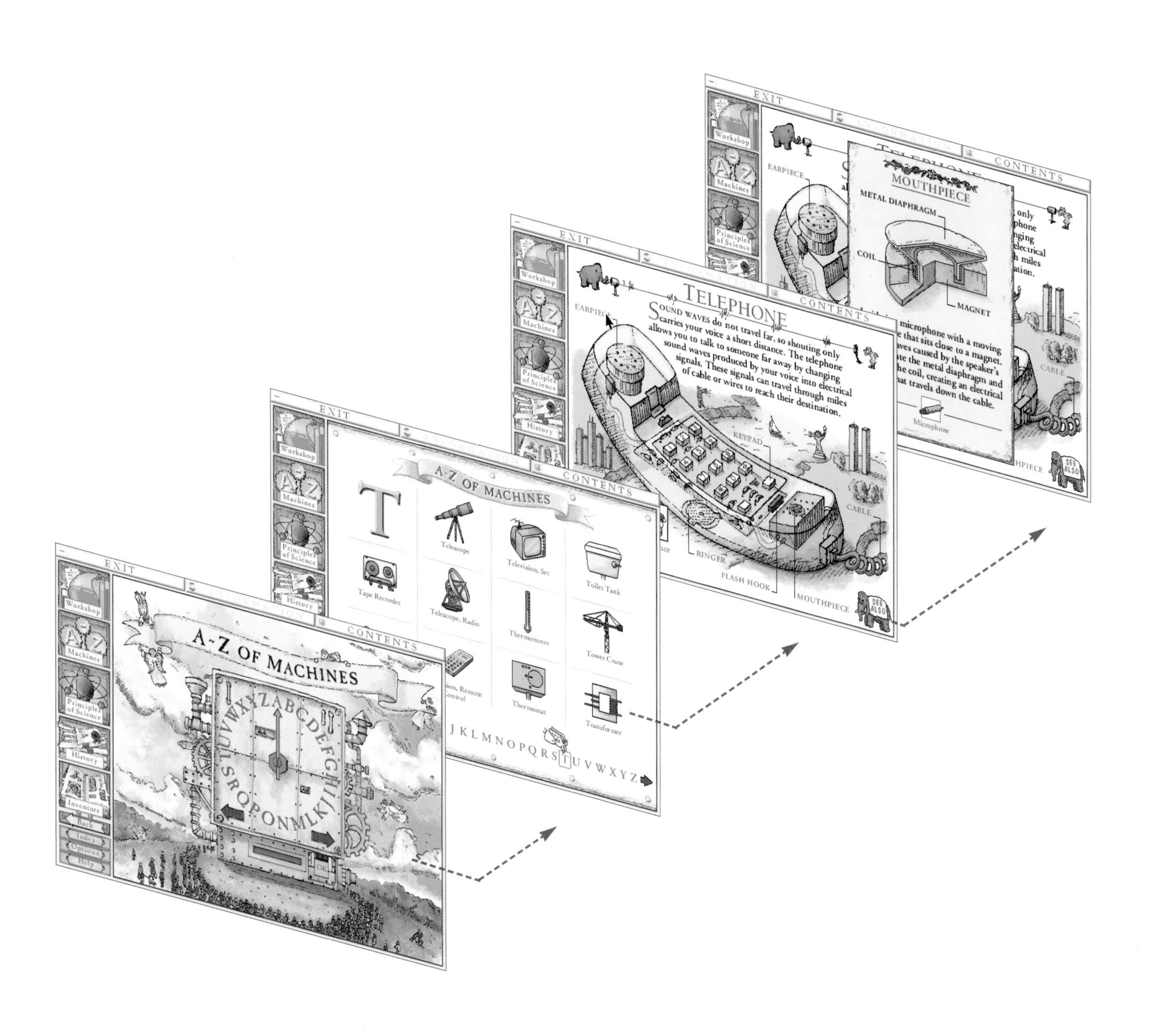

Unlike other titles based upon books, *The Way Things Work* is anything but shovelware. Using the strengths of the New Media—full-color animation, rich sound, and effective content pathways—Dorling Kindersley has developed a witty reinterpretation of the perennial bestseller. From telephones to space rockets, the 150 machines this title depicts will look familiar to readers—as will the artistic style—but the approach is far livelier than a book could ever be. It's the little things that win over the viewer: quirky animation sequences, witty asides, whimsical sound effects, and outlandish tales of eccentric inventors and their visionary brainchilds. *The Way Things Work* is a fun and informative romp through the principles of science and technology.

EXIT
INFORMATION
CONTENTS
Workshop
Machines
Principles of Science
History
Inventors
Back
Index
Options
Help
LASER
A LASER is a device that produces an intense beam of light. Unlike the light from a flashlight, the light from a laser carries a lot of energy. Laser beams can cut through metal, carry vast amounts of information, or be used by doctors to operate on your eyes.
Laser Light
MIRROR
GLASS TUBE
NEON AND HELIUM GASES
ANODE
SEMIREFLECTIVE MIRROR
CATHODE
How does it work?
PRINCIPLES OF SCIENCE
ELECTROMAGNETISM
SENSORS AND DETECTORS
GEARS AND BELTS
SPRINGS
SCREWS
INCLINED PLANES
PRESSURE
PHOTOGRAPHY
FRICTION
FLOATING
CAMS AND CRANKS
WHEELS
ELECTRICITY
PULLEYS
SOUND
LIGHT AND IMAGES
COMPUTERS
LEVERS
MAGNETISM
HEAT
TELECOMMUNICATIONS

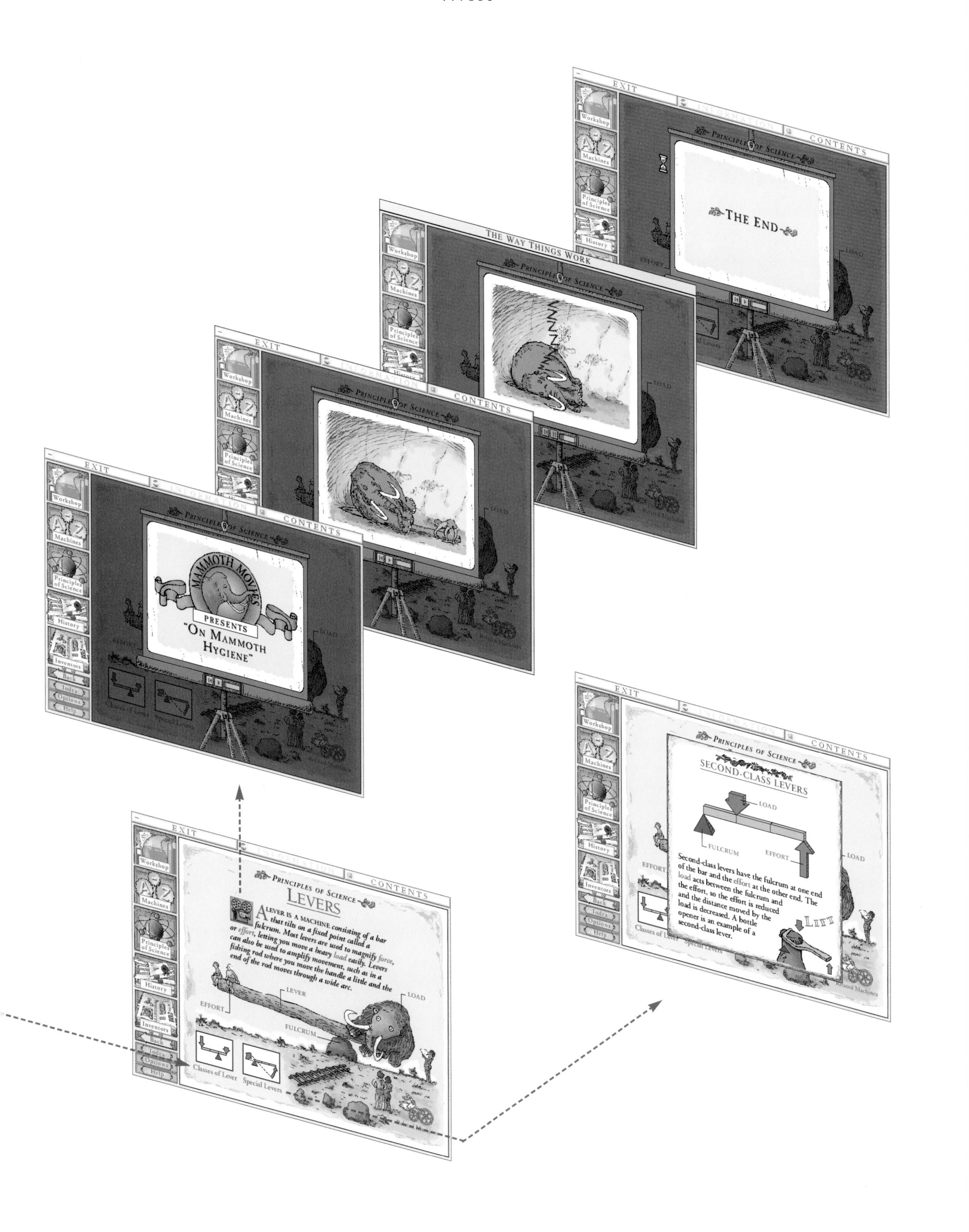
EXIT
INFORMATION
CONTENTS
THE WAY THINGS WORK
Workshop
Machines
Principles of Science
History
Inventors
Back
Index
Options
Help
Principles of Science
The End
Mammoth Movies
Presents
"On Mammoth Hygiene"
Levers
A lever is a machine consisting of a bar that tilts on a fixed point called a fulcrum. Most levers are used to magnify force, or effort, letting you move a heavy load easily. Levers can also be used to amplify movement, such as in a fishing rod where you move the handle a little and the end of the rod moves through a wide arc.
EFFORT
LEVER
LOAD
FULCRUM
Classes of Lever
Special Levers
Related Machines
Second-Class Levers
LOAD
FULCRUM
EFFORT
Second-class levers have the fulcrum at one end of the bar and the effort at the other end. The load acts between the fulcrum and the effort, so the effort is reduced and the distance moved by the load is decreased. A bottle opener is an example of a second-class lever.
LIFT

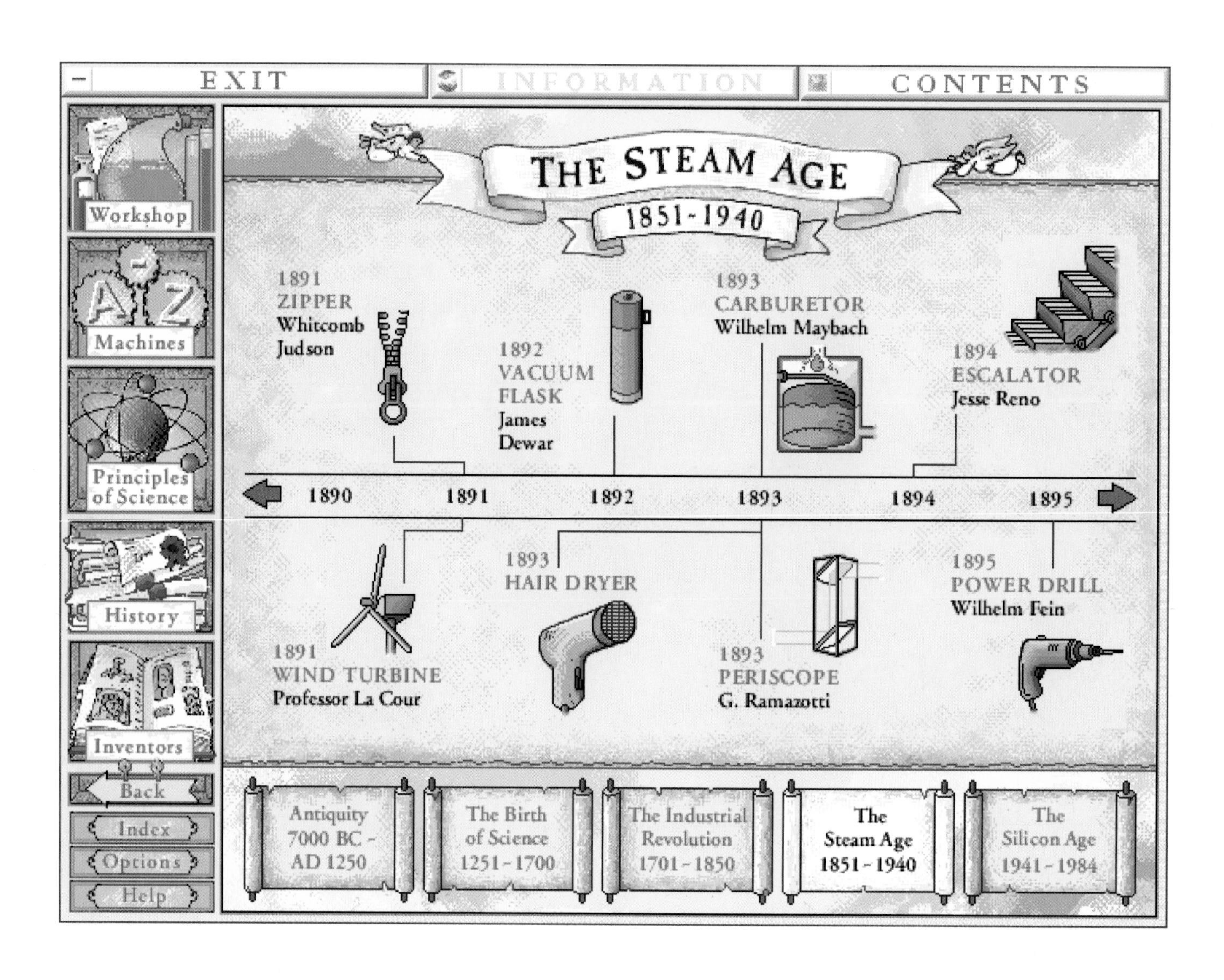
EXIT
INFORMATION
CONTENTS
THE STEAM AGE
1851-1940
Workshop
Machines
Principles of Science
History
Inventors
Back
Index
Options
Help
1891
ZIPPER
Whitcomb Judson
1892
VACUUM FLASK
James Dewar
1893
CARBURETOR
Wilhelm Maybach
1894
ESCALATOR
Jesse Reno
1890
1891
1892
1893
1894
1895
1891
WIND TURBINE
Professor La Cour
1893
HAIR DRYER
1893
PERISCOPE
G. Ramazotti
1895
POWER DRILL
Wilhelm Fein
Antiquity 7000 BC - AD 1250
The Birth of Science 1251 - 1700
The Industrial Revolution 1701 - 1850
The Steam Age 1851 - 1940
The Silicon Age 1941 - 1984

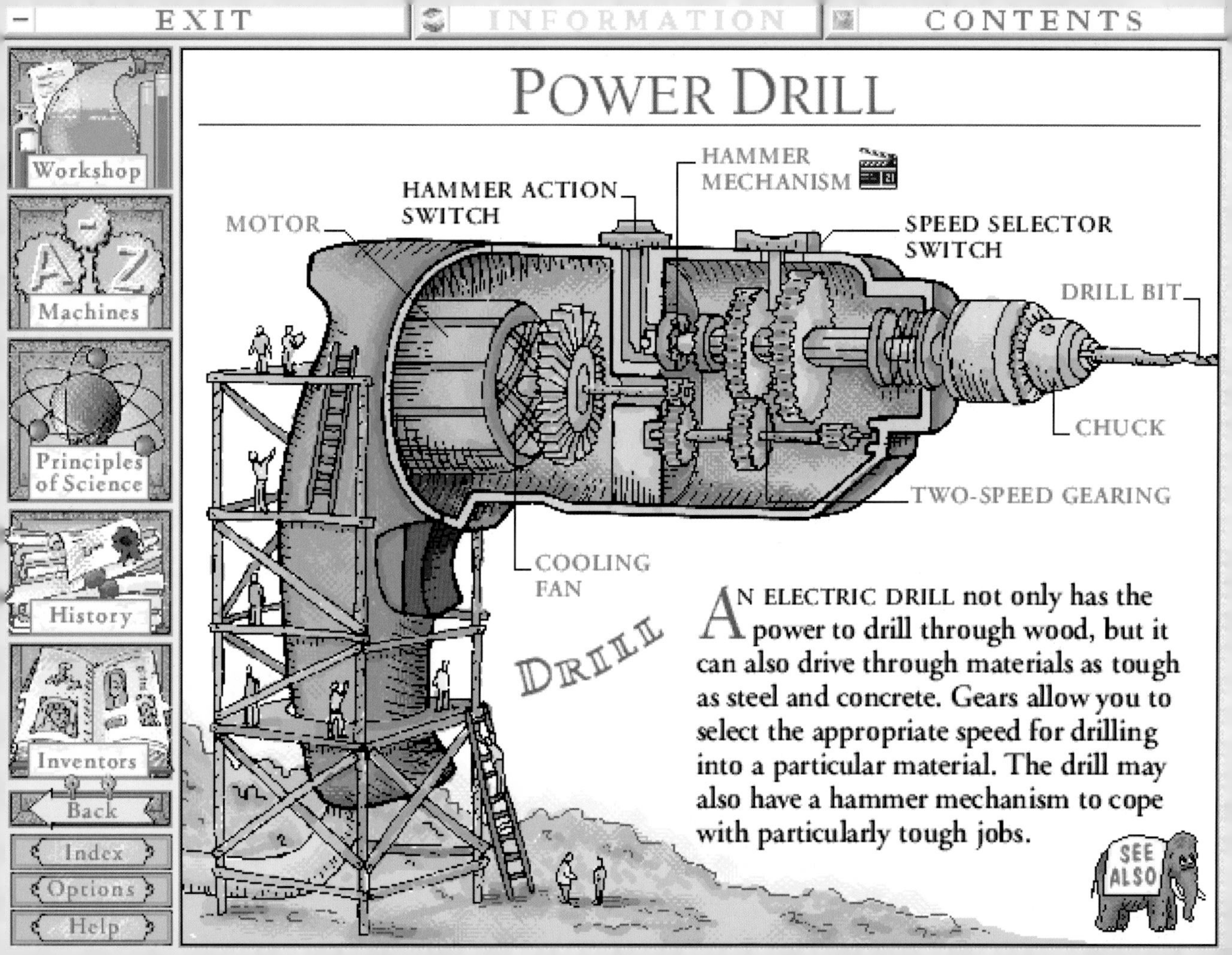
EXIT
INFORMATION
CONTENTS
Workshop
Machines
Principles of Science
History
Inventors
Back
Index
Options
Help
POWER DRILL
HAMMER MECHANISM
HAMMER ACTION SWITCH
MOTOR
SPEED SELECTOR SWITCH
DRILL BIT
CHUCK
TWO-SPEED GEARING
COOLING FAN
DRILL
AN ELECTRIC DRILL not only has the power to drill through wood, but it can also drive through materials as tough as steel and concrete. Gears allow you to select the appropriate speed for drilling into a particular material. The drill may also have a hammer mechanism to cope with particularly tough jobs.
SEE ALSO

ELRoy goes Bugzerk
GO!
CREDITS
copyright 1995 Headbone Interactive Inc., all rights reserved

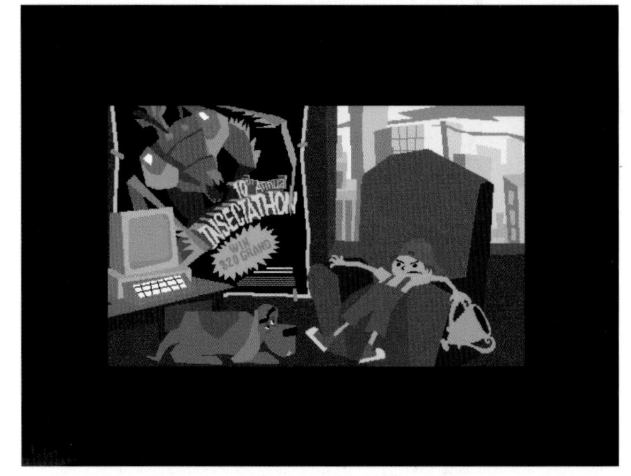
10th Annual
INSECTATHON
WIN
$20 GRAND

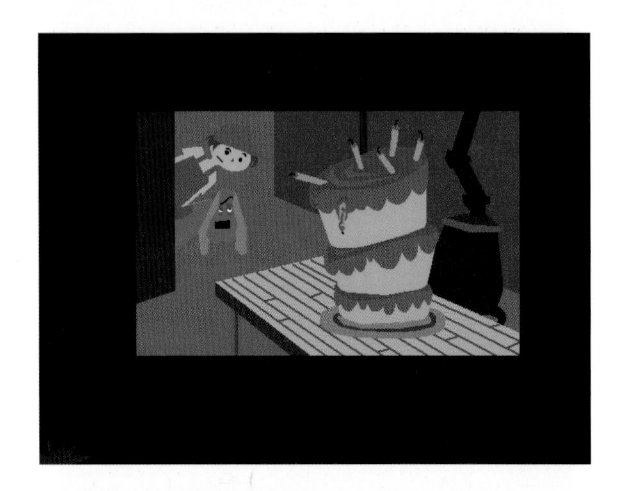

Elroy Goes Bugzerk is not just another ho-hum animated treasure hunt for kids. It stands out among its peers for its technical bravura and adolescent cheekiness. Our hero and his trusty bloodhound, Blue, set out on a joyride over hill and dale in search of the wily *Technoloptera,* the cyberbug of their dreams. Elroy's creators place blocky cartoon images amidst still photographs of barns and fields, a clever and effective juxtaposition of make-believe and reality that draws users into Elroy's world—and Elroy into the player's. An entertaining range of modules follows Elroy as he "aspirates," "accelerates," "spelunk-o-lates," "blink-er-ates," and "investigates." ■ While it might be true that, as the hard-boiled voice-over states, "Singing Egyptian Cockroaches are a dime-a-dozen in this town," Elroy is a decided rarity.

ELROY GOES BUGZERK

CLIENT / PUBLISHER headbone interactive, Inc.

DESIGN headbone interactive, Inc., Seattle, WA. Scott Hudson, creative director; Scott Hudson, interface design; Louica Callisti, Tim Bertram, Camille Nims, Lisa Bickerstaff, programmers; Alan Abrams, Francesca Lacagnine, photographers; Doug Brady, audio; Roman Laney, Chuck Gamble, Charlie Canfield, animators; Doug Brady, music composer; headbone interactive, Inc., new media production company.

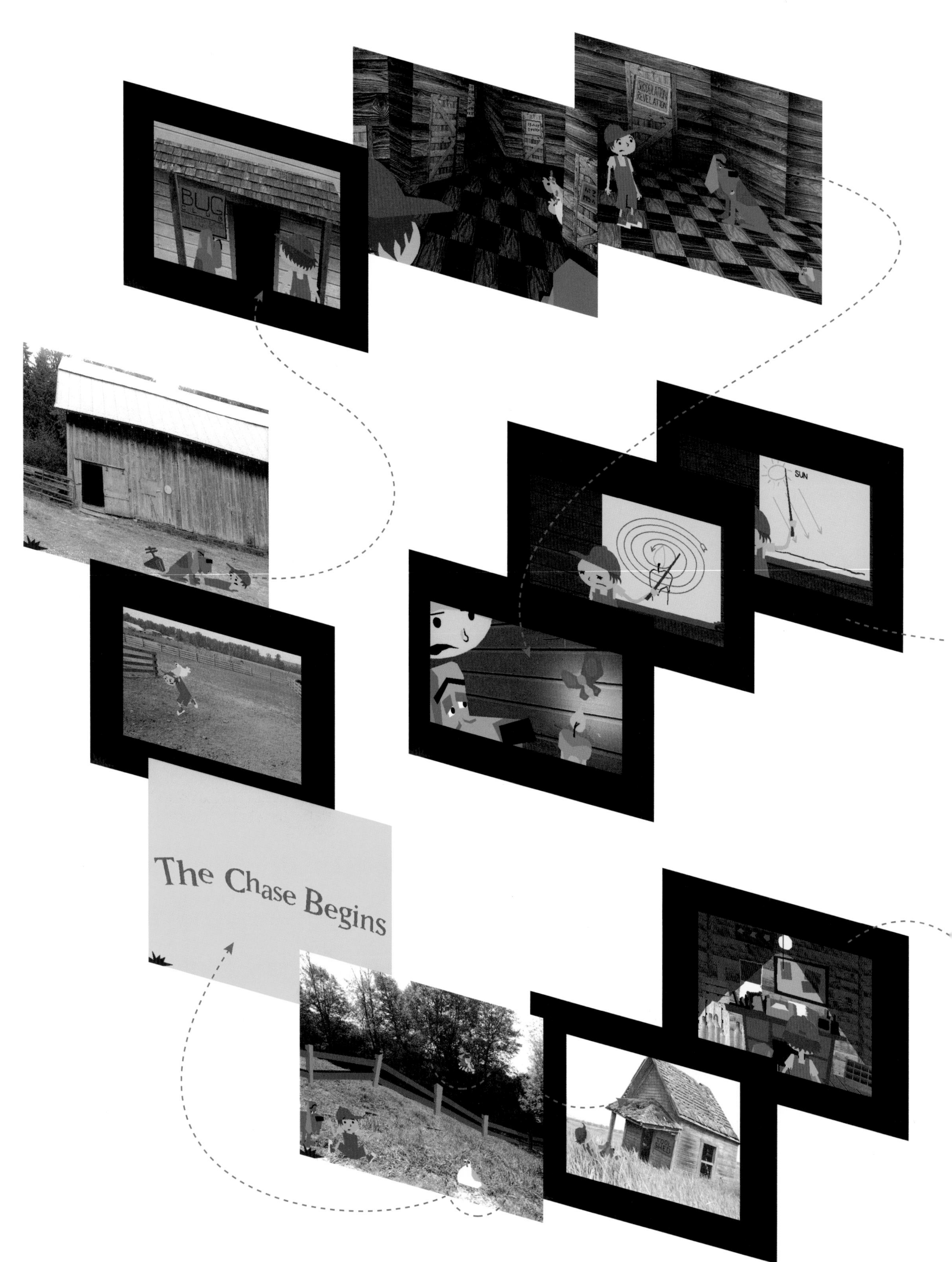
BUG
SUN
The Chase Begins

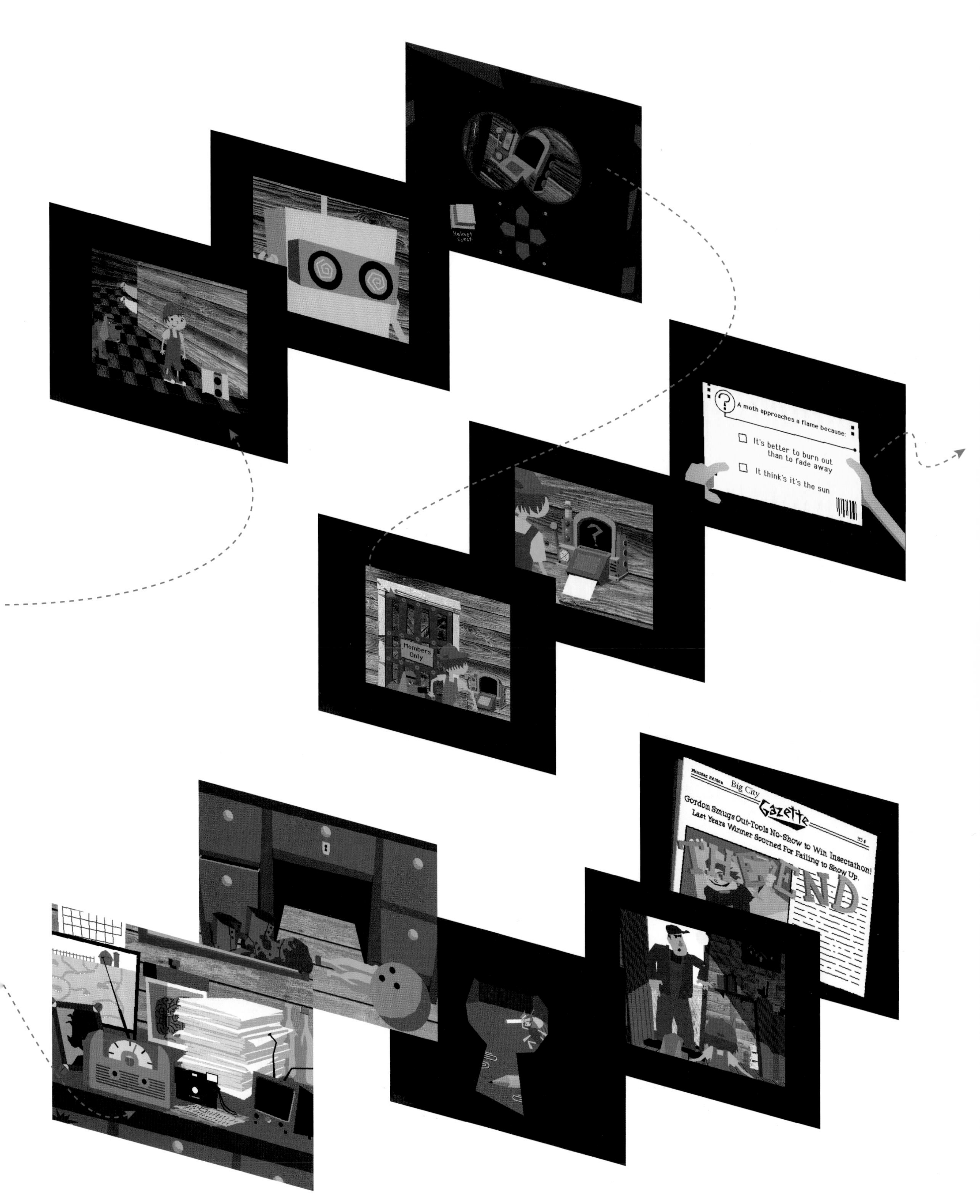
Helmet Eject
A moth approaches a flame because:
It's better to burn out than to fade away
It think's it's the sun
Members Only
Big City Gazette
Gordon Smugs Out-Tools No-Show to Win Insectathon!
Last Years Winner Scorned For Failing to Show Up.
THE END

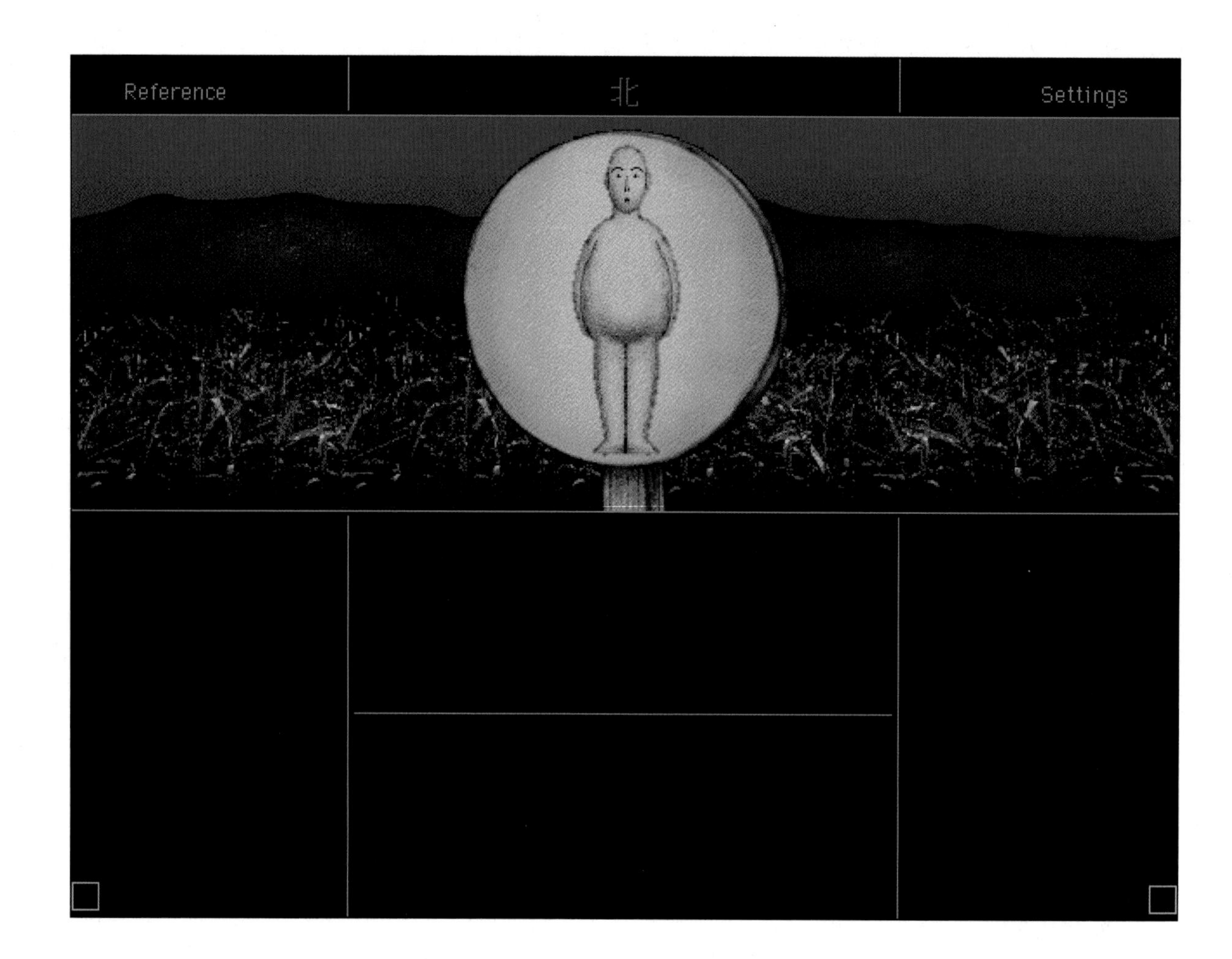

COSMOLOGY OF KYOTO

CLIENT / PUBLISHER SoftEdge

DESIGN SoftEdge, Kobe, Japan. Yoshio Kiso, art director; Koichi Mori, creative director; Shinnosuke Sugizaki and Sansei Kimura, interface designers; Koichi Mori and Hiroshi Onishi, writers; Takashi Kawahara, programmer; Yuri Kawata, graphic designer; Masahiro Nanbu, photographer; Yoshio Kiso, illustrator; Jun Okada, audio; Naomi Nakashima, animator; Yuko Anzai, music composer; Yoshinobu Asao, sound editor; Stephen Suloway, translator.

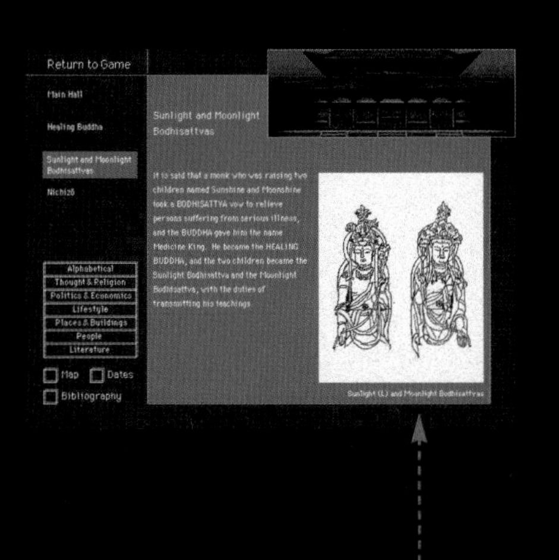

Direction
Shows the direction you are facing in the game, using Japanese characters. Click on this character to view a map showing your position and possessions.

Settings
Click here to select English or Japanese text, to turn subtitles off, or to set the volume.

Subtitles
Voice subtitles appear here when the subtitle function is turned on.

Karma Status
Your karma changes according to your actions in the game. When you die, your karma score determines where in the Six Realms of Existence you are reborn.

Possessions
The words displayed here show a new possession you can use in the game. Click once on a word to bring its icon to the screen, then click on the icon to use it in the game. For coins, click on the purse icon as many times as the number of coins you want to use. Then click on a coin to spend them. Clicking on the sword or arrow icon changes the pointer to an x or + mark. Position the mark with the mouse, and click to strike.

Reply Space
This space appears during an interactive conversation between you and a character in the game. Type in your replies.

Cash Status
Press this button to see how many coins you have at any point in the game.

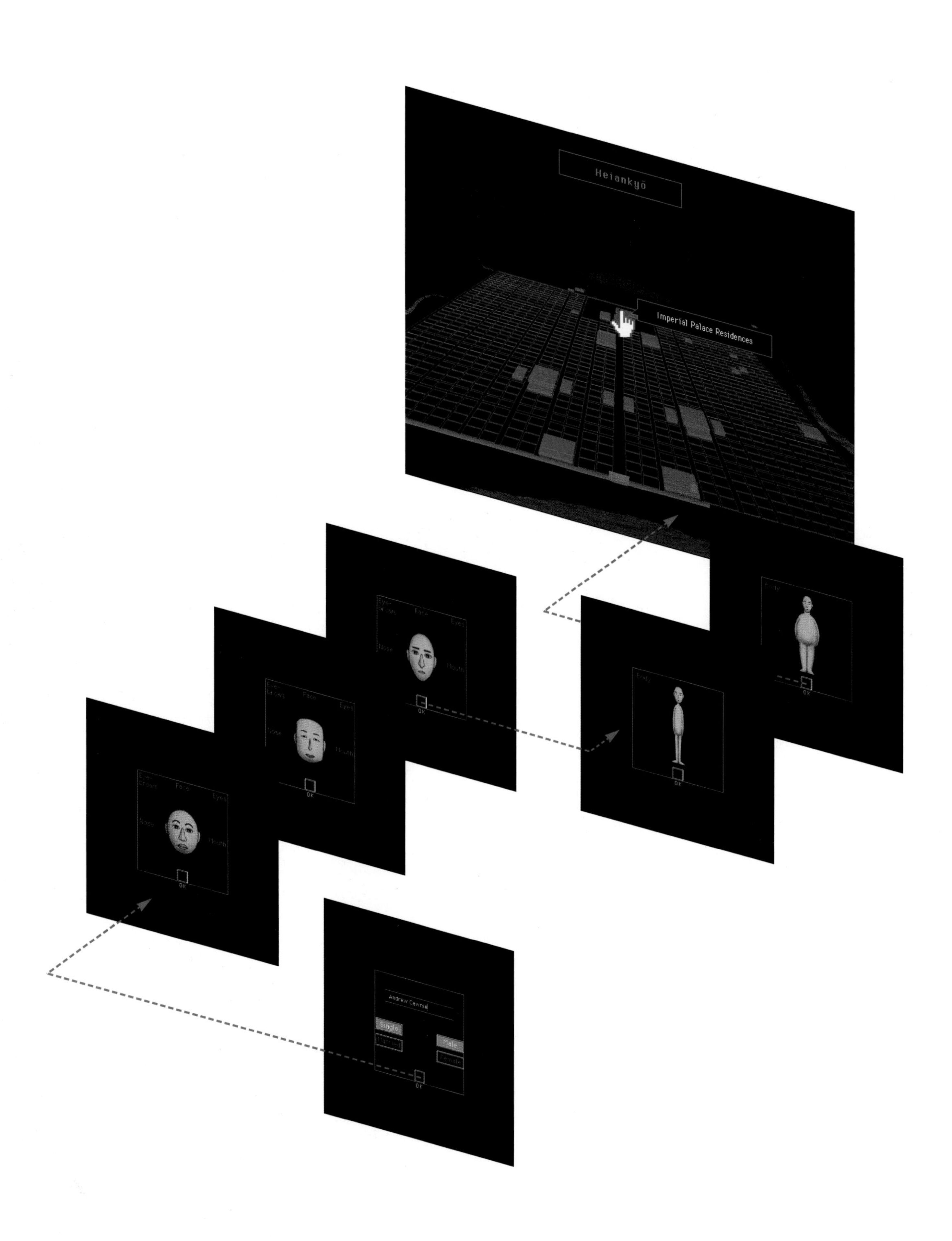
Heiankyō
Imperial Palace Residences
Andrew Cawrse
Single
Male
OK

Cosmology of Kyoto is beautiful in every sense, from its sophisticated concept and highly stylized aesthetics to its sinuous functionality and high entertainment and educational value. What's more, the implied spiritual dimensions of this work are astonishing. ■ This is the "backstage of history," in the creator's words, where players may enlarge their appreciation of a long-forgotten world obscured by a veil of years. The look and feel of this title promotes an eerie sense of historic incongruity: the juxtaposition of ancient folk art and costumes with a cutting-edge interface that splits the screen horizontally is stunning. ■ Players will find themselves buck-naked and penniless in a field of tall grass at the outskirts of 10th-century Kyoto. What to do? This is the player's first shot at rebirth—which will come complete with fresh reserves of karma, money, and clothing. Once outfitted, players will speak with the denizens at the city gate, explore ancient temples, rummage through the village market, and inevitably become embroiled in palace intrigue. But this is a world inhabited by ghosts and goblins, treacherous friends and angry warriors, so players know they must die—many times in all probability—and experience the torments of the Eight Hells. Billed as "historical entertainment," *Cosmology of Kyoto* is less a game in the traditional sense than a flawlessly rendered virtual environment.

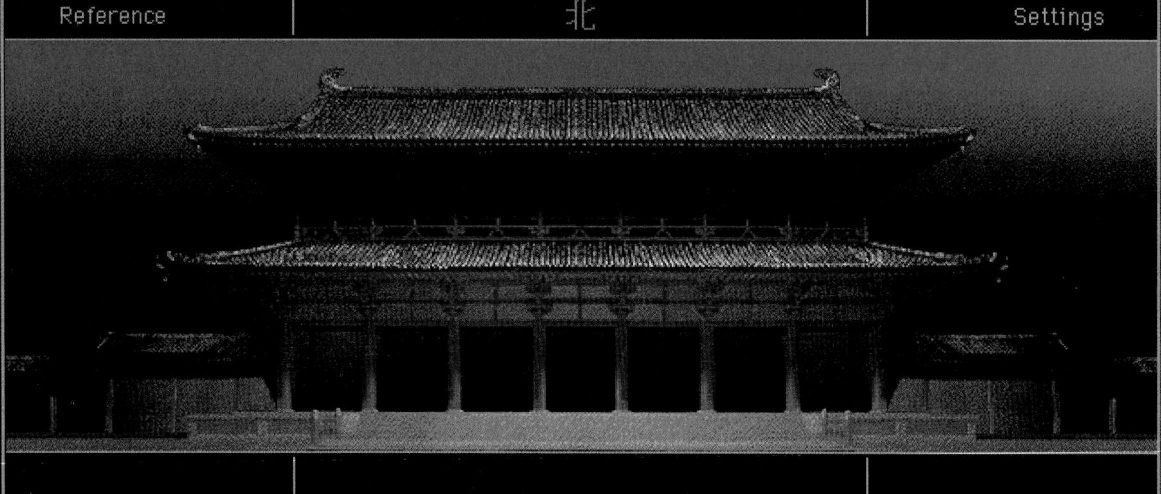
Reference
北
Settings

AMERICAN POETRY

THE NINETEENTH CENTURY

Click to Continue

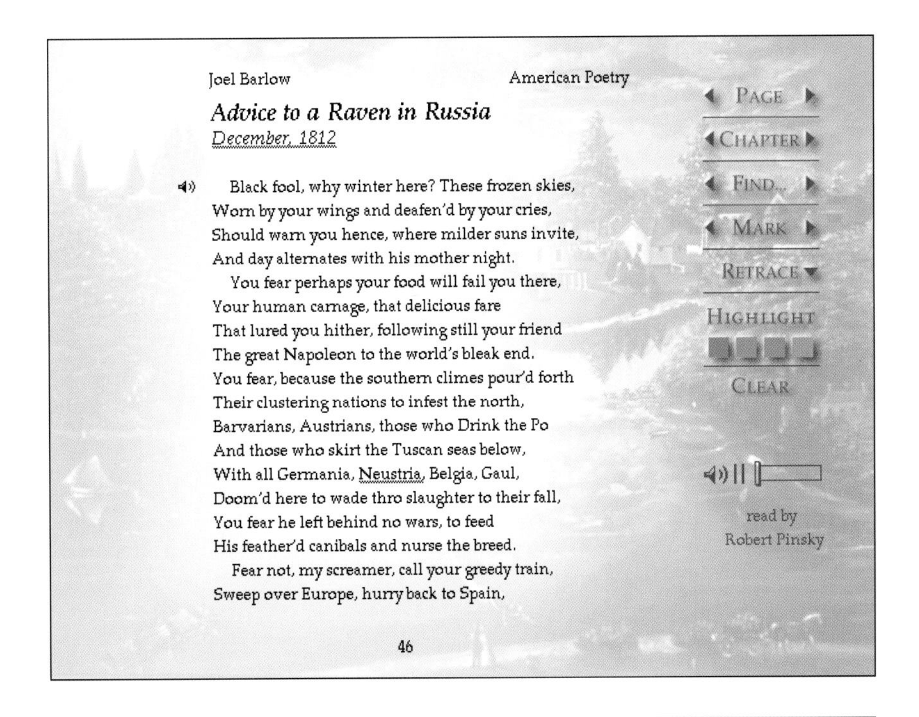

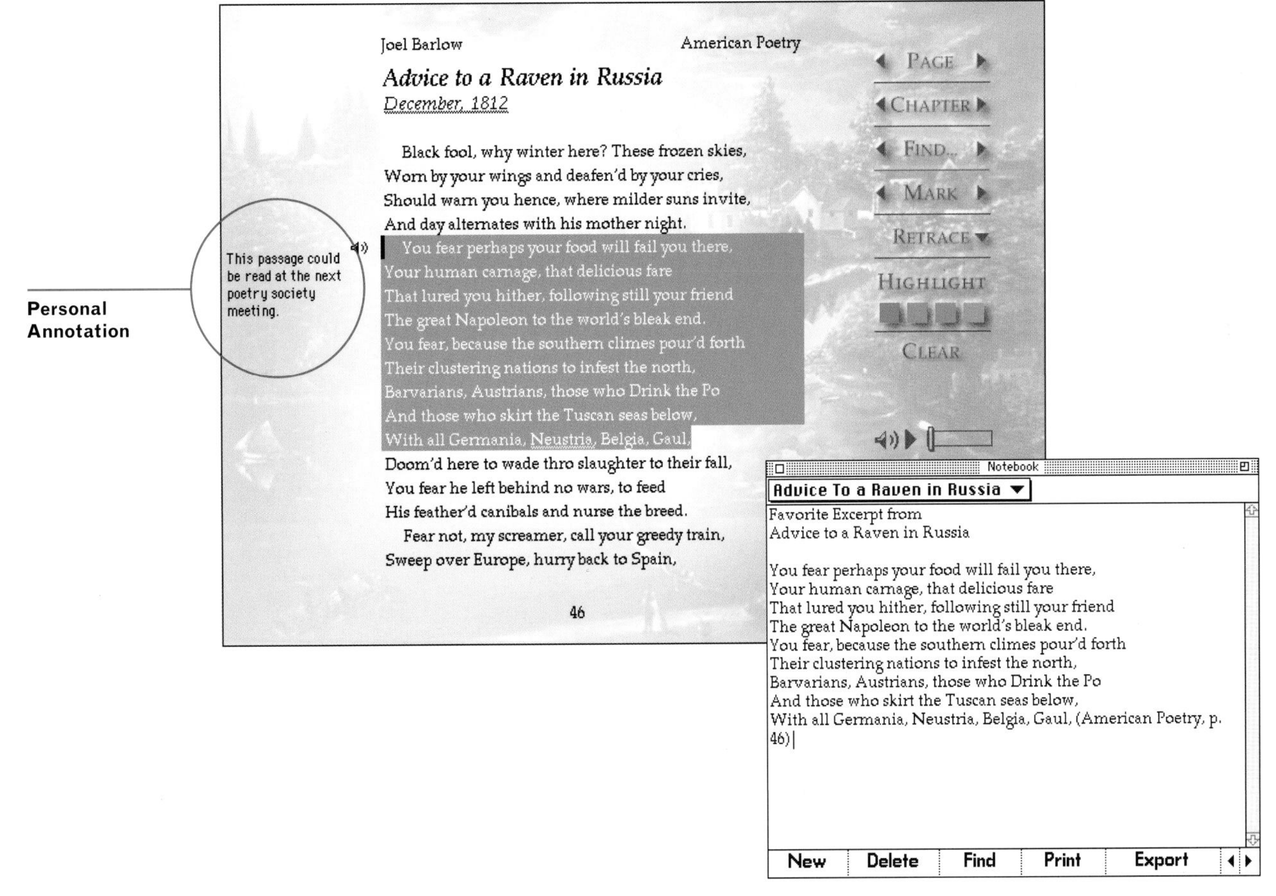

Voyager has filled this CD with a plethora of poetry, some of which users can choose to have read aloud by modern poets. The distinguishing design feature of *American Poetry: The Nineteenth Century* is the capacity for readers to annotate passages and leave electronic bookmarks to tag their place. They can also copy a passage out of a poem and paste it into a built-in notebook, to which annotations can also be pasted.

STOWAWAY! 

CLIENT / PUBLISHER Dorling Kindersley Multimedia

DESIGN Dorling Kindersley Multimedia, London, Great Britain. Christine Webs, editorial lead; Sally McKay, design lead; Tony Foo, Rebecca Painter and Flora Perreir, design; Kumi Akyoshi, Christian Batchlon, Henry Newton-Dunn and Virginia Russell, digital animation and imaging; Claudia Arron and Andy Moss, cel animation/illustration; Richard Howat and Patricia Grogan, editorial; Sid Wells and Patch McQuaid; Roy Margolis and Graham Westlake, software development; Tom Forge, senior technical lead; Clifford Rosney, managing editor; Susie Breen, managing art editor; Richard Plattt and Philip Wilkinson, writers.

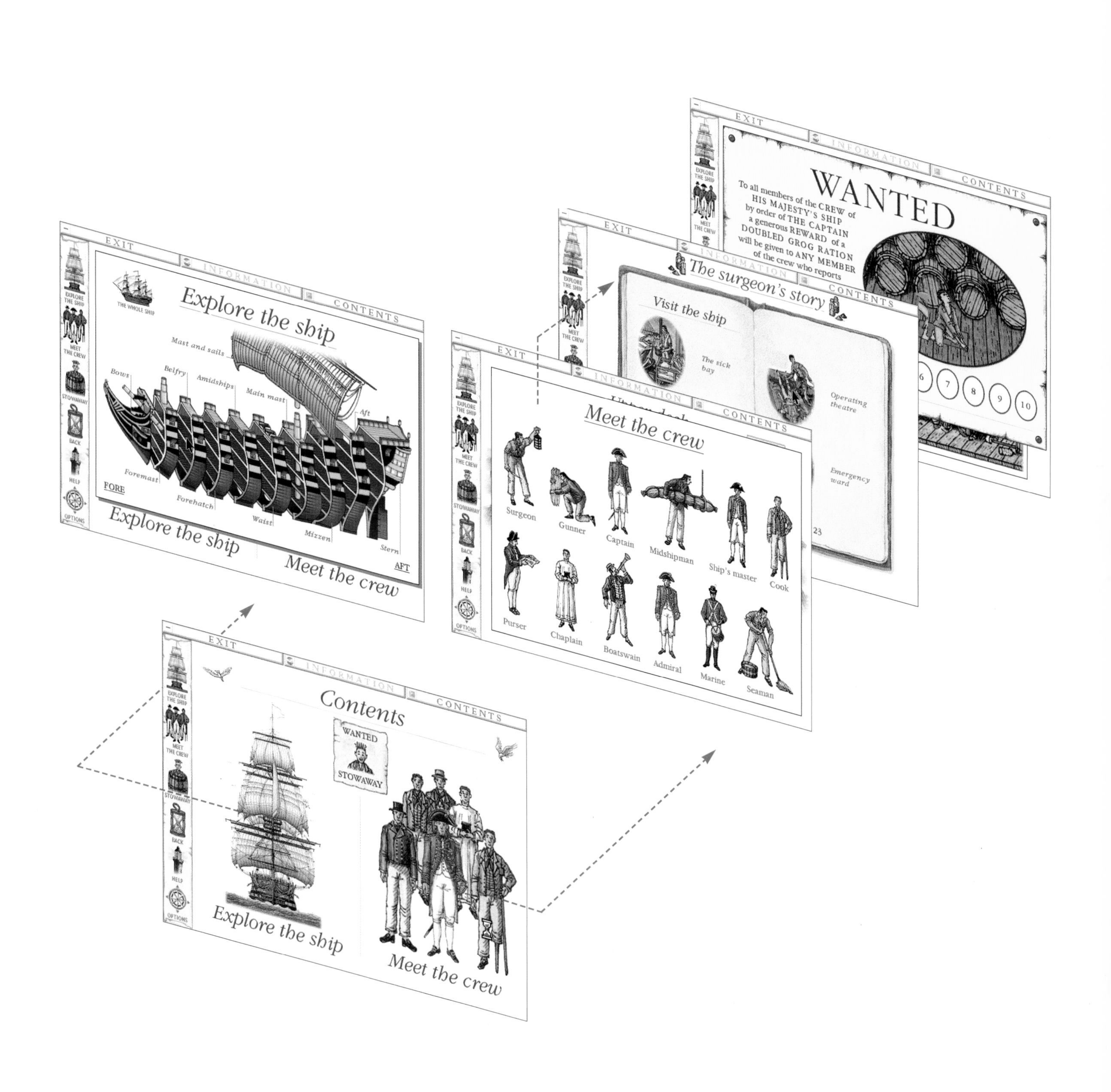
EXIT
INFORMATION
CONTENTS
Explore the ship
THE WHOLE SHIP
Mast and sails
Bows
Belfry
Amidships
Main mast
Aft
Foremast
Forehatch
Waist
Mizzen
Stern
FORE
AFT
Explore the ship
Meet the crew
EXPLORE THE SHIP
MEET THE CREW
STOWAWAY
BACK
HELP
OPTIONS
Meet the crew
Surgeon
Gunner
Captain
Midshipman
Ship's master
Cook
Purser
Chaplain
Boatswain
Admiral
Marine
Seaman
The surgeon's story
Visit the ship
The sick bay
Operating theatre
Emergency ward
23
WANTED
To all members of the CREW of
HIS MAJESTY'S SHIP
by order of THE CAPTAIN
a generous REWARD of a
DOUBLED GROG RATION
will be given to ANY MEMBER
of the crew who reports
6
7
8
9
10
Contents
WANTED
STOWAWAY
Explore the ship
Meet the crew

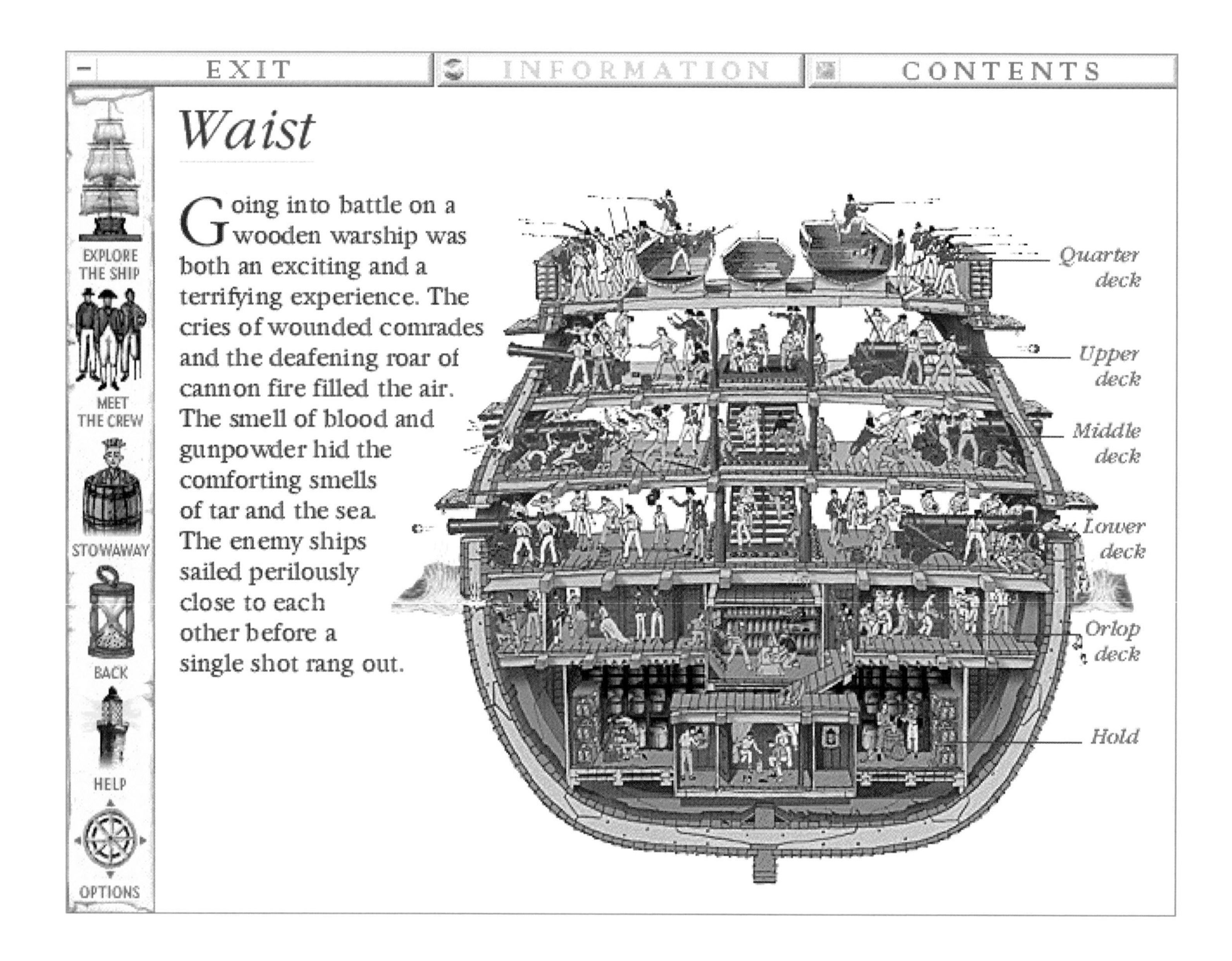

STOWAWAY! takes users on a thrilling voyage aboard one of Her Majesty's fleet of wooden warships from the 18th century. Users join a motley crew of sailors to explore life on the high seas, as well as to search for a stowaway hiding somewhere below the decks.

■ Stephen Biesty's stylish cross-sections of the ship are as pleasing to the eye as they are informative. The animations, for their part, are witty—and sometimes brutal, as with the segment that shows the ship's doctor sawing off the damaged leg of a sailor, who screams in agony throughout the cruel procedure. Navigation is a breeze with the clever ship icon that floats in the lower left-hand corner.

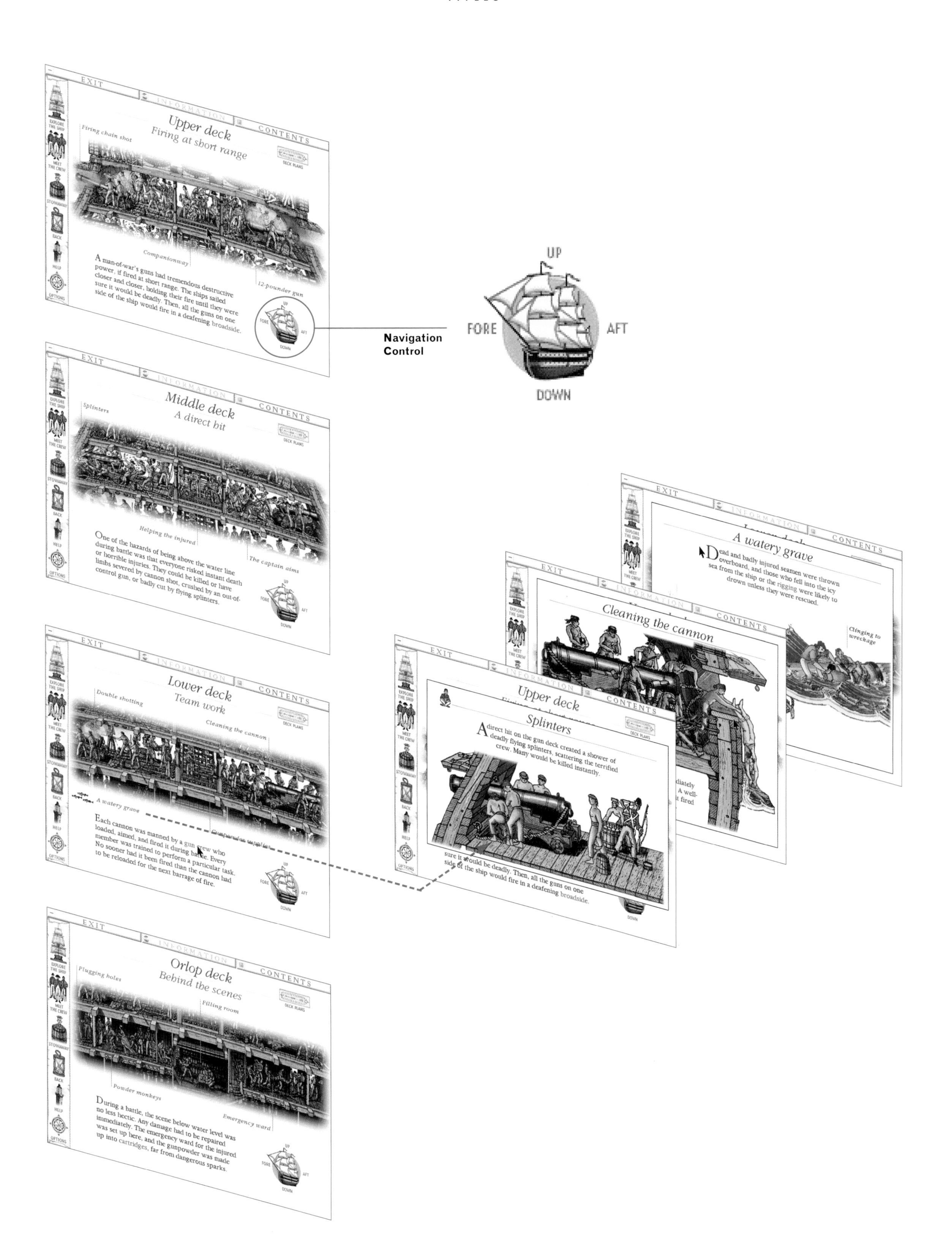
Upper deck
Firing at short range
A man-of-war's guns had tremendous destructive power, if fired at short range. The ships sailed closer and closer, holding their fire until they were sure it would be deadly. Then, all the guns on one side of the ship would fire in a deafening broadside.
Navigation Control
UP
FORE
AFT
DOWN
Middle deck
A direct hit
One of the hazards of being above the water line during battle was that everyone risked instant death or horrible injuries. They could be killed or have limbs severed by cannon shot, crushed by an out-of-control gun, or badly cut by flying splinters.
Lower deck
Team work
Each cannon was manned by a gun crew who loaded, aimed, and fired it during battle. Every member was trained to perform a particular task. No sooner had it been fired than the cannon had to be reloaded for the next barrage of fire.
Orlop deck
Behind the scenes
During a battle, the scene below water level was no less hectic. Any damage had to be repaired immediately. The emergency ward for the injured was set up here, and the gunpowder was made up into cartridges, far from dangerous sparks.
A watery grave
Dead and badly injured seamen were thrown overboard, and those who fell into the icy sea from the ship or the rigging were likely to drown unless they were rescued.
Cleaning the cannon
Splinters
A direct hit on the gun deck created a shower of deadly flying splinters, scattering the terrified crew. Many would be killed instantly.

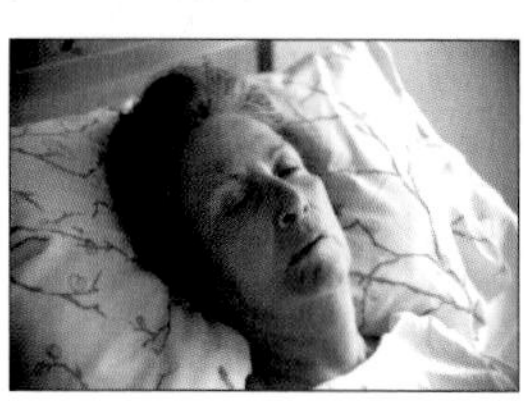

I PHOTOGRAPH TO REMEMBER/FOTOGRAFIO PARA RECORDAR

CLIENT / PUBLISHER The Voyager Company

DESIGN The Voyager Company, New York, NY. Pedro Meyer, photographer; Thomas Luehrsen, producer; Brock La Porte, programming; Manuel Rocha, music; Pedro Meyer, narration; Michael Draghi, Morgan Holly and Curtis Wong, audio production; Rebekah Behrendt and Brian Speight, production assistance.

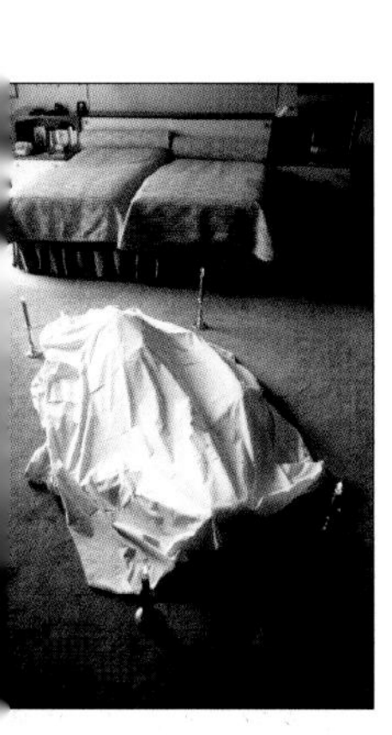

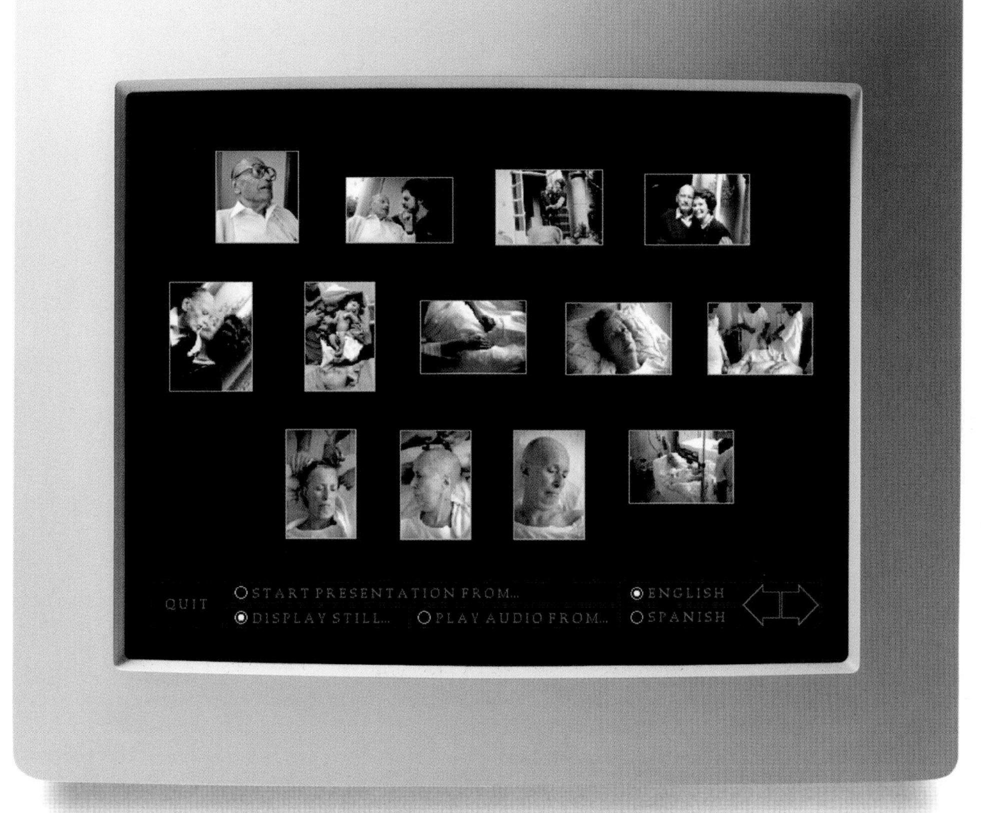

I Photograph to Remember/Fotografio Para Recordar documents the last years in the lives of photographer Pedro Meyer's parents. Combining almost 100 black-and-white photographs with music and narration (the viewer can choose English or Spanish), Meyer has created a most unusual title: a personal reflection on family and mortality.

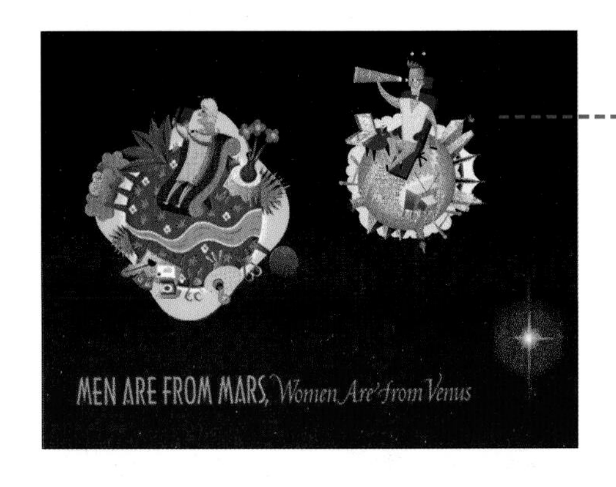

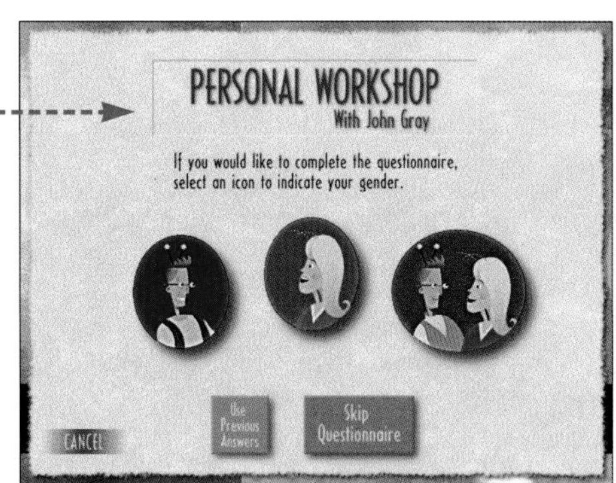

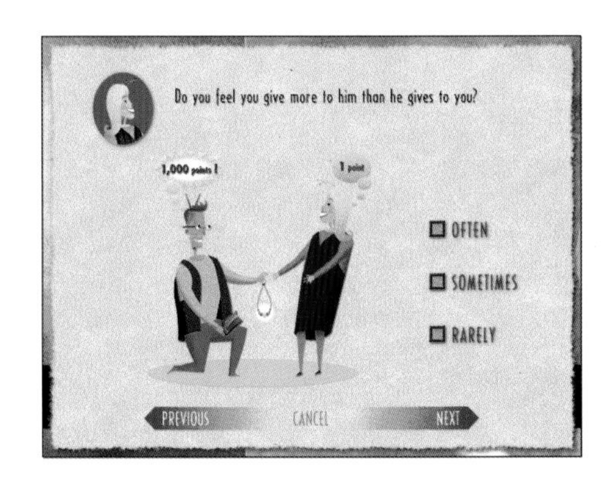

MEN ARE FROM MARS, WOMEN ARE FROM VENUS

CLIENT / PUBLISHER HarperCollins Interactive.

DESIGN Medior Incorporated, San Mateo, CA. Medior Incorporated, design and production; Nancy Dickenson, executive producer. Based on the book by John Gray.

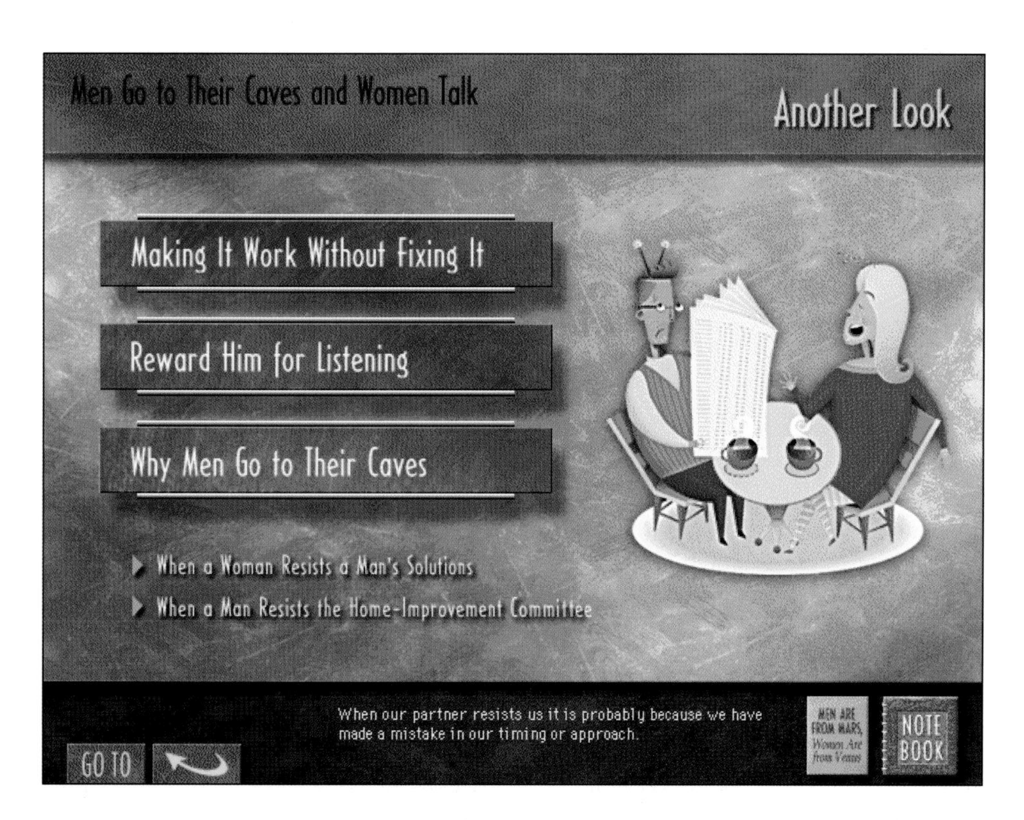

HarperCollins Interactive adapted this paper-publishing phenomenon into a CD filled with interactive therapy sessions. What is special about this title is that its designers succeeded where others have failed: developing practical and eye-pleasing dialogue boxes.

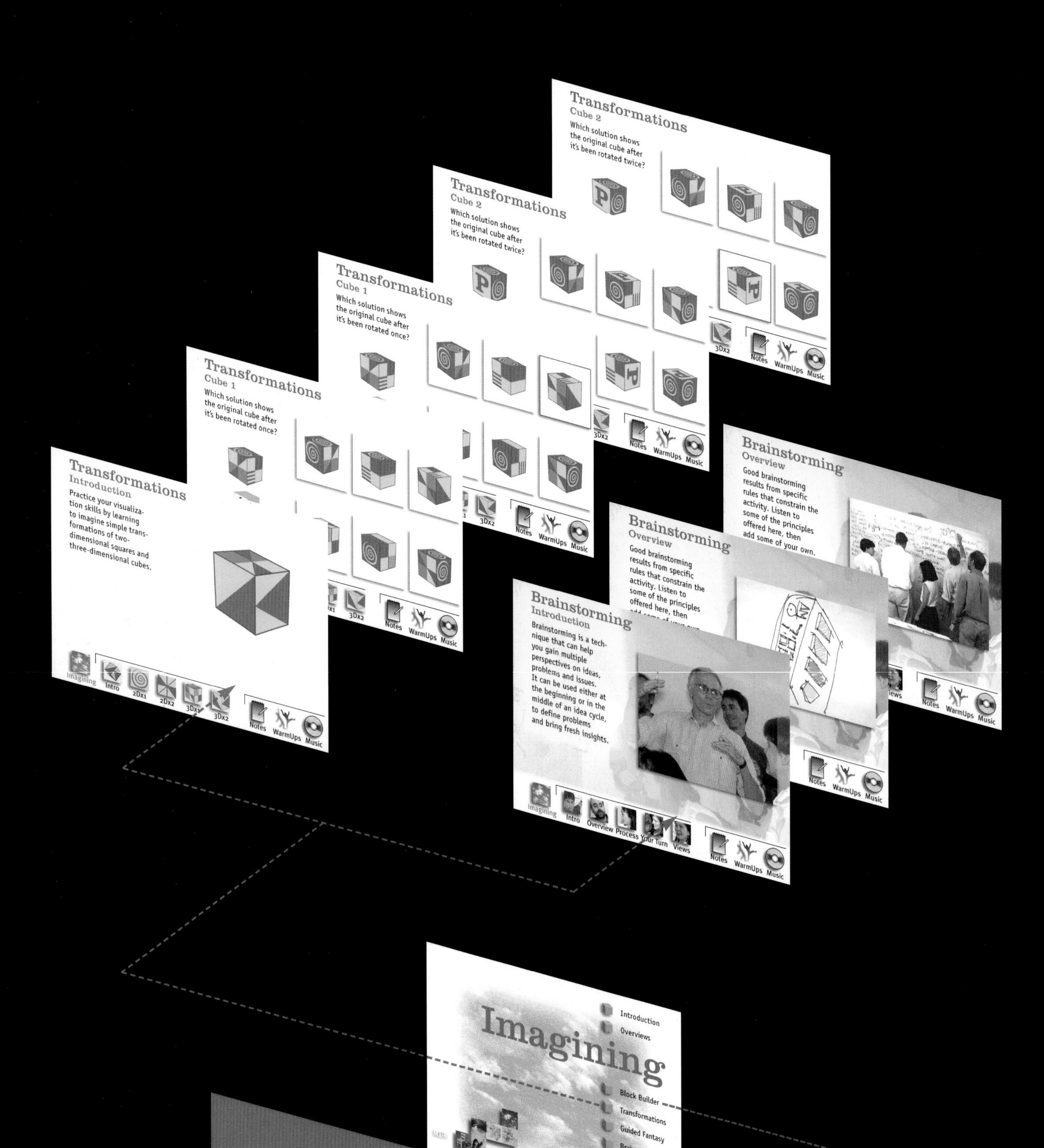

Transformations
Cube 2
Which solution shows the original cube after it's been rotated twice?
Transformations
Cube 2
Which solution shows the original cube after it's been rotated twice?
Transformations
Cube 1
Which solution shows the original cube after it's been rotated once?
Transformations
Cube 1
Which solution shows the original cube after it's been rotated once?
Transformations
Introduction
Practice your visualization skills by learning to imagine simple transformations of two-dimensional squares and three-dimensional cubes.
Imagining
Intro
2Dx1
2Dx2
3Dx1
3Dx2
Notes
WarmUps
Music
Brainstorming
Overview
Good brainstorming results from specific rules that constrain the activity. Listen to some of the principles offered here, then add some of your own.
Brainstorming
Overview
Good brainstorming results from specific rules that constrain the activity. Listen to some of the principles offered here, then
Brainstorming
Introduction
Brainstorming is a technique that can help you gain multiple perspectives on ideas, problems and issues. It can be used either at the beginning or in the middle of an idea cycle, to define problems and bring fresh insights.
Imagining
Intro
Overview
Process
Your Turn
Views
Notes
WarmUps
Music

Imagining
Introduction
Overviews
Block Builder
Transformations
Guided Fantasy
Brainstorming
Magic Theater

VizAbility™
Imagining
Seeing
Drawing
Diagramming
Environment
Culture
Introduction
Orientation
Quit

izAbility is one of a new generation of hybrid multi-
nedia titles that are part game/part self-teaching
ool/part productivity application. The intent is to
each users how to use their eyes in productive and
reative ways. Playful and enlightening, *VizAbility's* exercises and puzzles show users how to identify objects out of context, recognize hidden patterns, accurately describe objects seen in a flash, build three-dimensional objects that cast complex shadows upon multiple surfaces, understand how to balance positive and negative space, and other valuable techniques. Multi-layered and appropriate to all skill and age levels, *VizAbility* has real guts as well as a pretty face.

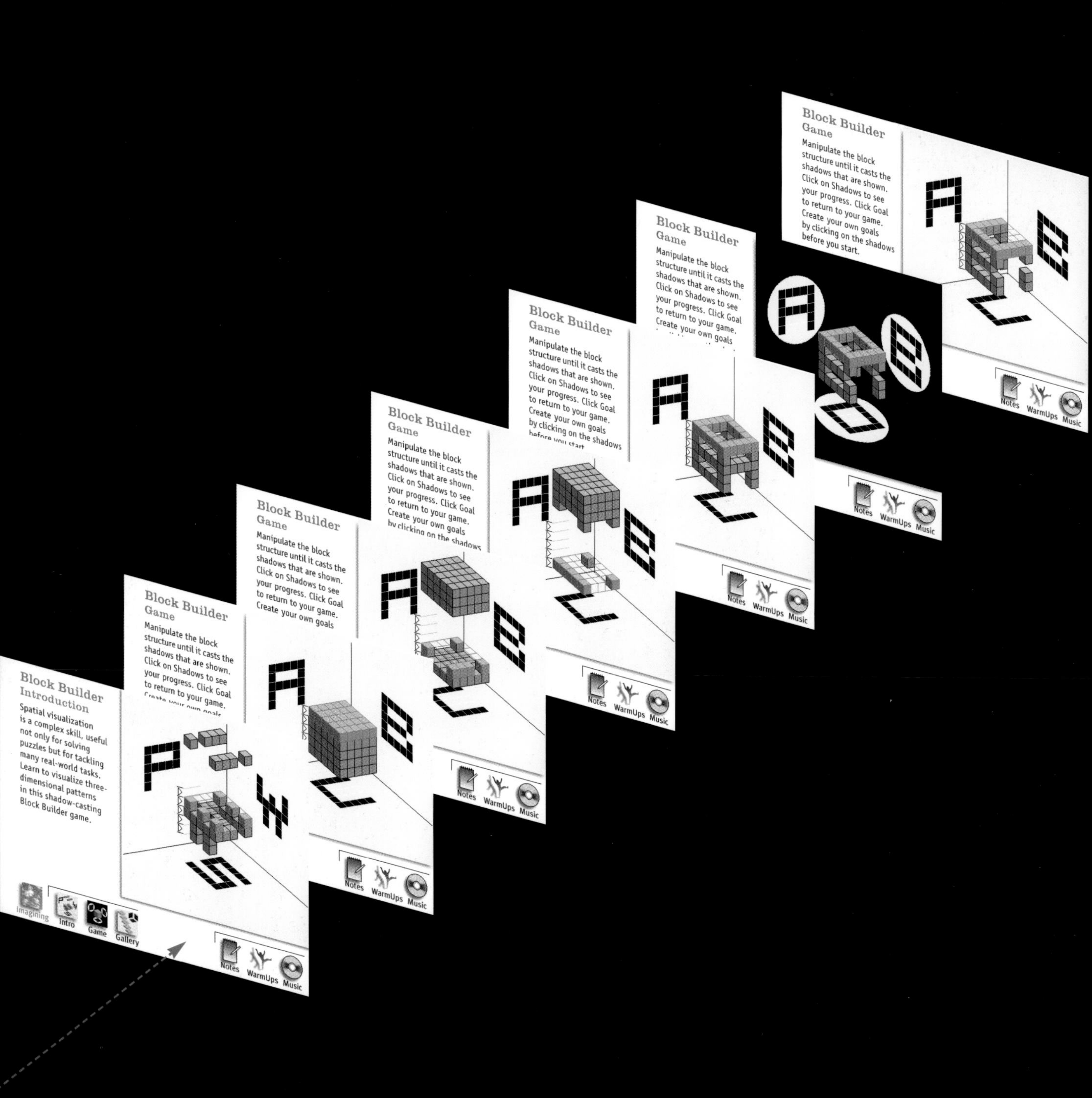

V I Z A B I L I T Y

CLIENT / PUBLISHER PWS Publishing.

DESIGN MetaDesign, San Francisco, CA. Kristina Hooper Woolsey and Bill Hill, executive producers; Kristina Hooper Woolsey, Scott Kim and Gayle Curtis, authors; MetaDesign, developer; Bill Purdy, producer; Cindy Rink, associate producer; Terry Irwin and Jeff Zwerner, creative direction; Wendy Slick, video direction/producer; Marabeth Harding, programming; Don Ahrens, digital video design; Jym Warhol,

Hidden Pictures
B&W
Find the small piece in the big picture and click on it.
Next
Grid
Answer
Pieces
Hits
Misses
New
Notes
WarmUps
Music
Hidden Pictures
Color
Find the small piece in the big picture and click on it.
Seeing
Intro
B&W
Color
Hidden Pictures
Introduction
We usually see objects in context, noticing just enough about their shape and form to identify them. But if we take the time to really look, we can discover a wealth of detail in the most ordinary things.
Attributes
Introduction
We are pattern seekers, uniting or separating objects according to their visual attributes, such as striped vs. solid, or blue vs. red. Learning to group objects into more subtle categories—such as striped vs. square—can increase both our visual and mental flexibility.
Letters
Shapes
Objects
Introduction
Overviews
Seeing
Flash Sketching
Eye Tracking
Hidden Pictures
Attributes
Seeing Objects
VizAbility™
Imagining
Seeing
Environment
Culture
Introduction
Orientation
Quit

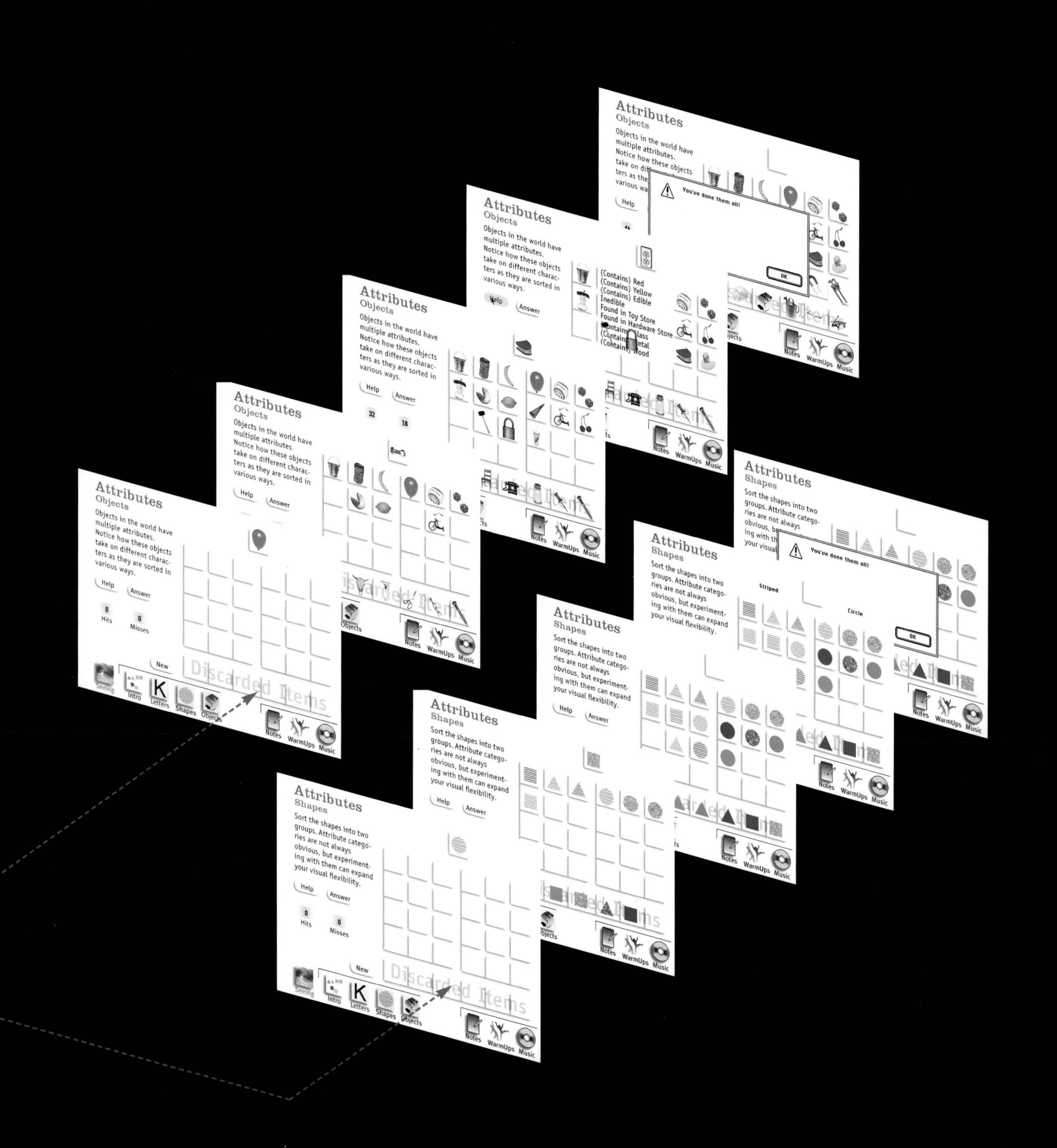

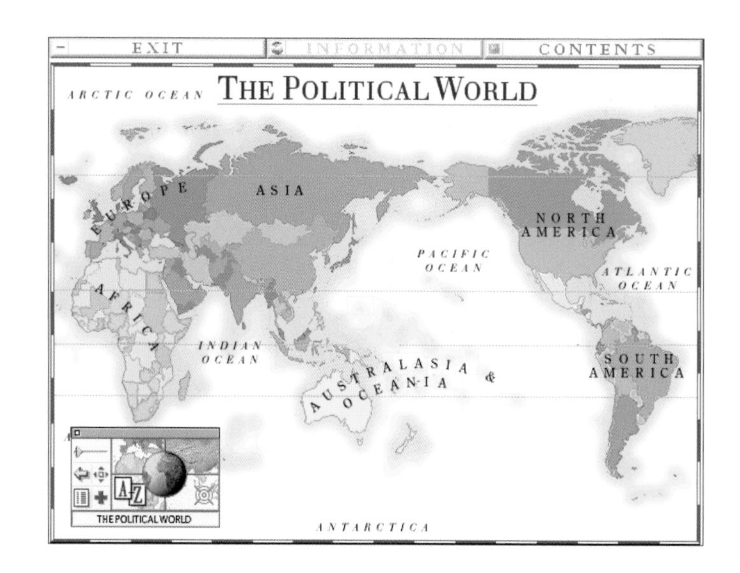

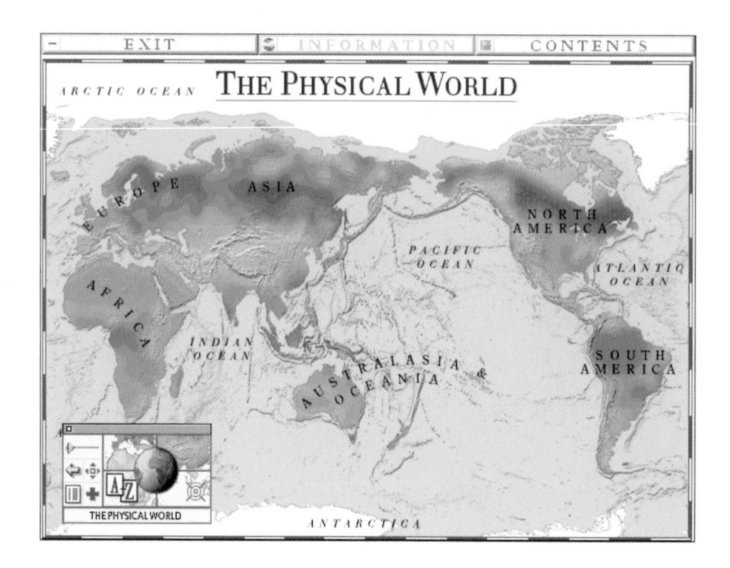

WORLD REFERENCE ATLAS 

CLIENT/COMPANY Dorling Kindersley Multimedia

DESIGN Dorling Kindersley Multimedia, London, Great Britain. Helen Dowling, editorial lead; Pippa Hurst and Andy Walker, design leads; Patrick Boyle, production supervisor; Rebecca Painter, Panos Pantelatos and Virginia Rusell, designers; Robert Mitchell, editor; Christian Bacheor, custom tools designer; Alen Charitids, Mark Logue and Paul Lamb of I.E., Claire Fisher (Chrysalis), video processing; Sid Wells, Ian Hawkridge, Patch McQuaid, audio production; Roy Margolis, software manager; Beverley Mitchell, Nick Ager, Kevin Wells, Brian Burton-Cundall, Neil Gallager and Mike Medhurst, software developers; Iain Pusey, additional production support; Andrea Pinnington, managing editor; Susie Breen, design manager; Isabel Whitfield, product testing supervisor; Henrik Bramens and Scott McKibben, product testing coordinators.

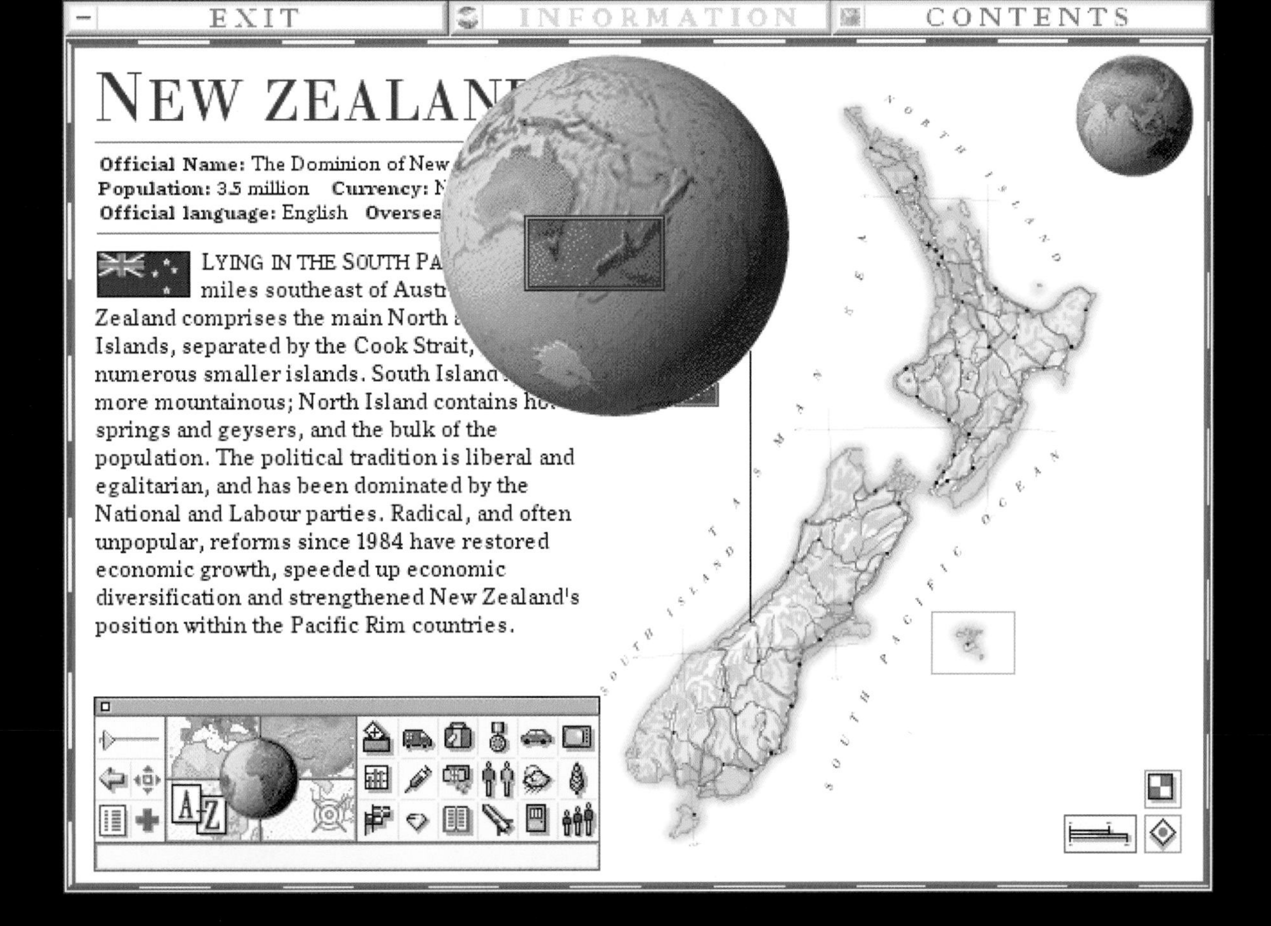

This title does everything the book version does—and more. Putting to shame similar titles, the *World Reference Atlas* sports a highly visual and attractive interface that will make any user feel like Magellan. With a spin of the globe, the user lands anywhere from Aukland or Oakland; once there, the user can click on the navigation panel to view still photographs or video clips, study demographic tables, or read a brief history of the country in question. The maps and ancillary data are fairly detailed, and are appropriate for home, school, or office use.

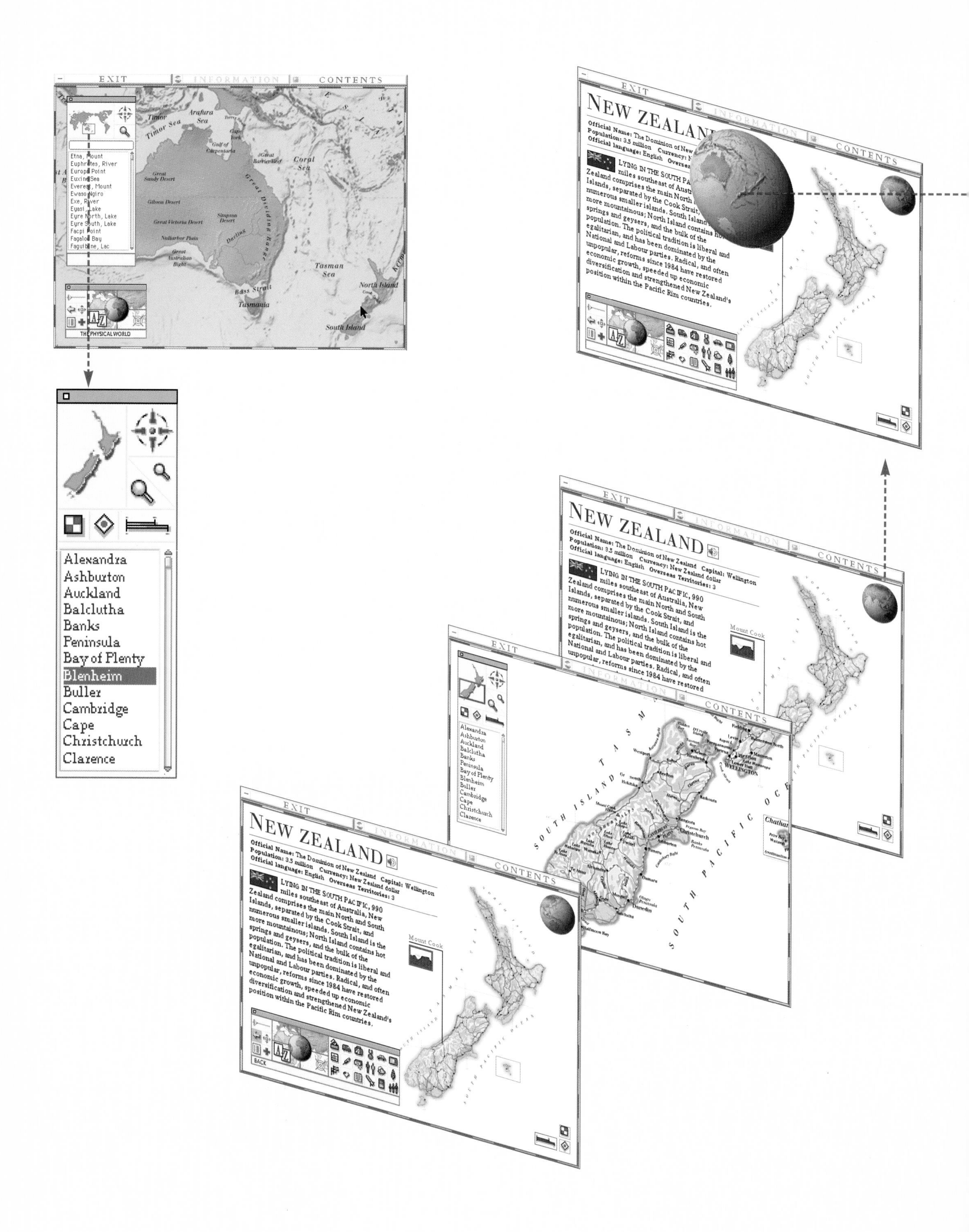
EXIT
INFORMATION
CONTENTS
Etna, Mount
Euphrates, River
Europa Point
Euxine Sea
Everest, Mount
Ewaso Ngiro
Exe, River
Eyasi, Lake
Eyre North, Lake
Eyre South, Lake
Facpi Point
Fagalo Bay
Fagutine, Lac
Timor Sea
Arafura Sea
Coral Sea
Great Sandy Desert
Gibson Desert
Great Victoria Desert
Nullarbor Plain
Great Dividing Range
Tasman Sea
Bass Strait
Tasmania
North Island
South Island
THE PHYSICAL WORLD
Alexandra
Ashburton
Auckland
Balclutha
Banks
Peninsula
Bay of Plenty
Blenheim
Buller
Cambridge
Cape
Christchurch
Clarence
NEW ZEALAND
Official Name: The Dominion of New Zealand Capital: Wellington
Population: 3.5 million Currency: New Zealand dollar
Official language: English Overseas Territories: 3
LYING IN THE SOUTH PACIFIC, 990 miles southeast of Australia, New Zealand comprises the main North and South Islands, separated by the Cook Strait, and numerous smaller islands. South Island is the more mountainous; North Island contains hot springs and geysers, and the bulk of the population. The political tradition is liberal and egalitarian, and has been dominated by the National and Labour parties. Radical, and often unpopular, reforms since 1984 have restored economic growth, speeded up economic diversification and strengthened New Zealand's position within the Pacific Rim countries.
Mount Cook
BACK
SOUTH ISLAND
SOUTH PACIFIC OCEAN
Christchurch
Dunedin
WELLINGTON

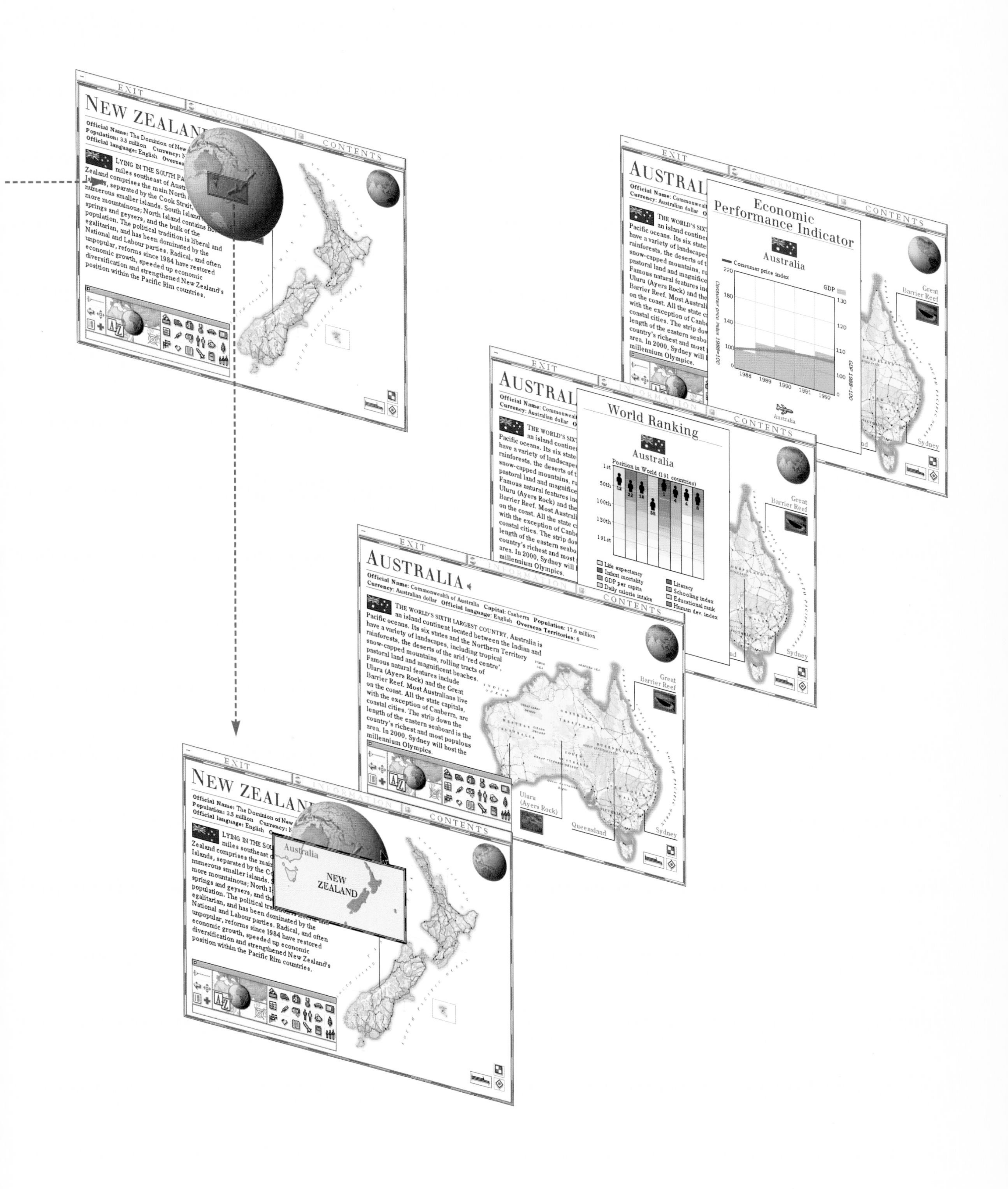
EXIT
INFORMATION
CONTENTS
NEW ZEALAND
AUSTRALIA
Official Name: Commonwealth of Australia Capital: Canberra Population: 17.6 million
Currency: Australian dollar Official language: English Overseas Territories: 6
THE WORLD'S SIXTH LARGEST COUNTRY, Australia is an island continent located between the Indian and Pacific oceans. Its six states and the Northern Territory have a variety of landscapes, including tropical rainforests, the deserts of the arid 'red centre', snow-capped mountains, rolling tracts of pastoral land and magnificent beaches. Famous natural features include Uluru (Ayers Rock) and the Great Barrier Reef. Most Australians live on the coast. All the state capitals, with the exception of Canberra, are coastal cities. The strip down the length of the eastern seaboard is the country's richest and most populous area. In 2000, Sydney will host the millennium Olympics.
Great Barrier Reef
Uluru (Ayers Rock)
Queensland
Sydney
World Ranking
Australia
Position in World (191 countries)
Life expectancy
Infant mortality
GDP per capita
Daily calorie intake
Literacy
Schooling index
Educational rank
Human dev. index
Economic Performance Indicator
Australia
Consumer price index
GDP
1988
1989
1990
1991
1992
Australia
NEW ZEALAND

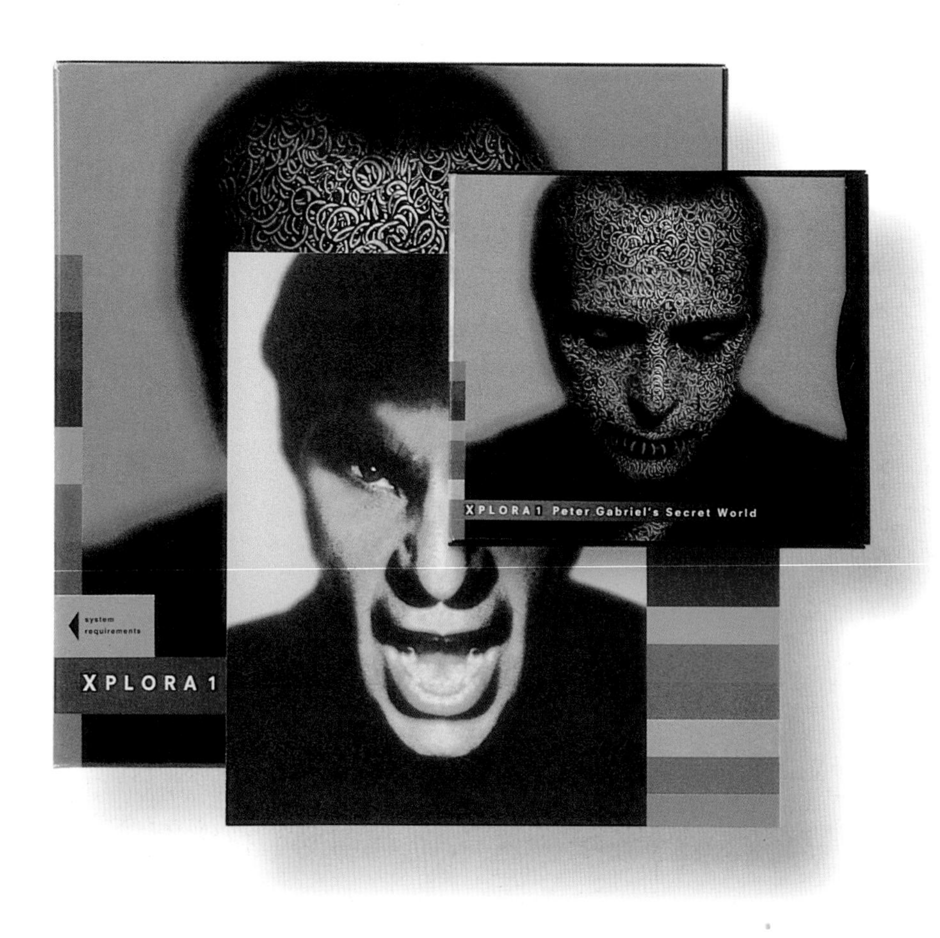

XPLORA1: PETER GABRIEL'S SECRET WORLD

CLIENT / PUBLISHER Peter Gabriel Ltd. and Real World Multimedia Ltd.

DESIGN Real World Multimedia and Brilliant Media, Inc., Great Britian. Peter Gabriel, Steve Nelson, Micheal Colson, Nichola Bruce and Mike Large, concept and artistic direction; Peter Gabriel, Mike Large and David Eno, executive producers; Real World Multimedia and Brilliant Media, Inc., new media production company.

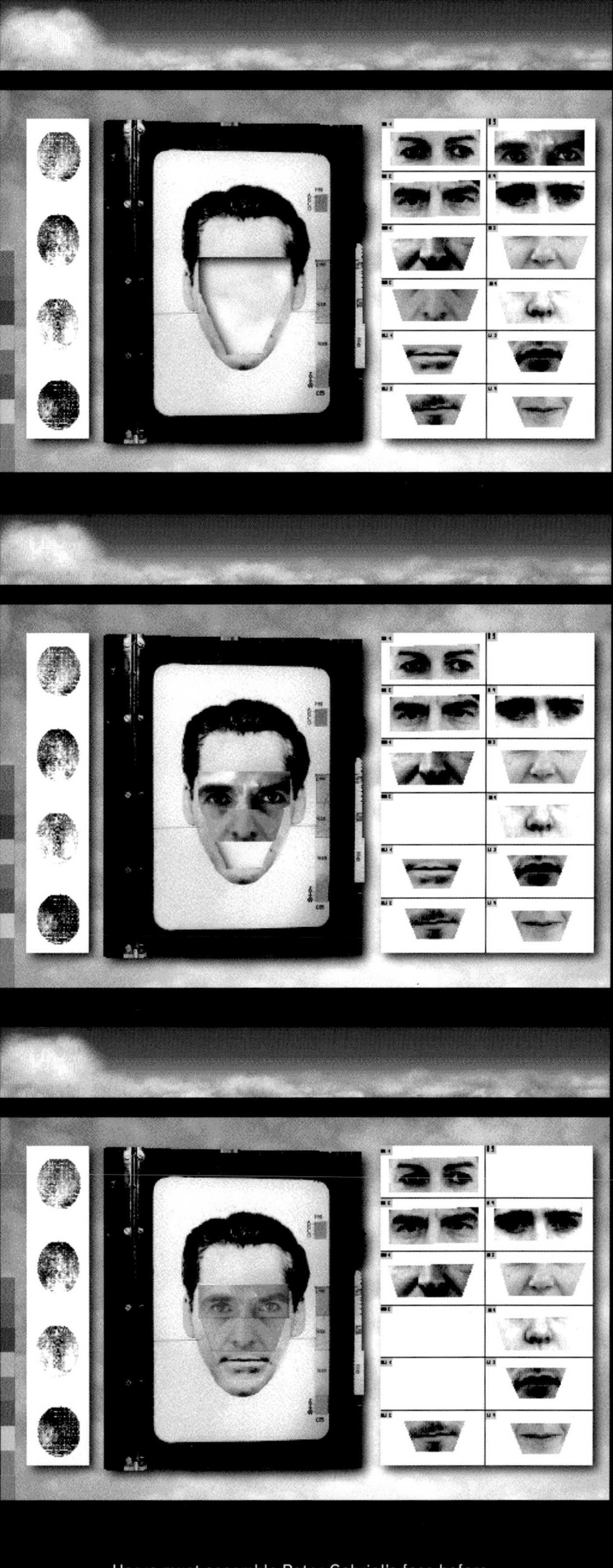

Users must assemble Peter Gabriel's face before entering the CD. Once there, they are presented with numerous text, audio, and animation navigational cues.

EXPLORE
WATCH
RESUME
QUIT

To gain access to certain areas of the CD, users must collect items—a passport, a backstage pass—which they deposit in a briefcase.

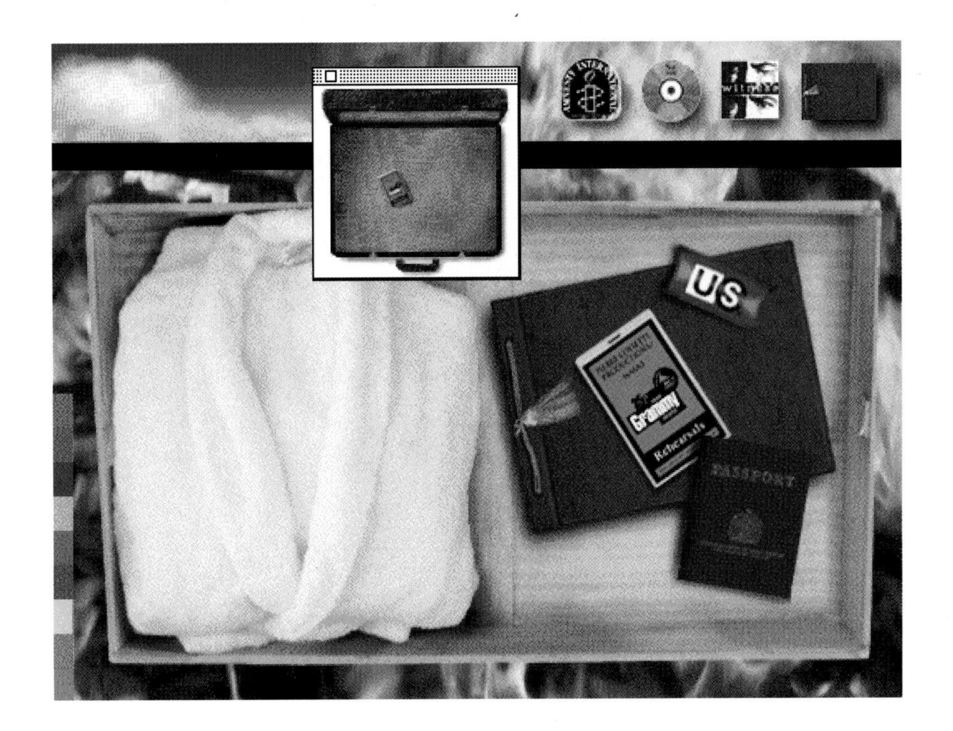

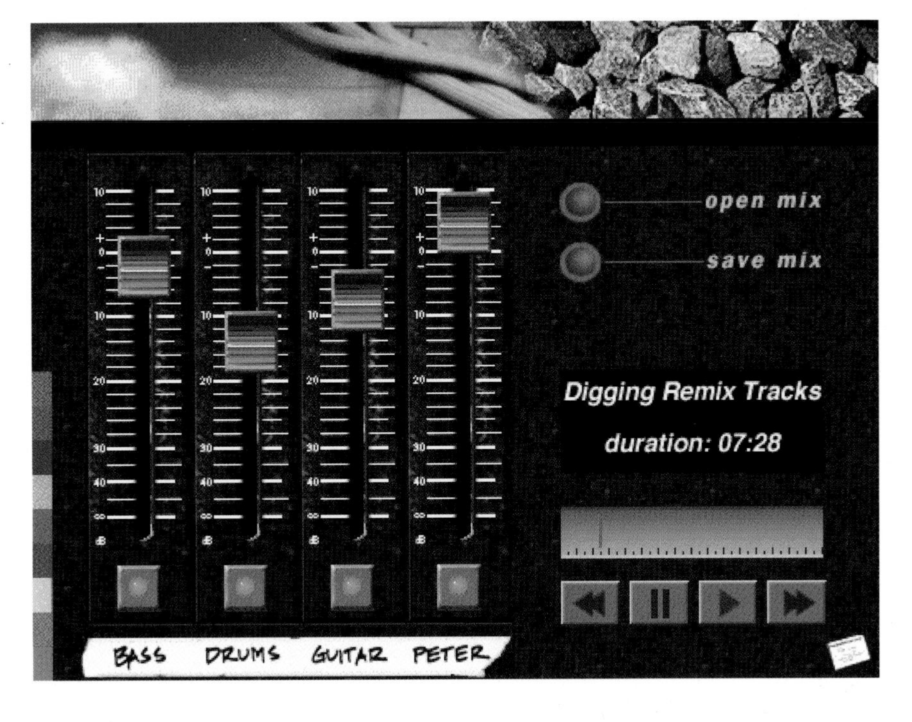

Users can fiddle with the sound on certain songs by using a handy mouse-controlled mixer, which controls voice, drums, guitar, and bass.

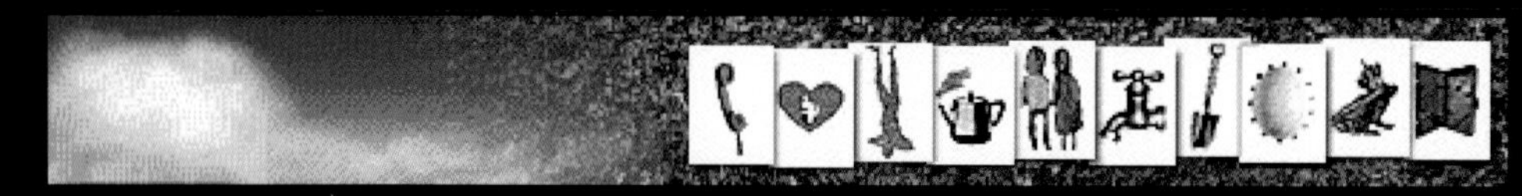

Users can click on color bars that reside in the lower left-hand corner and which provide background on songs from Gabriel's *US* album or else send users to previous menus.

Archetypal images appear—a globe, a lion, a drum, a Chinese coin—which serve as gateways to the title. Click on the globe icon, for instance, and users can watch videos of musicians from a variety of countries play and sing; each location also boasts a virtual instrument—a pipe or a drum—that users can play with a mouse.

With *ScruTiny in the Great Round,* New York artists Tennessee Rice Dixon and Jim Gasperini have created an interactive dream of interwoven moving images, metaphoric icons, audible symbols, poetry, fascinating animation, and fine music. It is a highly textured interactive experience that turns the user's computer into a tool for spiritual enlightenment, as well as a piece of kinetic art. ■ Users manipulate the screen with a changing cursor that appears as a moon (which explores the feminine, rhythmic cycle of life), a sun (which relates the linear, masculine perspective); a bird or fish cursor allows the user to move between scenes of rich collage that quickly infuse with flowing images and three-dimensional elements that morph smoothly and convincingly. It is a hypnotic interactive experience that allows users to interact time and again without replicating earlier experiences. ■ One sequence caused an egg to crack open, spilling out a field of stars; a sand dollar then appeared, which morphed into a naked infant drifting through the heavens; the child transformed into a fish that swam across the screen, which in turn morphed back into the shape of the shell, then back to the baby. All the while, the baby (and the user) are soothed by the voice of a mother reciting a simple lullaby. Soon enough, the cursor turned into the arm of the baby, and by sweeping this arm across the screen, the user painted over the night sky with another interactive collage. A cybernetic acid trip.

SCRUTINY IN THE GREAT ROUND

CLIENT/PUBLISHER Calliope Media

DESIGN Calliope Media, Santa Monica, CA. Tennessee Rice Dixon and Jim Gasperini, design and production; Charlie Morrow, audio and music composer.

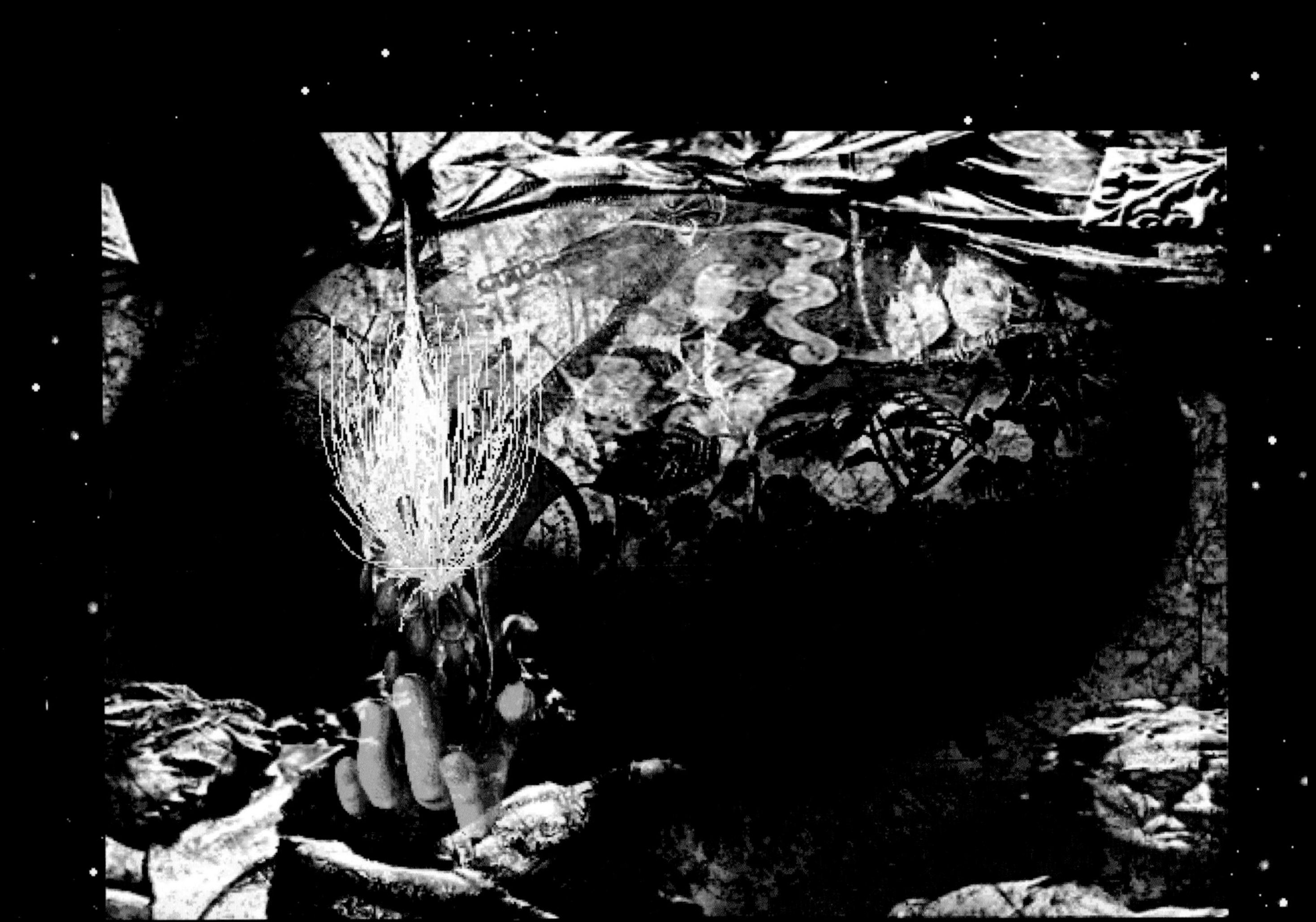

Fruit Scar
Pith

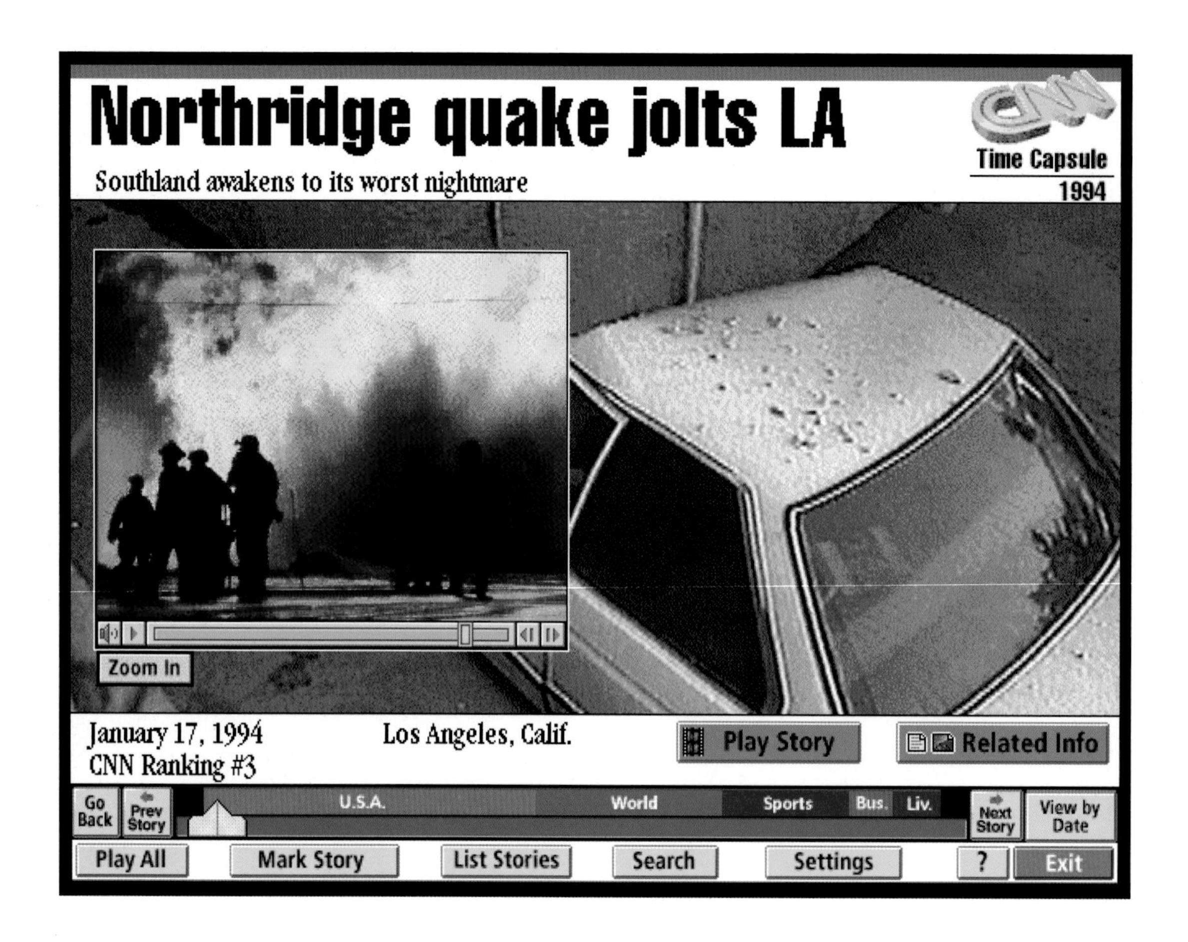

CNN TIME CAPSULE

CLIENT / PUBLISHER Vicarious

DESIGN Vicarious, Redwood City, CA. Greg Gretsch, art director; Paul Bauersfield and Fred Malouf, programmers, Chris Kruger, graphic designer; Vicarious, new media production company.

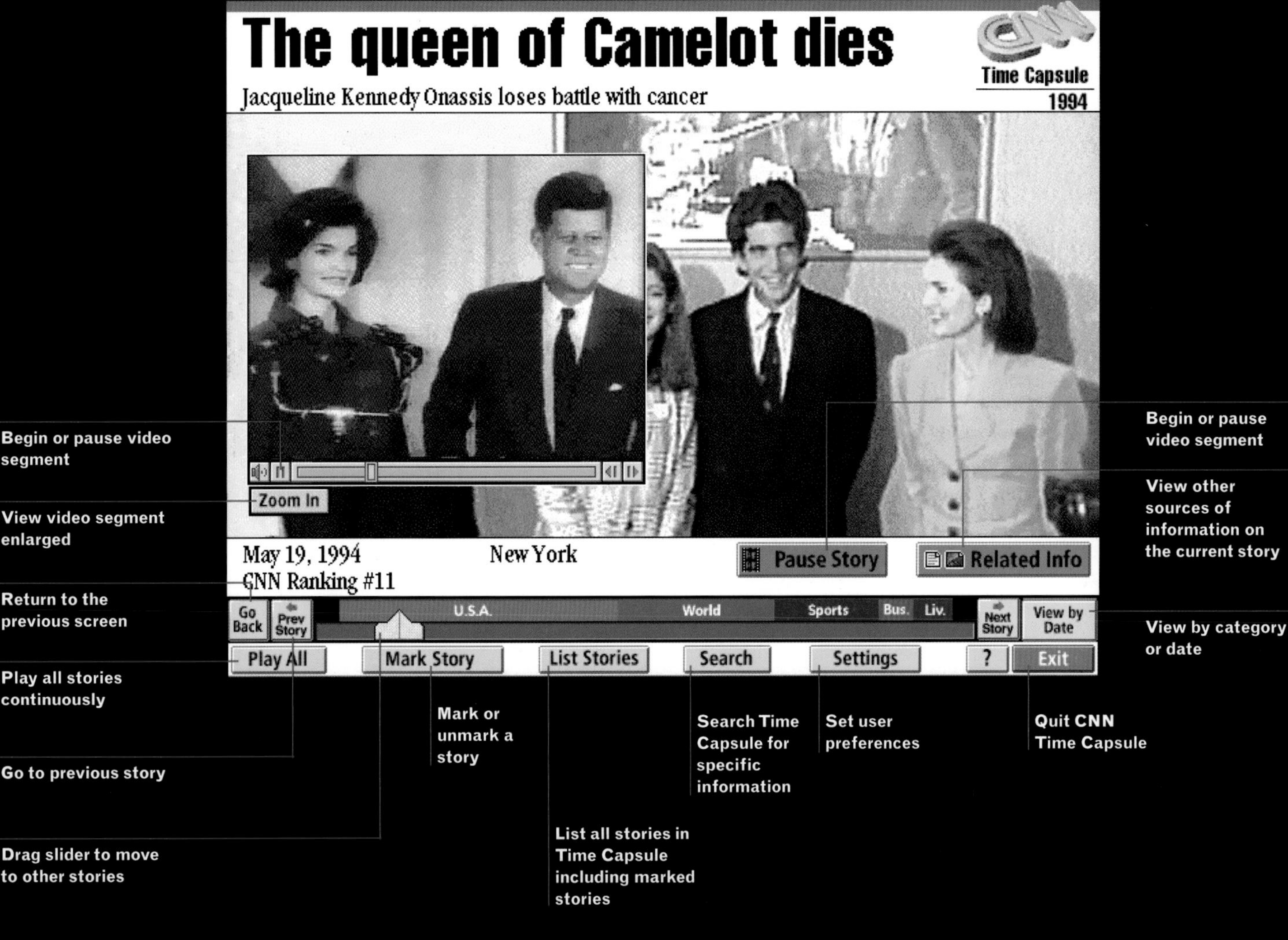

This *CNN Time Capsule* reviews the year's most newsworthy stories by way of a snappy, user-friendly interface. Video clips from the Cable News Network can be compared with political cartoons from papers around the globe, as well as reprints from *USA Today* and *US News and World Report.* Content can be accessed through a time-line, a powerful search function, and a smart cross-referencing system. What makes this a serious research tool rather than mere entertainment are its easy-to-use export and printing functions.

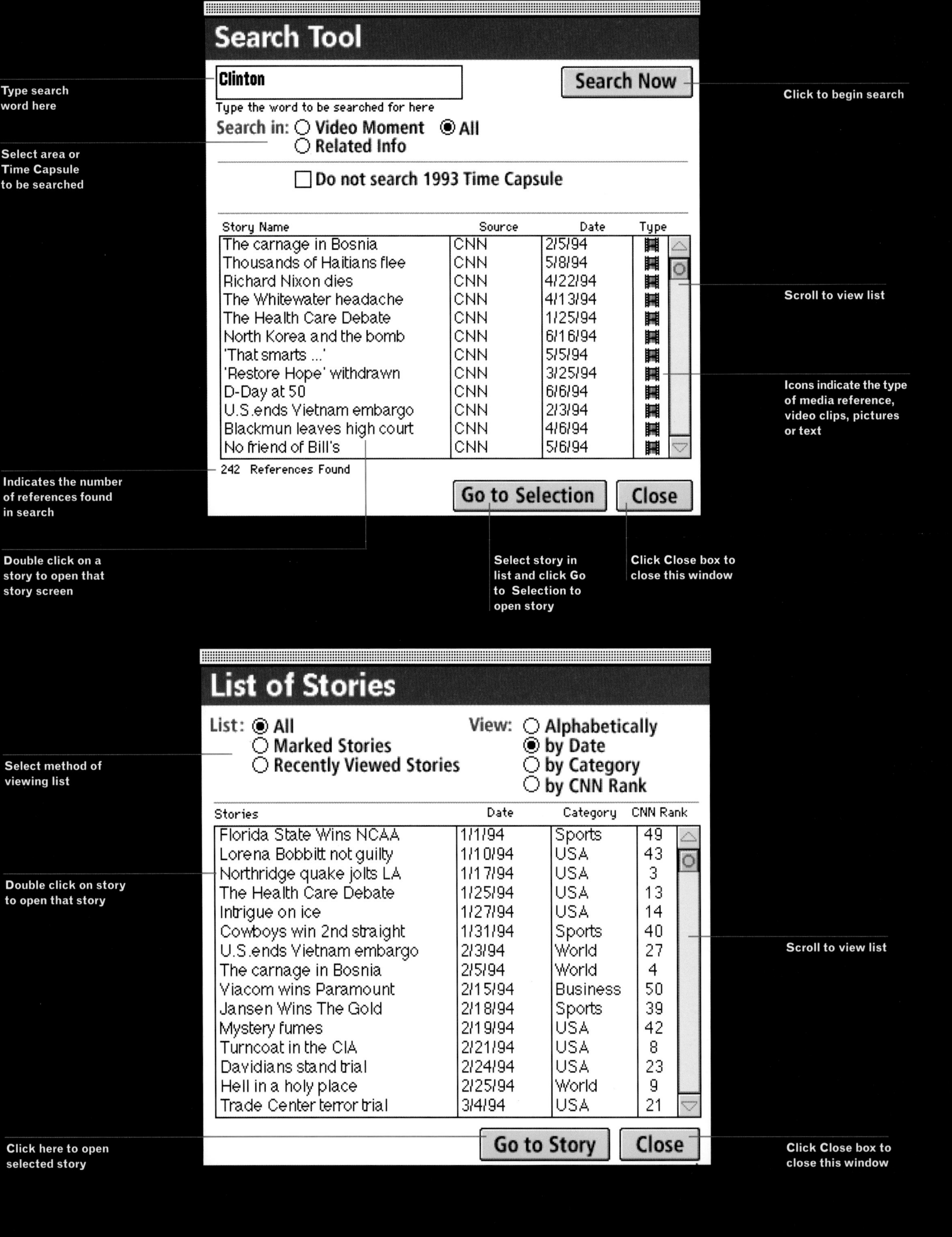
Search Tool
Clinton
Search Now
Type the word to be searched for here
Search in: Video Moment All
Related Info
Do not search 1993 Time Capsule
Story Name Source Date Type
The carnage in Bosnia CNN 2/5/94
Thousands of Haitians flee CNN 5/8/94
Richard Nixon dies CNN 4/22/94
The Whitewater headache CNN 4/13/94
The Health Care Debate CNN 1/25/94
North Korea and the bomb CNN 6/16/94
'That smarts ...' CNN 5/5/94
'Restore Hope' withdrawn CNN 3/25/94
D-Day at 50 CNN 6/6/94
U.S.ends Vietnam embargo CNN 2/3/94
Blackmun leaves high court CNN 4/6/94
No friend of Bill's CNN 5/6/94
242 References Found
Go to Selection
Close
Type search word here
Select area or Time Capsule to be searched
Indicates the number of references found in search
Double click on a story to open that story screen
Select story in list and click Go to Selection to open story
Click Close box to close this window
Click to begin search
Scroll to view list
Icons indicate the type of media reference, video clips, pictures or text
List of Stories
List: All
Marked Stories
Recently Viewed Stories
View: Alphabetically
by Date
by Category
by CNN Rank
Stories Date Category CNN Rank
Florida State Wins NCAA 1/1/94 Sports 49
Lorena Bobbitt not guilty 1/10/94 USA 43
Northridge quake jolts LA 1/17/94 USA 3
The Health Care Debate 1/25/94 USA 13
Intrigue on ice 1/27/94 USA 14
Cowboys win 2nd straight 1/31/94 Sports 40
U.S.ends Vietnam embargo 2/3/94 World 27
The carnage in Bosnia 2/5/94 World 4
Viacom wins Paramount 2/15/94 Business 50
Jansen Wins The Gold 2/18/94 Sports 39
Mystery fumes 2/19/94 USA 42
Turncoat in the CIA 2/21/94 USA 8
Davidians stand trial 2/24/94 USA 23
Hell in a holy place 2/25/94 World 9
Trade Center terror trial 3/4/94 USA 21
Go to Story
Close
Select method of viewing list
Double click on story to open that story
Click here to open selected story
Scroll to view list
Click Close box to close this window

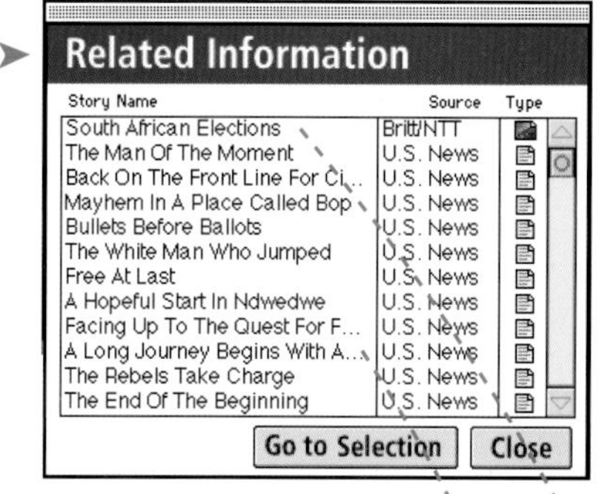

U.S.NEWS & WORLD REPORT

May 16, 1994

A Long Journey Begins With A Dance Step

No image sums up the joy, relief and hope felt by millions of South Africans better than that of 75-year-old Nelson Mandela dancing at the African National Congress's victory party last week. Gone was the dour, frowning, often hectoring Mandela of news conferences, interviews and debates. Instead, South Africa saw its new president-elect as a funky father of the nation, a beaming septuagenarian doing his own, stiff-armed version of the toyi-toyi, a warlike stomp that is synonymous with black protest against apartheid...

...priate for a nation that is ...fter decades of crippling ...dela turned to the sober ...iorities -- forging a united ...ng-oppressed people ...we build an atmosphere ...bber stamps," Mandela

...Setup Print Close

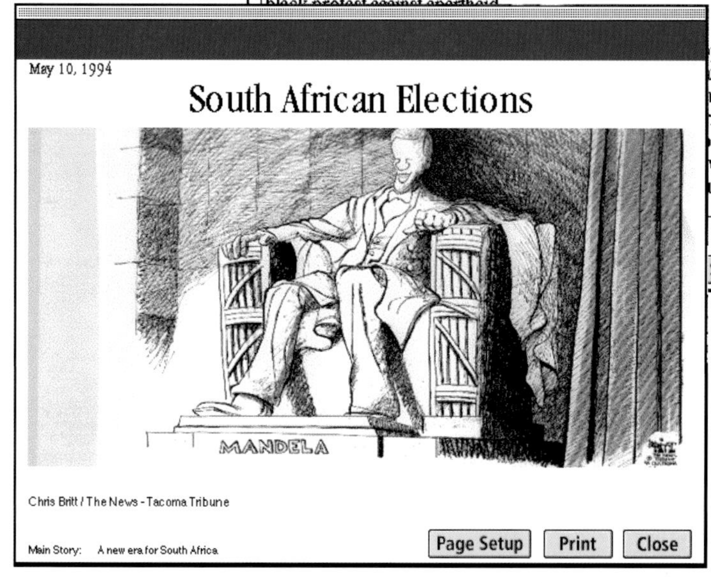

"This is not a disk, this is a building in the shape of a disk; it is a maze." So exhorts the slightly sinister voice that guides players through *The Riddle of the Maze.* Indeed, many players find this interactive game thoroughly engrossing, owing largely to the designers' application of a simple concept—a maze—to New Media. ■ Players enter a house by clicking on the front door. Once inside the antechamber, they must choose one of four doors, which leads to rooms with more doors, seemingly endless loops, or worse. Users are directed to pick up animated clues along the way so that they may answer riddles, the proper answers to which will help them advance. ■ The objective is to cut the shortest path possible to the 45th door, where a riddle awaits. Though the shortest path involves passing through only 16 doors, virtually all players eventually stumble into the room of lost souls, their eyes straining into the darkness. This portends the close of the game—at least for the losers. *The Riddle of the Maze* can be frustrating, but players have been warned. As the guide cautions, "Everything can be a clue, but not all clues can be trusted."

THE RIDDLE OF THE MAZE

CLIENT / PUBLISHER Fathom Pictures

DESIGN Fathom Pictures Inc., Sausalito, CA. Hennie Farrow, art director; Christopher Manson, illustrator; Colin Andrews, producer.

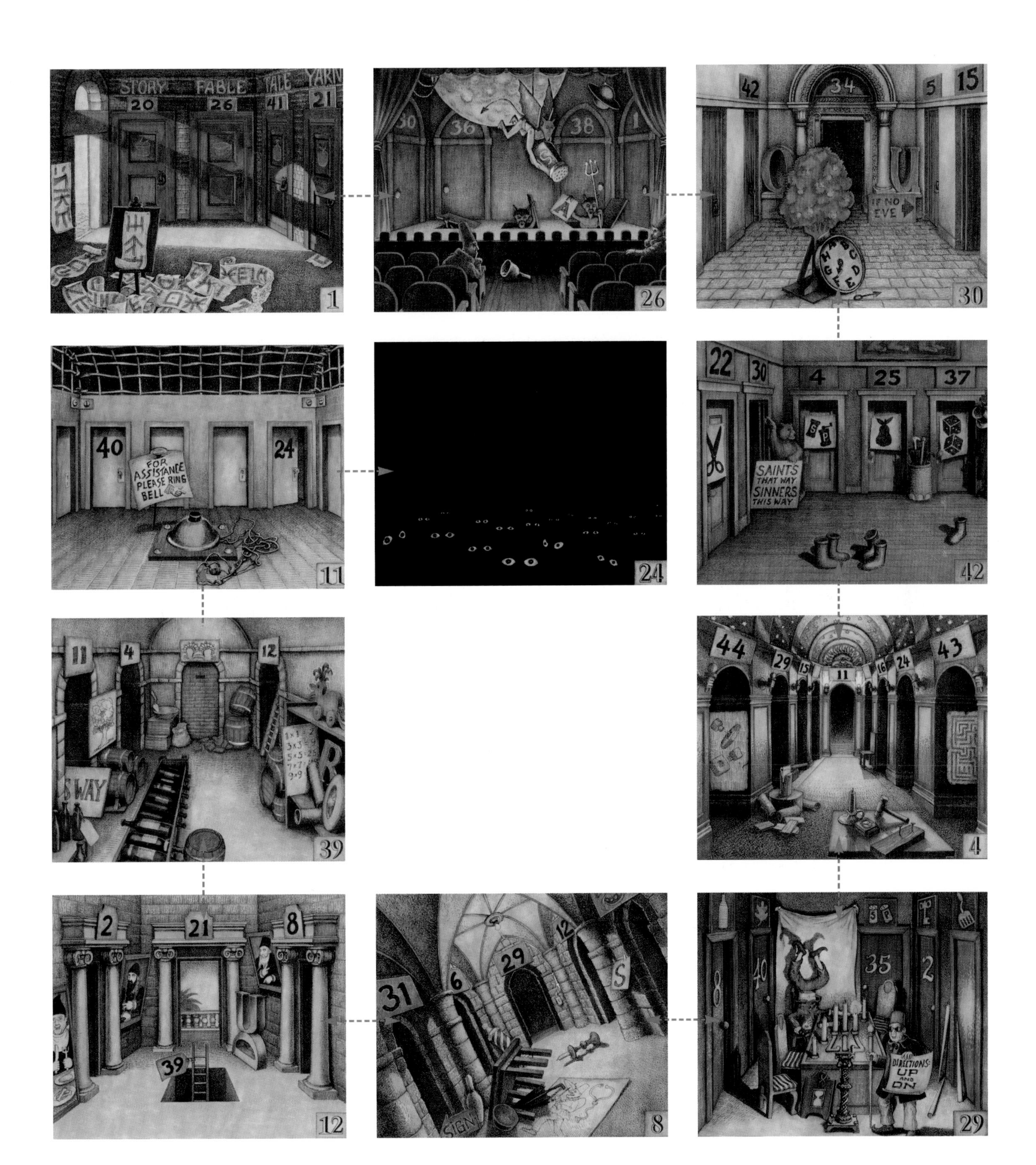

STORY FABLE TALE YARN
20 26 41 21
1
30 36 38 1
26
42 34 5 15
IF NO EVE
30
40 24
FOR ASSISTANCE PLEASE RING BELL
11
24
22 30 4 25 37
SAINTS THAT WAY SINNERS THIS WAY
42
11 4 12
1×1 3×3 5×5 7×7 9×9
39
44 29 15 11 16 24 43
4
2 21 8
39
12
31 6 29 12
S
SIGN
8
8 40 35 2
DIRECTIONS: UP AND ON
29

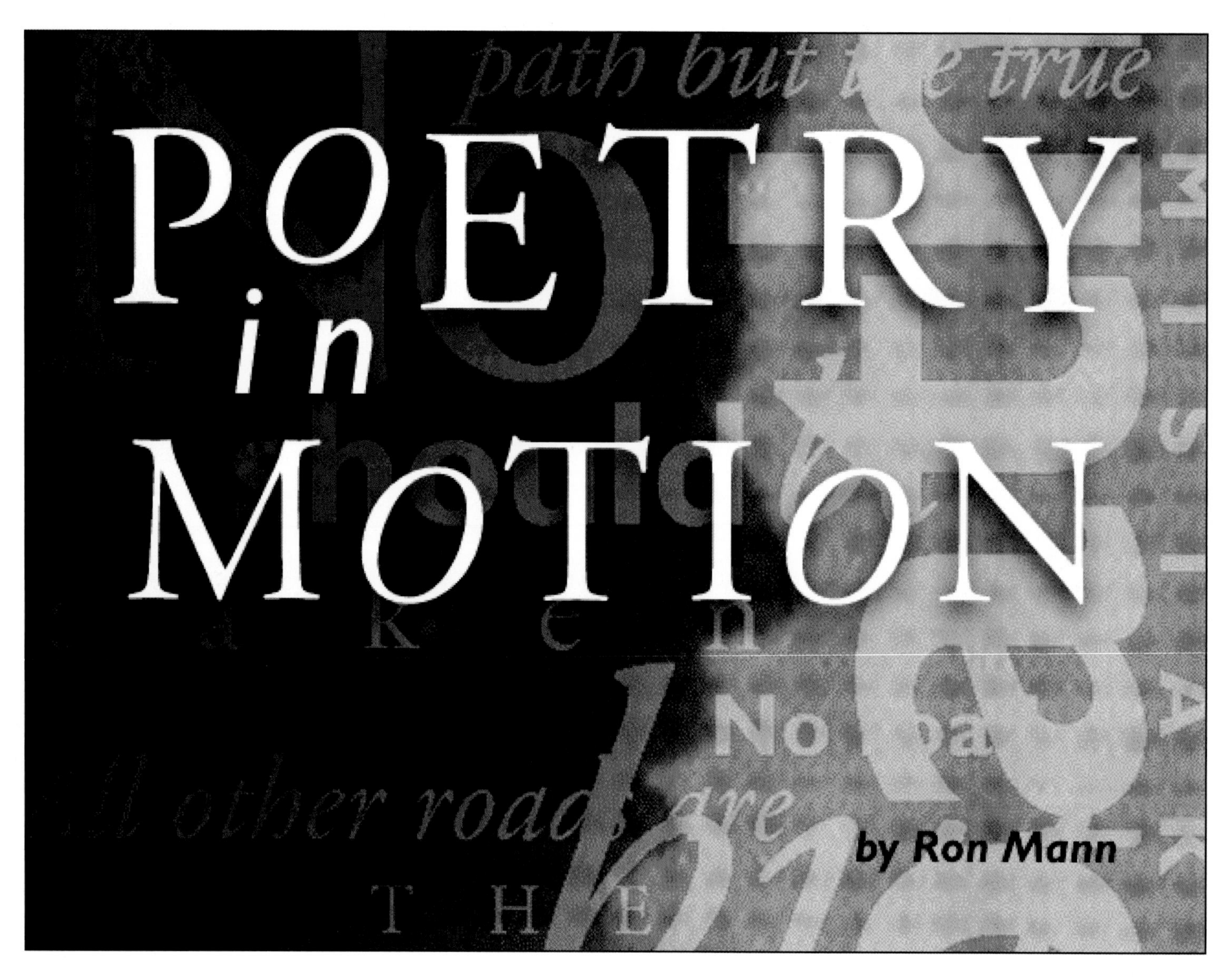

This is the new media's answer to the K-Tel pop anthologies, only it features the words of 25 contemporary poets, from Amiri Baraka to Tom Waits. Viewers haven't experienced multimedia until they double-click on the Allen Ginsberg module of this exceptional title. Here they watch a compressed video clip of a locker-room lecture he delivers on the subject of revolutionary poetry. Viewers can read Ginsberg's poem, "Capitol Air," as they view the ancient yet spry Beat poet belt out his poem with a punk band backing him up and a mosh pit of poetry fans flailing about at his feet.

POETRY IN MOTION

CLIENT / PUBLISHER The Voyager Company

DESIGN The Voyager Company, New York, NY. Ron Mann, art director; Peter Girardi, interface designer; Ron Mann, introduction writer; Colin Holgate, programmer; Ron Mann, video director; Peter Girardi, graphic designer; Rex Arthur, audio; Cristina Merlo, producer.

Performance

Interview

Allen Ginsberg

"Capitol Air"

I don't like Nationalist Supremacy White or Black
I don't like the Narcs & the Mafia marketing Smack
The General bullying Congress in his tweed vest
The President building up his Armies East & West

I don't like Argentine police assassinating Jews
Government Terrorist takeover Salvador news
I don't like Zionists acting Nazi Storm Troop
Palestine Liberation cooking Israel into Moslem soup

I don't like the Crown's Official Secrets Act
You can get away with murder in the Government that's a
 fact
Security cops teargassing radical kids
In Switzerland or Czechoslovakia God Forbids

In America it's Attica in Russia it's Lubianka Wall
In China if you disappear you wouldn't know yourself at all

Performance

Anne Waldman

"Makeup on Empty Space"

Look what thoughts will do Look what words will do
from nothing to the face
from nothing to the root of the tongue
from nothing to speaking of empty space
I bind the ash tree
I bind the yew
I bind the willow
I bind uranium
I bind the uneconomical unrenewable energy of uranium
dash the uranium to empty space
I bind the color red I seduce the color red to empty space
I put the sunset in empty space
I take the blue of his eyes and make an offering to empty
 space
renewable blue
I take the green of everything coming to life, it grows &
climbs into empty space
I put the white of the snow at the foot of empty space

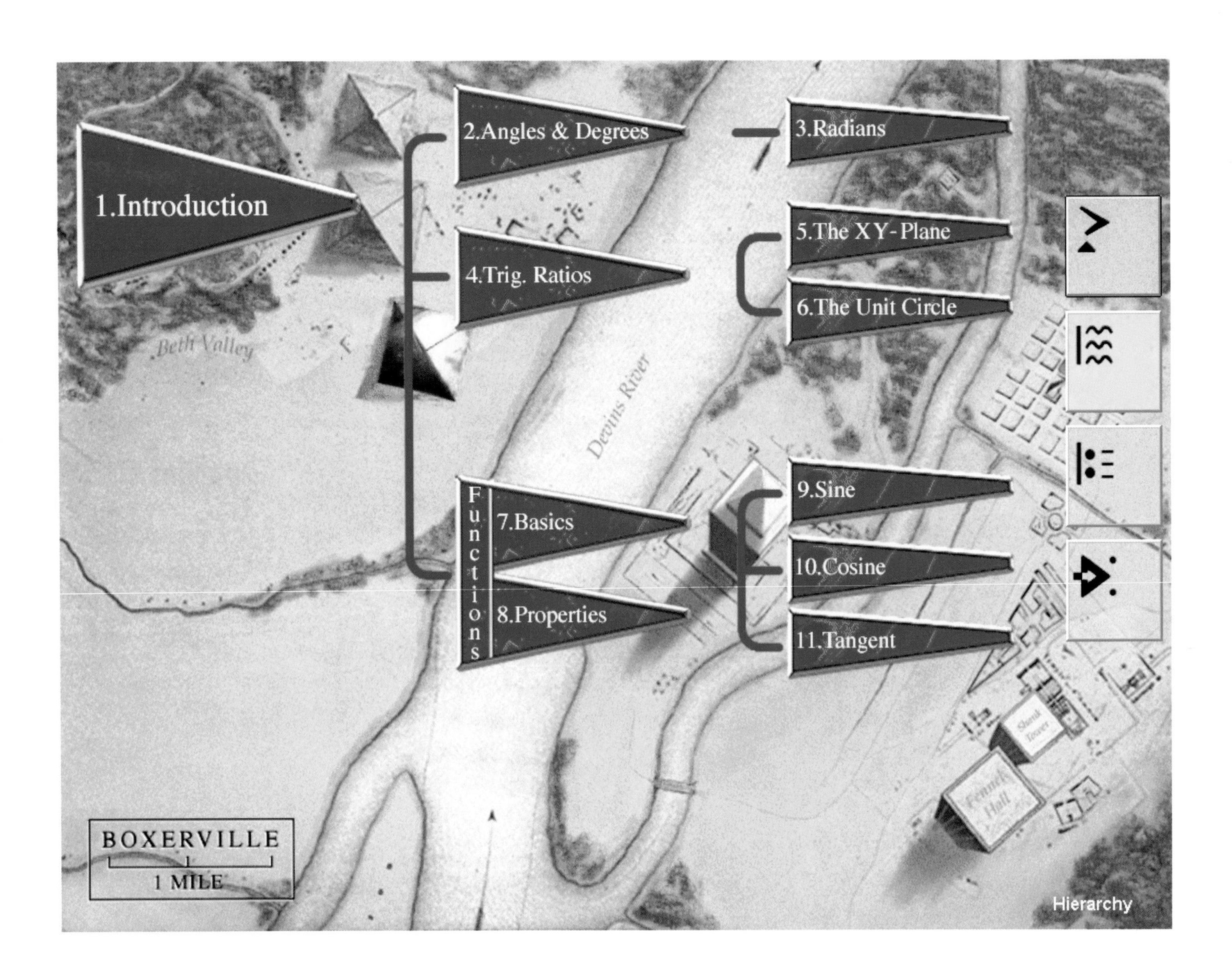

BOXER TRIGONOMETRY

CLIENT / PUBLISHER Boxer Inc.

DESIGN Boxer Inc., Charlottesville, VA. Peter Devins, art director; Colin Prepscius and Eric Rath, interface designers; Dave Shuster, Corey Brady, Seth Oldham and Diana Perdue, writers; Eric Rath, Colin Prepscius, Anu Thakkar and Tom DeWire, programmers; Beth Hollen, Sam Shank and Chris Nelson, graphic designers; Eric Rath, animator.

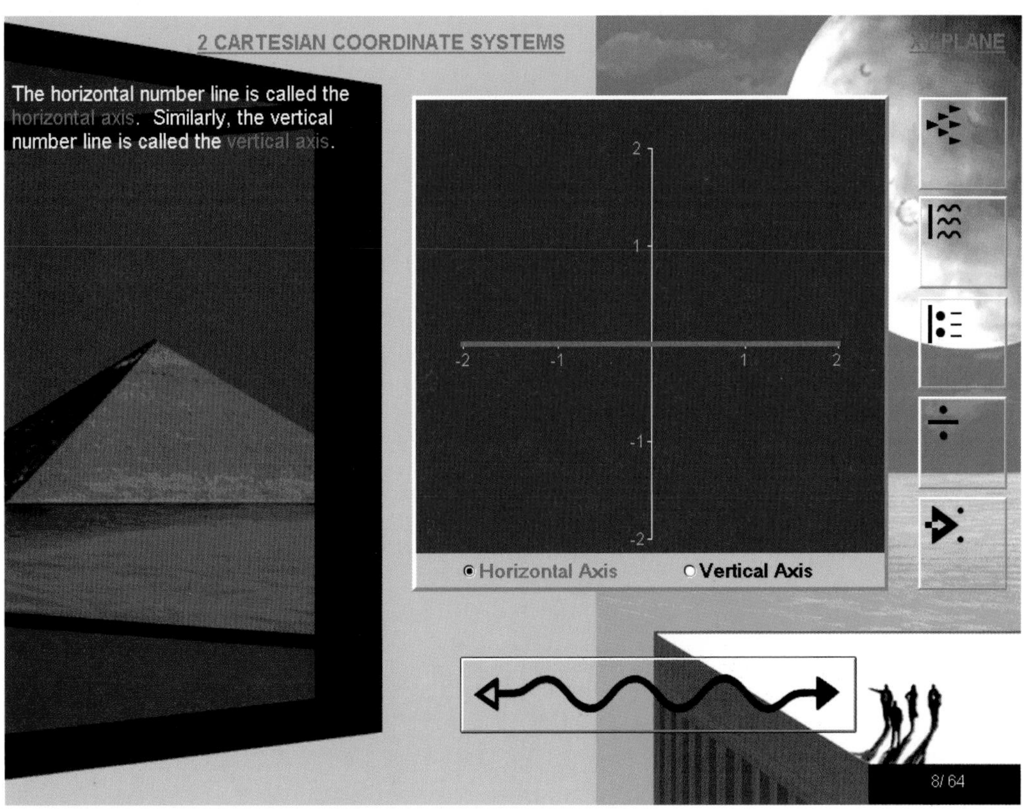

The tone and images of this do-it-yourself trigonometry course embrace a refreshingly wry tone, though they never descend into cuteness—a common design flaw of educational titles. Anyone old enough to learn trigonometry will appreciate the clean and icon-oriented approach to design and navigation of this title, even if its help icon is not a cuddly animated rabbit. ■ Boxer Trigonometry is the first title in the Boxer Math series, which includes Algebra, Geometry, Trigonometry, and Calculus. Covering everything from angles and degrees to sines and cosines, this title sports compelling real-world examples of trigonometric problems, set in desolate Dali-esque landscapes. Students learn mathematical principles, such as the axes of the XY-plane, and are invited to manipulate these principles on Cartesian planes, ask questions of the cyber-teacher, or consult a glossary. Students may then apply these principles to the everyday problems of Boxerville, the title's mythical mathematical wonderland.

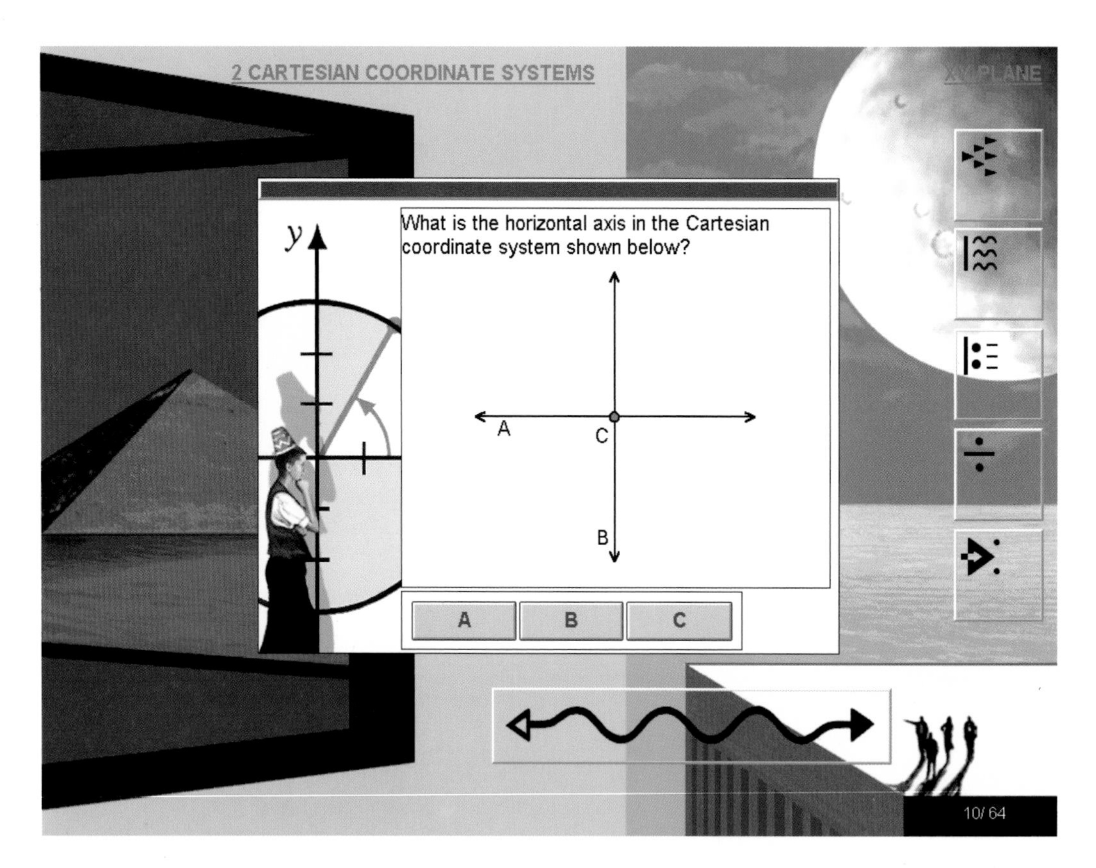
2 CARTESIAN COORDINATE SYSTEMS
What is the horizontal axis in the Cartesian coordinate system shown below?
A
C
B
A
B
C
10/ 64

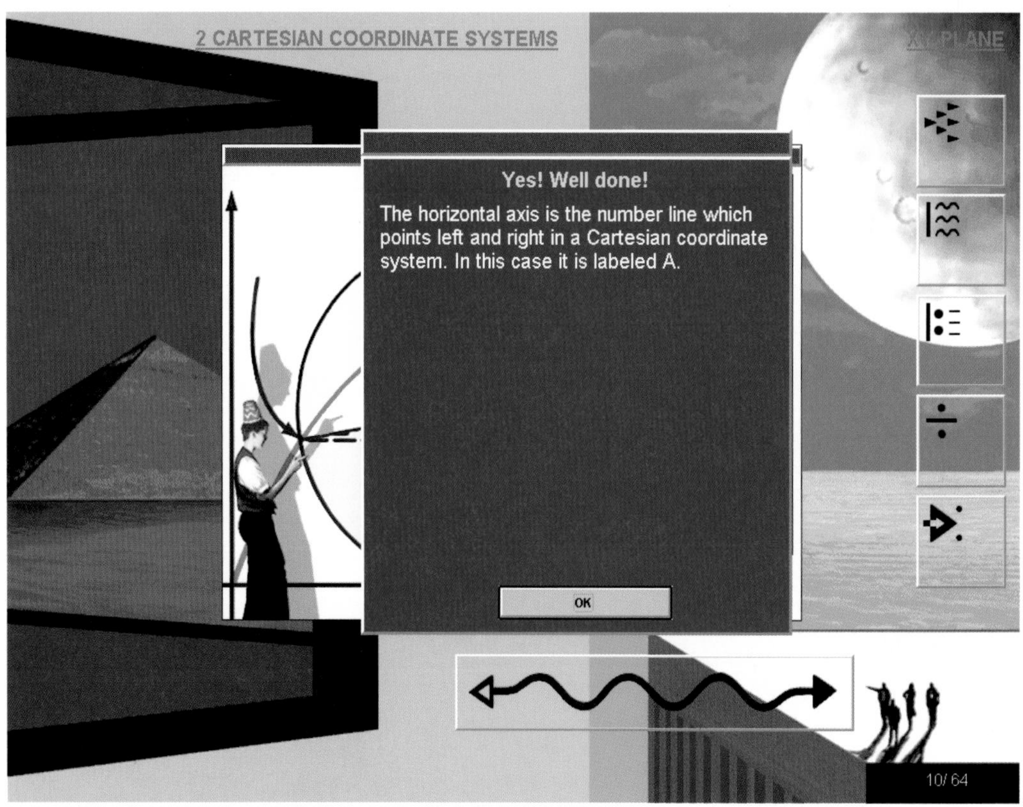
2 CARTESIAN COORDINATE SYSTEMS
Yes! Well done!
The horizontal axis is the number line which points left and right in a Cartesian coordinate system. In this case it is labeled A.
OK
10/ 64

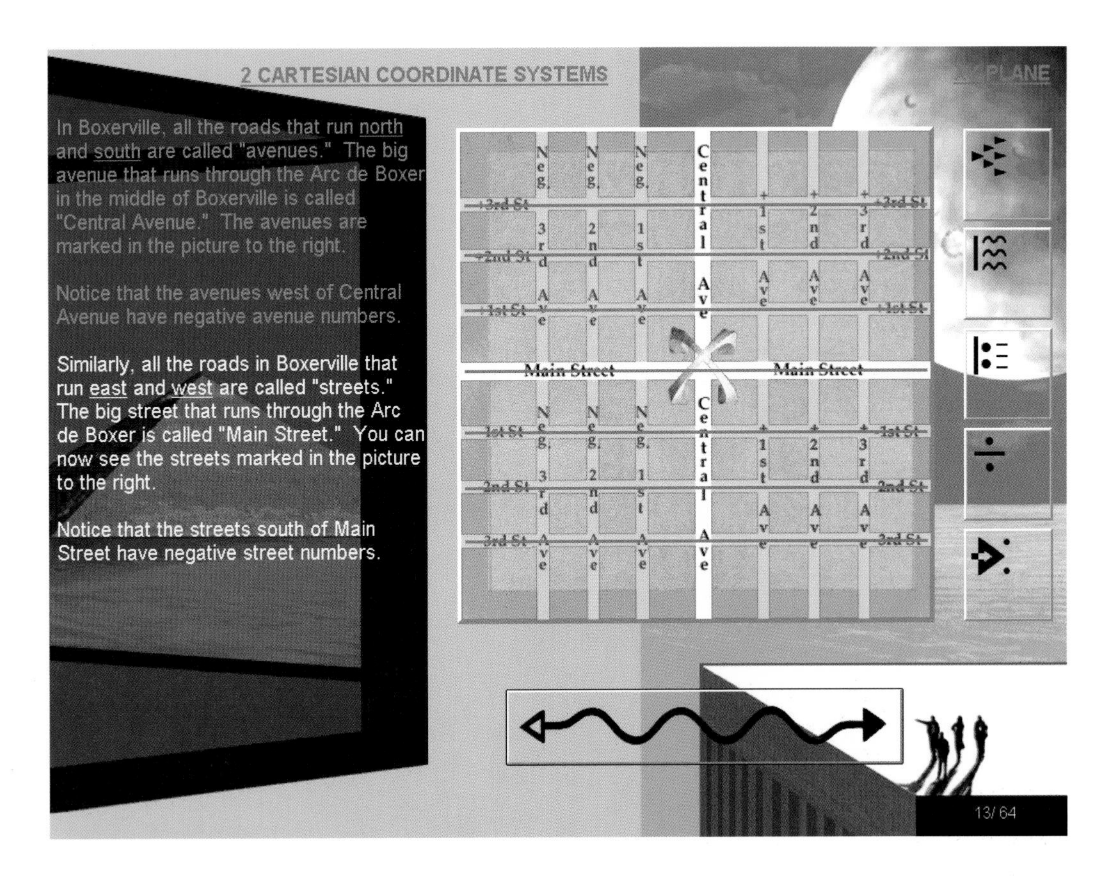
2 CARTESIAN COORDINATE SYSTEMS
In Boxerville, all the roads that run north and south are called "avenues." The big avenue that runs through the Arc de Boxer in the middle of Boxerville is called "Central Avenue." The avenues are marked in the picture to the right.
Notice that the avenues west of Central Avenue have negative avenue numbers.
Similarly, all the roads in Boxerville that run east and west are called "streets." The big street that runs through the Arc de Boxer is called "Main Street." You can now see the streets marked in the picture to the right.
Notice that the streets south of Main Street have negative street numbers.
Main Street
13/ 64

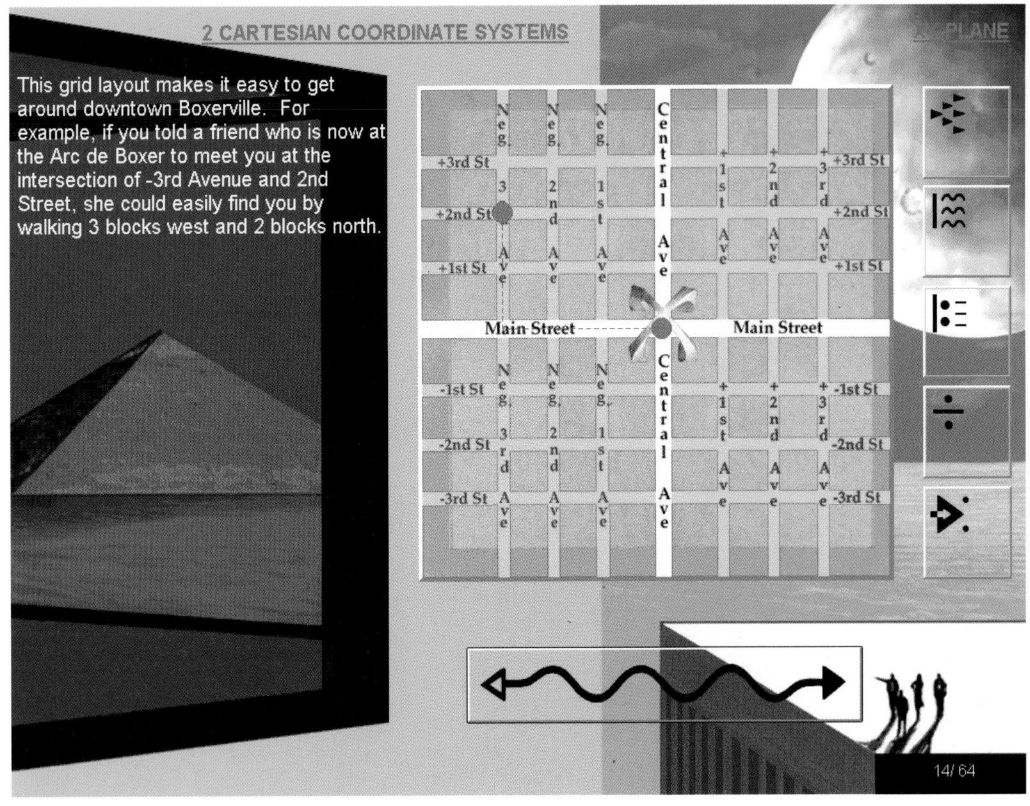
2 CARTESIAN COORDINATE SYSTEMS
This grid layout makes it easy to get around downtown Boxerville. For example, if you told a friend who is now at the Arc de Boxer to meet you at the intersection of -3rd Avenue and 2nd Street, she could easily find you by walking 3 blocks west and 2 blocks north.
+3rd St
+2nd St
+1st St
Main Street
-1st St
-2nd St
-3rd St
14/ 64

In Haruhiko Shono's *Alice,* users explore a museum filled with bizarre paintings, fanciful furniture, mysterious *objets d'art,* and whimsical characters created by Kuniyoshi Kaneko, all the while being serenaded by an impressive range of compositions inked by Kazuhiko Kato. Like Lewis Carroll's favorite little girl, users follow a bespeckeled rabbit through a world of surreal images, enigmatic messages, bizarre sounds, and unnerving experiences. Cabinets spring from puddles of water, and butterflies flutter out from open cabinet doors: do you follow the flight of the butterflies or do you dig deeper into the cabinet? Though the ostensible goal is to pick up clues that will help find a way out of this curious museum of anachronistic wonders, users may never wish to return to world of the mundane again.

ALICE 

CLIENT/PUBLISHER Synergy Interactive

DESIGN Synergy Interactive, San Francisco, CA. Haruhiko Shono, art director; Haruhiko Shono, interface designer; Hirokazu Nabekura, writer; Hideyuki Aida and Koji Katayama, programmers; Haruhiko Shono, digital video director; Haruhiko Shono, graphic designer; Yasuo Ichige and Isamu Ichige, photographers; Kuniyoshi Kaneko, illustrator; Takeshi Tanaka, audio; Haruhiko Shono, animator; Kazuhiko Kato, music composer; Makoto Sekikawa and Harumi Kato, sound editor; Masanori Awata, executive producer; Eri Osada, assistant producer.

LIFE

THE PAJAMA GAME

12
1
2
3
4
5
6
7
8
9
10
11

INTRODUCTION

Making MAUS

1 Why a CD-ROM?

2 Interviewing Vladek

3 Defining THE PAGE

4 Researching THE PAGE

5 Refining THE PAGE

6 Complaining about the screen

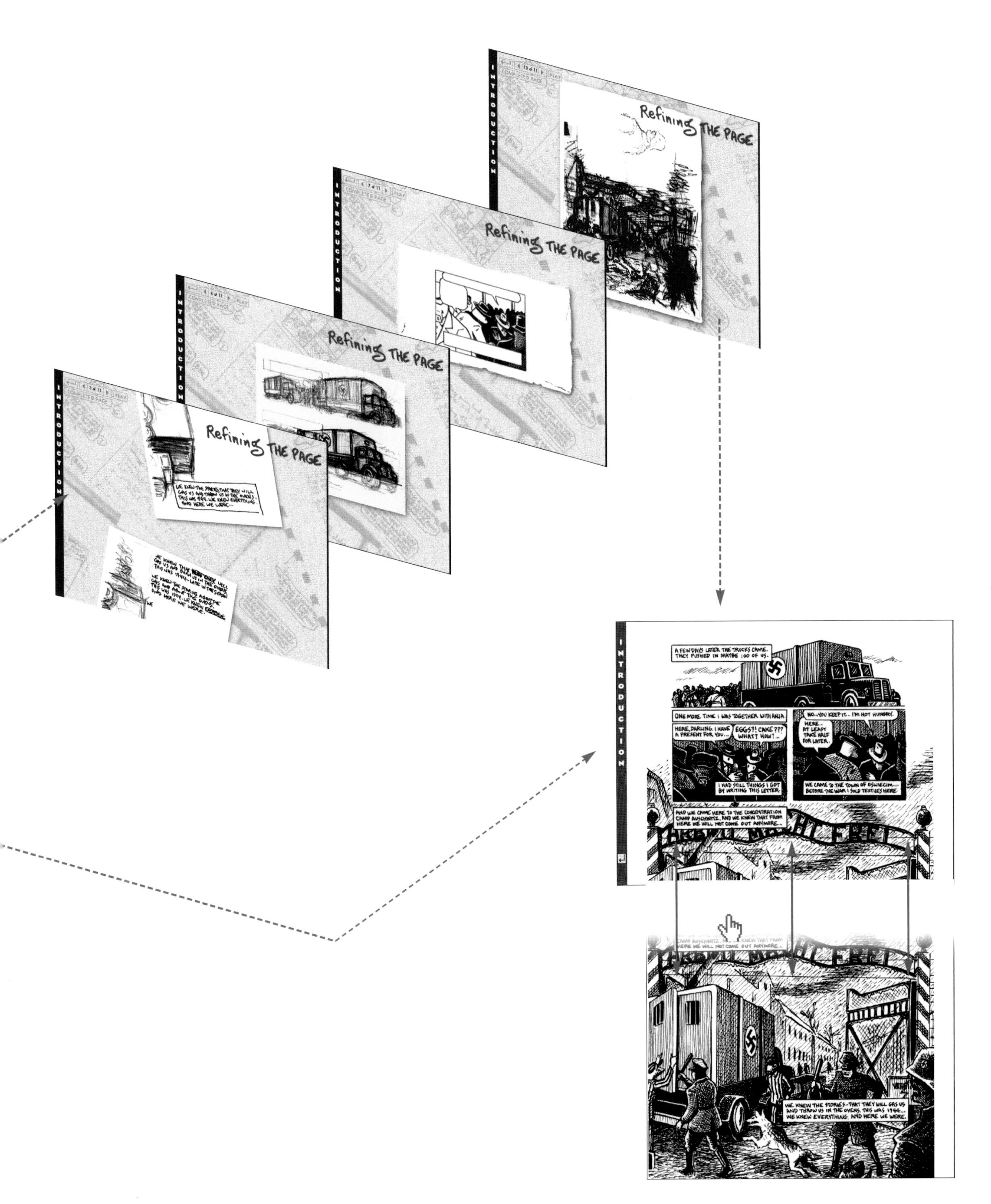
INTRODUCTION
Refining THE PAGE
INTRODUCTION
Refining THE PAGE
INTRODUCTION
Refining THE PAGE
INTRODUCTION
Refining THE PAGE
INTRODUCTION
A FEW DAYS LATER THE TRUCKS CAME. THEY PUSHED IN MAYBE 100 OF US.
ONE MORE TIME I WAS TOGETHER WITH ANJA.
HERE, DARLING. I HAVE A PRESENT FOR YOU...
EGGS?! CAKE??? WHAT? HOW?...
I HAD STILL THINGS I GOT BY WRITING THIS LETTER.
NO...YOU KEEP IT... I'M NOT HUNGRY.
HERE... AT LEAST TAKE HALF FOR LATER.
WE CAME TO THE TOWN OF OSWIECIM... BEFORE THE WAR I SOLD TEXTILES HERE.
AND WE CAME HERE TO THE CONCENTRATION CAMP AUSCHWITZ, AND WE KNEW THAT FROM HERE WE WILL NOT COME OUT ANYMORE...
WE KNEW THE STORIES—THAT THEY WILL GAS US AND THROW US IN THE OVENS. THIS WAS 1944... WE KNEW EVERYTHING. AND HERE WE WERE.

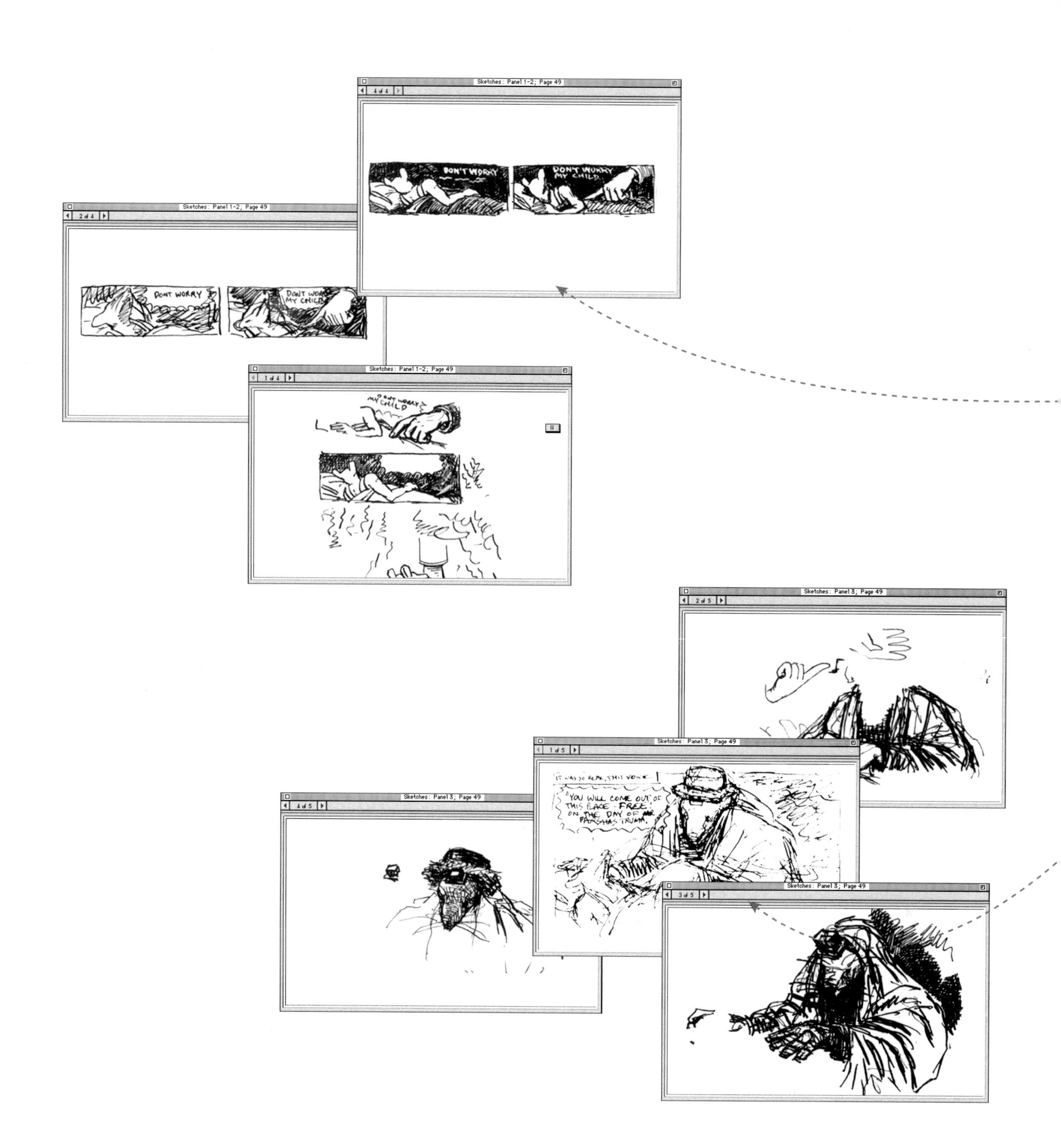
Sketches: Panel 1-2; Page 49
2 of 4
DONT WORRY
DONT WORRY MY CHILD
Sketches: Panel 1-2; Page 49
4 of 4
DON'T WORRY
DONT WORRY MY CHILD
Sketches: Panel 1-2; Page 49
1 of 4
DONT WORRY MY CHILD
Sketches: Panel 3; Page 49
2 of 5
Sketches: Panel 3; Page 49
4 of 5
Sketches: Panel 3; Page 49
1 of 5
"YOU WILL COME OUT OF THIS PLACE - FREE! ON THE DAY OF
Sketches: Panel 3; Page 49
3 of 5

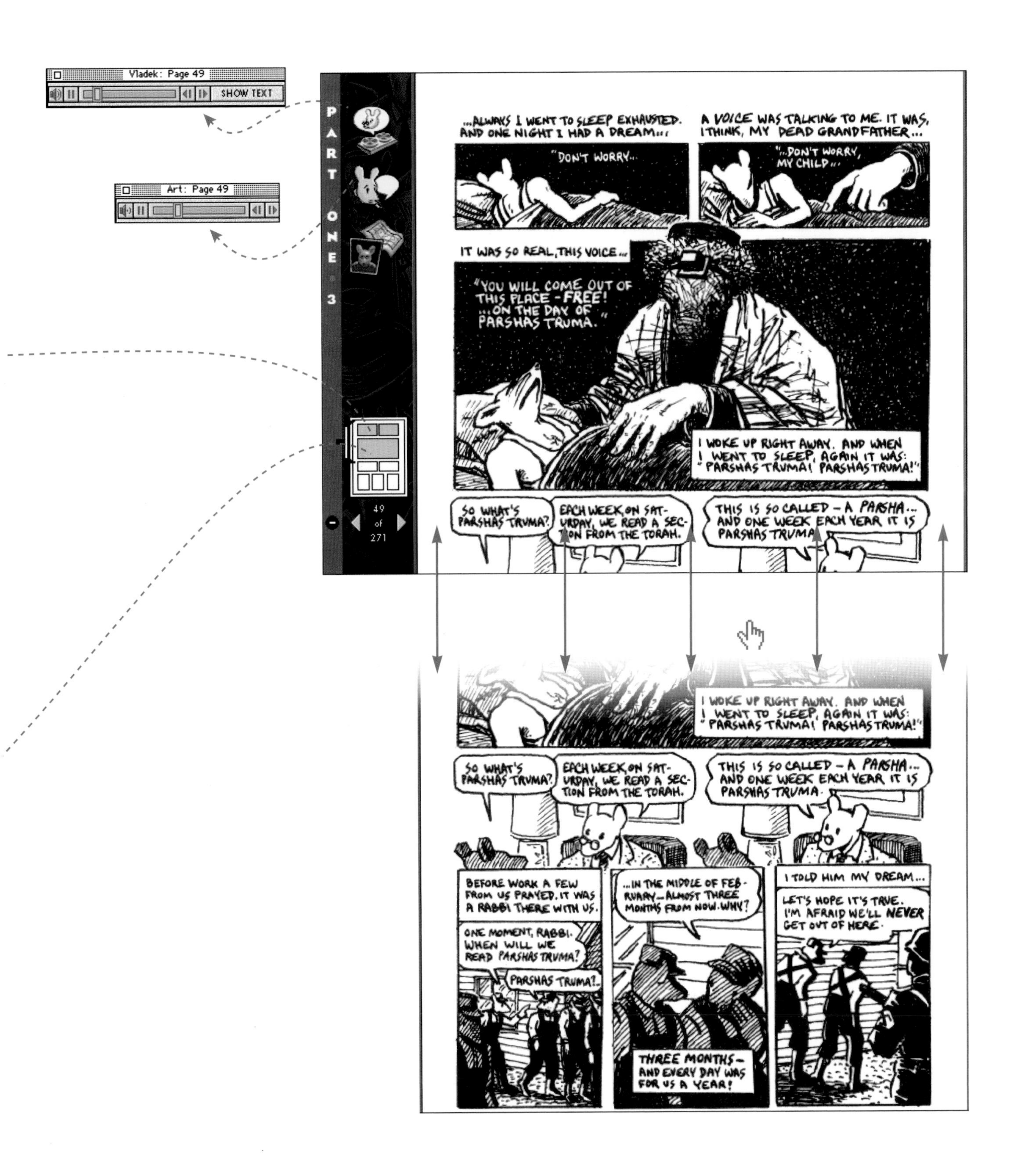
Vladek: Page 49
SHOW TEXT
Art: Page 49
PART ONE 3
49 of 271
...ALWAYS I WENT TO SLEEP EXHAUSTED. AND ONE NIGHT I HAD A DREAM...
"DON'T WORRY..
A VOICE WAS TALKING TO ME. IT WAS, I THINK, MY DEAD GRANDFATHER...
"...DON'T WORRY, MY CHILD...
IT WAS SO REAL, THIS VOICE...
"YOU WILL COME OUT OF THIS PLACE - FREE! ...ON THE DAY OF PARSHAS TRUMA."
I WOKE UP RIGHT AWAY. AND WHEN I WENT TO SLEEP, AGAIN IT WAS: "PARSHAS TRUMA! PARSHAS TRUMA!"
SO WHAT'S PARSHAS TRUMA?
EACH WEEK ON SATURDAY, WE READ A SECTION FROM THE TORAH.
THIS IS SO CALLED - A PARSHA... AND ONE WEEK EACH YEAR IT IS PARSHAS TRUMA.
BEFORE WORK A FEW FROM US PRAYED. IT WAS A RABBI THERE WITH US.
ONE MOMENT, RABBI. WHEN WILL WE READ PARSHAS TRUMA?
PARSHAS TRUMA?..
...IN THE MIDDLE OF FEBRUARY... ALMOST THREE MONTHS FROM NOW. WHY?
THREE MONTHS - AND EVERY DAY WAS FOR US A YEAR!
I TOLD HIM MY DREAM...
LET'S HOPE IT'S TRUE. I'M AFRAID WE'LL NEVER GET OUT OF HERE.

The Complete MAUS CD-ROM presents Volumes I and II of the Pulitzer Prize-winning comics that document the genocide and persecution of Polish and German Jews during the years surrounding the Second World War, while also providing viewers the historical and structural details behind the book.

■ The pages of *MAUS* are linked to preliminary sketches, alternate drafts, archival photographs, and drawings made by concentration camp prisoners. Also included are two hours of original audio interviews of Art Spiegelman and his father (which served as the basis for the original comic book), as well as audio and video commentary by Art Spiegelman on the making of *MAUS* and critical commentary on the form, ideas, and history behind it. These features can be accessed any time by clicking on a navigation bar, as well as a family tree, which allows viewers to explore other areas of the title.

Mr. Zylberberg

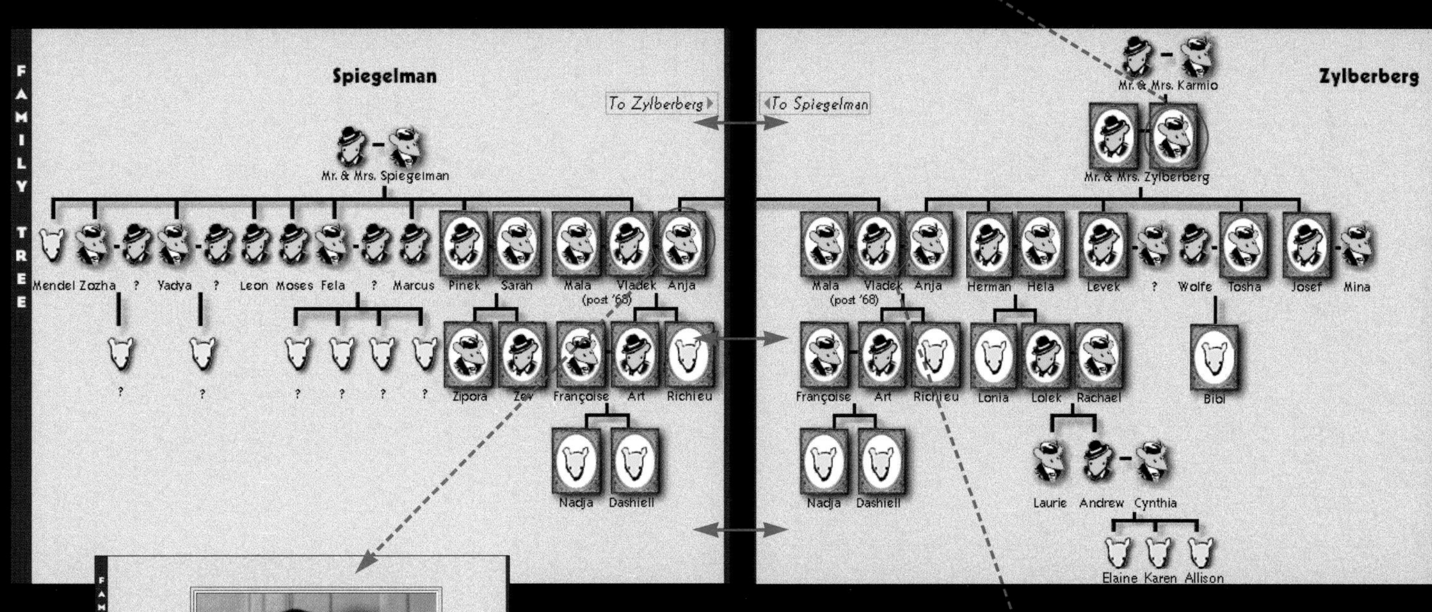

Anja & Vladek

Anja, Richieu & Vladek

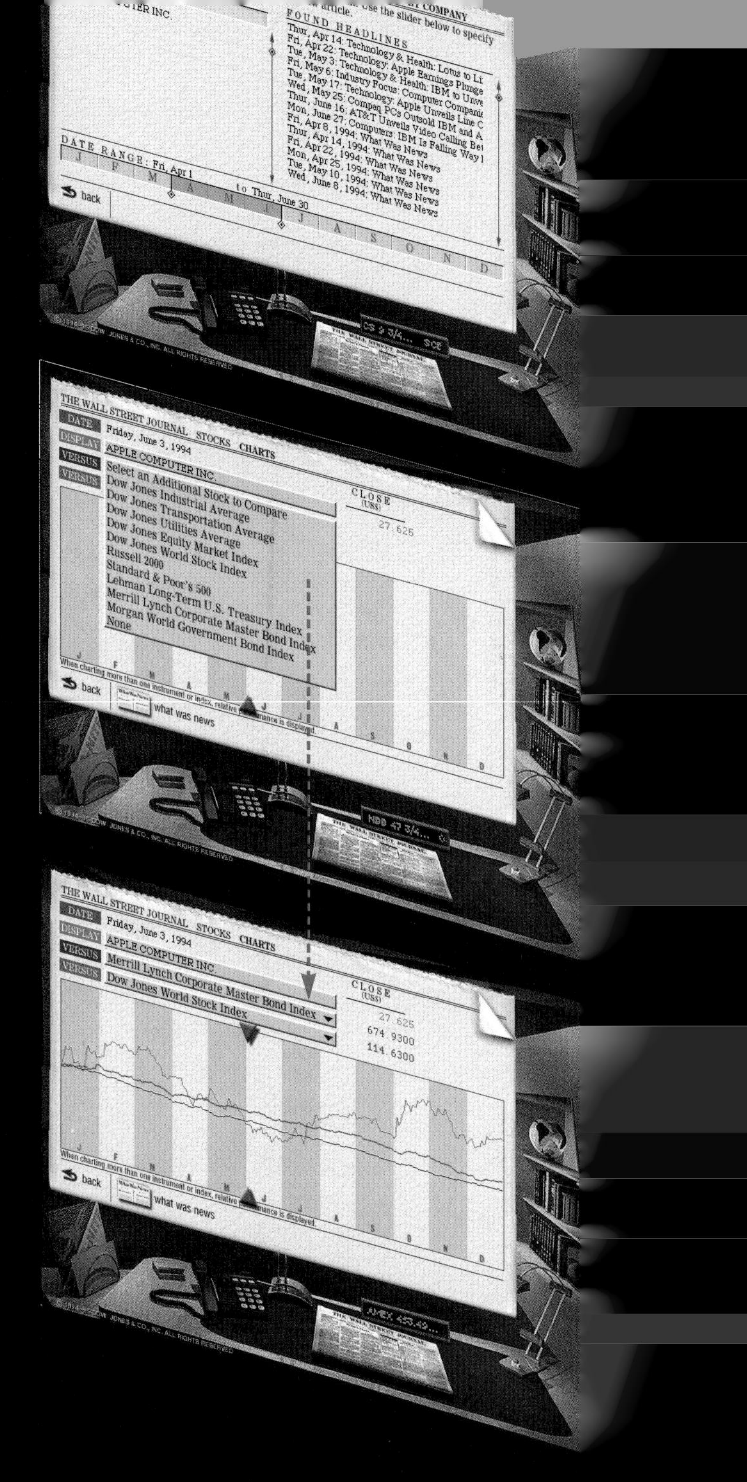

THE WALL STREET JOURNAL REVIEW OF MARKETS AND FINANCE

CLIENT / PUBLISHER The Wall Street Journal

DESIGN Magnet Interactive, Washington, DC. Chuck Seelye, art director; Paul Cofrancesco and Drew Williams, interface designer; Bernd Jachnicen, Waldren

This title is remarkably rich and robust, and the information is highly contextualized and conveniently layered. While the design emulates that of America's redoubtable journal of finance, navigation opportunities are as smart and lively as any New Media package around. Users can conduct detailed searches of economic data by company, industry, word, or date, then analyze the top stories of the day to determine whether a stock went haywire because of some subtle industry-wide trend or simply because the Administration released a set of pessimistic economic indicators that week. Particularly impressive is the title's ability to instantly plot the performance of a company's stock, U.S. Treasury bonds, the Dow Jones Industrial Average, and heating prices, then to layer them one on top of the other. The speed with which *The Wall Street Journal of Markets and Finance* compiles such data comparisons on the fly is often astonishing.

This imaginatively designed and tastefully illustrated title launches you on a whirlwind tour of global history. The user interface is a roll-top desk, the features of which change depending upon the period of history in question. The user can click on these, or else on tool bars to call up photographs of archaeological sites, listen to the music of a lute, watch animated sequences of an Aztec ritual, or watch video clips of Martin Luther King, Jr. The user can also click on hot words or desktop objects to find brief biographies or descriptions of unfamiliar terms. While not encyclopedic by any stretch, this title is in the style of all Dorling Kindersley products, which always pare down copy and illustrations to fit onto a single screen, thus reducing or eliminating the need for scrolling.

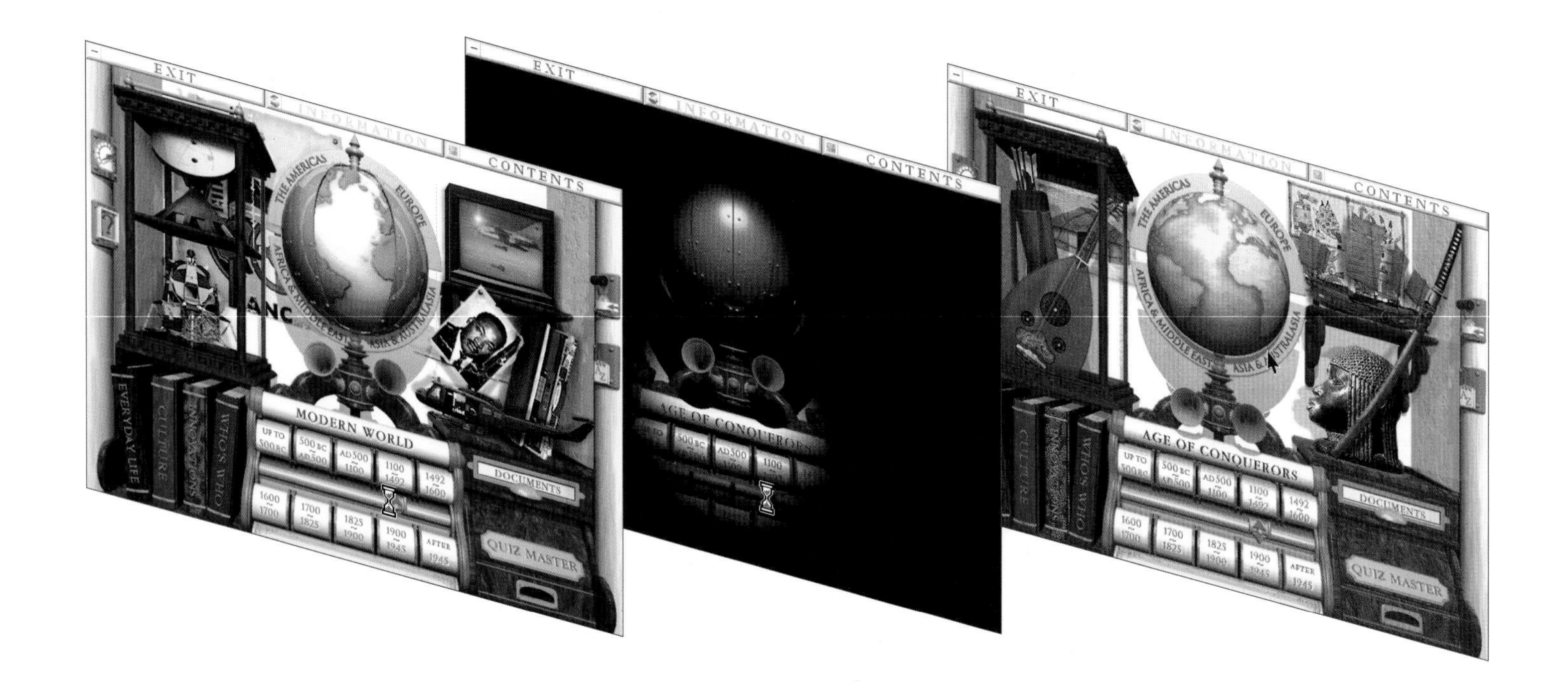

HISTORY OF THE WORLD

CLIENT / PUBLISHER Dorling Kindersley Multimedia

DESIGN Dorling Kindersley Multimedia, London Great Britain. Corinne Roberts and Deirdre Headon, editorial leads; Emma Ainsworth and Frank Cawley, design leads; Ian Callow, production coordinator; Emily Hill, Andrea Horth, Scott Stedman and Anthony Whitehorn, editorial; Amanda Carroll, Frank Cawley, Richard Clemson, Christian Nouyou, Samantha Webb and Wilfrid Wood, design; Rik Greenland and Christian Nouyou, interface design; Sharon Bambaji and Loise Wass, production supervisors; Raljih McArdel, software development; Rik Greenland, Douglas Miller, Dougall Muir, Christian Nouyou, Patrick Schirvanian and Alastair Wardle, digital animation and imaging; Andy Moss, cel animation; Isabel Whitfield, product testing; Ian Callow, video compilation; Sid Wells, Patch McQuaid and Ian Hawkridge, audio production; Richard Williams and Robert Dinwiddle, managing editors; Caroline Murry and Simon Webb, Managing art editors; Roy Margolis, software development manager; Adrian Gilbert, R.G. Grant, Nina Hathaway, Margaret Mulvihill and Philip Wilkinson, writers.

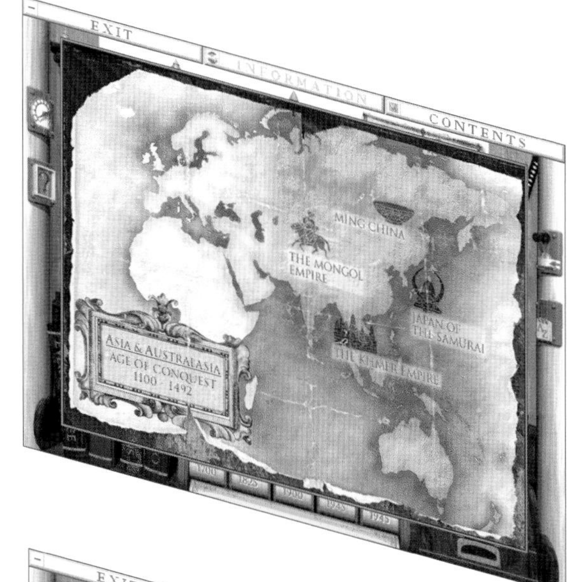
EXIT
INFORMATION
CONTENTS
MING CHINA
THE MONGOL EMPIRE
JAPAN OF THE SAMURAI
ASIA & AUSTRALASIA
AGE OF CONQUEST
1100 - 1492

EXIT
INFORMATION
CONTENTS
MONGOL EMPIRE
THE MONGOLS were nomadic people who roamed over the steppes of Central Asia. By 1206 Genghis Khan was leader of these tribesmen and had united them into a ruthless army. By the end of the 1200s, the Mongols ruled the largest land empire ever known.
ASIA
Bow
EXPERT RIDERS
Mongol warriors could fire arrows at full gallop.
Protective silk shirt
Arrows
Harness
Saddle
MONGOL CONQUESTS
SEE ALSO
KUBLAI KHAN'S COURT
MONGOL LIFESTYLE
KEY DATES
FACT FILE
YURTS
NEXT

EXIT
INFORMATION
CONTENTS
EVERYDAY LIFE
CLOTHING
FOOD
FOOD
EVERYDAY LIFE
Hunting and Gathering
Ancient Egyptian Food
Classical Feasts
Rice
Corn in the Americas
Medieval Kitchen
Spices
Pepper
Sugar
Tea
Thanksgiving Day
Preserving Foods
MEDICINE

EXIT
INFORMATION
CONTENTS
MONGOL CONQUESTS
BY THE TIME Genghis Khan died in 1227, it took almost a year to ride from one end of his empire to the other and back. His successors conquered still more land.
PERSIA
CHINA
THE EMPIRE EXPANDS
1211
1224
1237
1260
SEE ALSO
NEXT

EXIT
INFORMATION
CONTENTS
CORN IN THE AMERICAS
CLOTHING
FOOD
EVERYDAY LIFE
SEE ALSO
THE AZTECS
THE MAYAS
THE TOLTECS
THE OLMECS
TEOTIHUACAN
THE INCAS
Mayas ate tortillas (pancakes)
over an open fire.
CORN PLANT
a hot sauce made from chili peppers and tomatoes.
SEE ALSO
MEDICINE

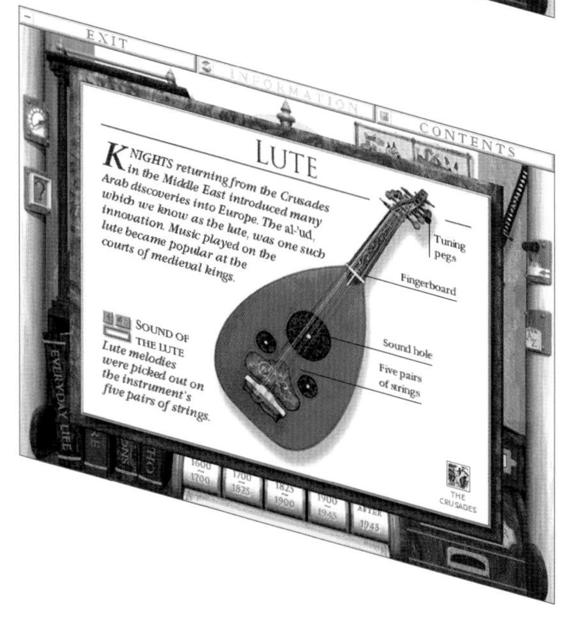
EXIT
INFORMATION
CONTENTS
LUTE
KNIGHTS returning from the Crusades in the Middle East introduced many Arab discoveries into Europe. The al-'ud, which we know as the lute, was one such innovation. Music played on the lute became popular at the courts of medieval kings.
Tuning pegs
Fingerboard
Sound hole
Five pairs of strings
SOUND OF THE LUTE
Lute melodies were picked out on the instrument's five pairs of strings.
EVERYDAY LIFE
1600 – 1700
1700 – 1825
1825 – 1900
1900 – 1945
AFTER 1945
THE CRUSADES

PASSAGE TO VIETNAM

CLIENT / PUBLISHER Against All Odds Productions and Interval Research

DESIGN Against All Odds Productions, Sausalito, CA. Rick Smolan, producer, director of Interval Research, Palo Alto, CA; Megan Wheeler, art director; Pico Iyer, Stanley Karnow, Peter Saidel and Colin Leinster, writers; Shawn McKee, programmer; Rick Smolan, digital video director; Megan Wheeler, graphic designer; Megan Wheeler, illustrator; Aaron Singer, audio; Megan Wheeler, animator; Aaron Singer, sound editor. 70 International Photojournalists including Bruno Barbey,Yanni Arthus-Bertrand, Randy Olson, Vu Dat and Radhika Chalasani, photographers. Ad Hoc Interactive, interface designer and new media production company. Rebo Associates, Karen Mullarkey and Pat Weatherford, video directors. Celestial Harmonies "Music of Vietnam" Volumes 1 and 2, music composers.

To move the map up or down use the compass arrows.
(You can also move the cursor to the top of your screen or the bottom.)

Click on a location on the map, then check the compass to see what information is available.

RED RIVER
Ha Giang
Cao Bang
CHINA
Sapa
Tuyen Quang
Bac Thai Province
Yen Bai
Lang Son
Vinh Phu Province
Quang Ninh Province
Dien Bien Phu
Son La Province
Ha Tay Province
Ha Bac Province
Hanoi
Ha Long Bay
Hoa Binh
Haiphong
Cat Ba Island
Nam Ha Province
Ninh Binh
Thanh Hoa Province
GULF OF TONKIN
LAOS
HAINAN
Vinh
MEKONG RIVER
VIENTIANE
Quang Binh Province
Quang Tri Province
Hue
Danang
Hoi An
Reunification Express
Binh Dinh Province
Gia Lai Province
CAMBODIA
Dac Lac Province
Nha Trang
Dalat
Phan Rang
Song Be Province
PHNOM PENH
Tay Ninh
Bien Hoa
Phan Thiet
Ho Chi Minh City
Dong Thap Province
My Tho
Vung Tau
An Giang Province
Can Tho
Kien Giang Province
Tra Vinh
Soc Trang Province
Minh Hai Province

Photographers...

Monica Almeida
Yann Arthus-Bertrand
Bruno Barbey
Nicole Bengiveno
P.F. Bentley
Torin Boyd
Radhika Chalasani
Paul Chesley

done

biography
virtual gallery
photos by this photographer

N
E
W
S

PHOTOGRAPHERS ASSIGNED TO THIS LOCATION.

VIEW PHOTOGRAPHS TAKEN IN THIS REGION.

Map

Photo by Bruno Barbey
Cat Ba Island

phers
bey
us-Bertrand
us-Bertrand
on

Photographs
Above: Denise Rocca
Right: Michael Yamashita

This rich and robust title is a do-it-yourself photographic documentary expedition through the cities and rice paddies of Vietnam. Users can navigate through *Passage to Vietnam* by scrolling up and down a map of the country, or else by using a handy navigational tool called the Quebe, which provides users easy access to specific photographs or videos, information on what is depicted, and background on the photographers who contributed work to this title. The information is well layered, there is a bookmarking feature that allows users to return to their favorite areas, and there is a printing capability built in. In addition to the many impressive technical features, the images themselves are often stunning.

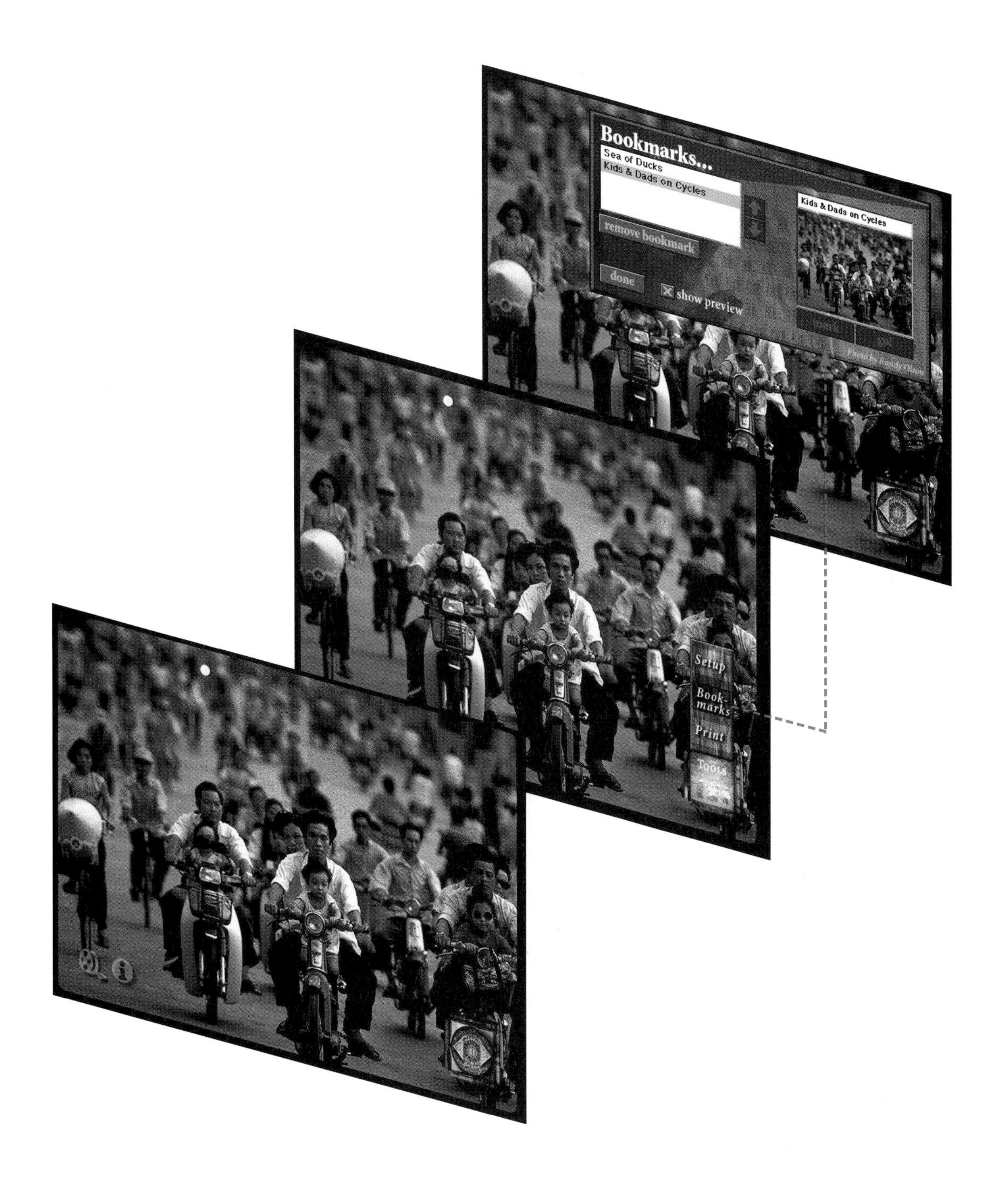

The Quebe is a three-dimensional interface tool developed for exploring *Passage to Vietnam.* The user can spin it around in any direction. Each of the six sides allows users to access different areas of this CD-ROM. This navigation device is available everywhere in this title.

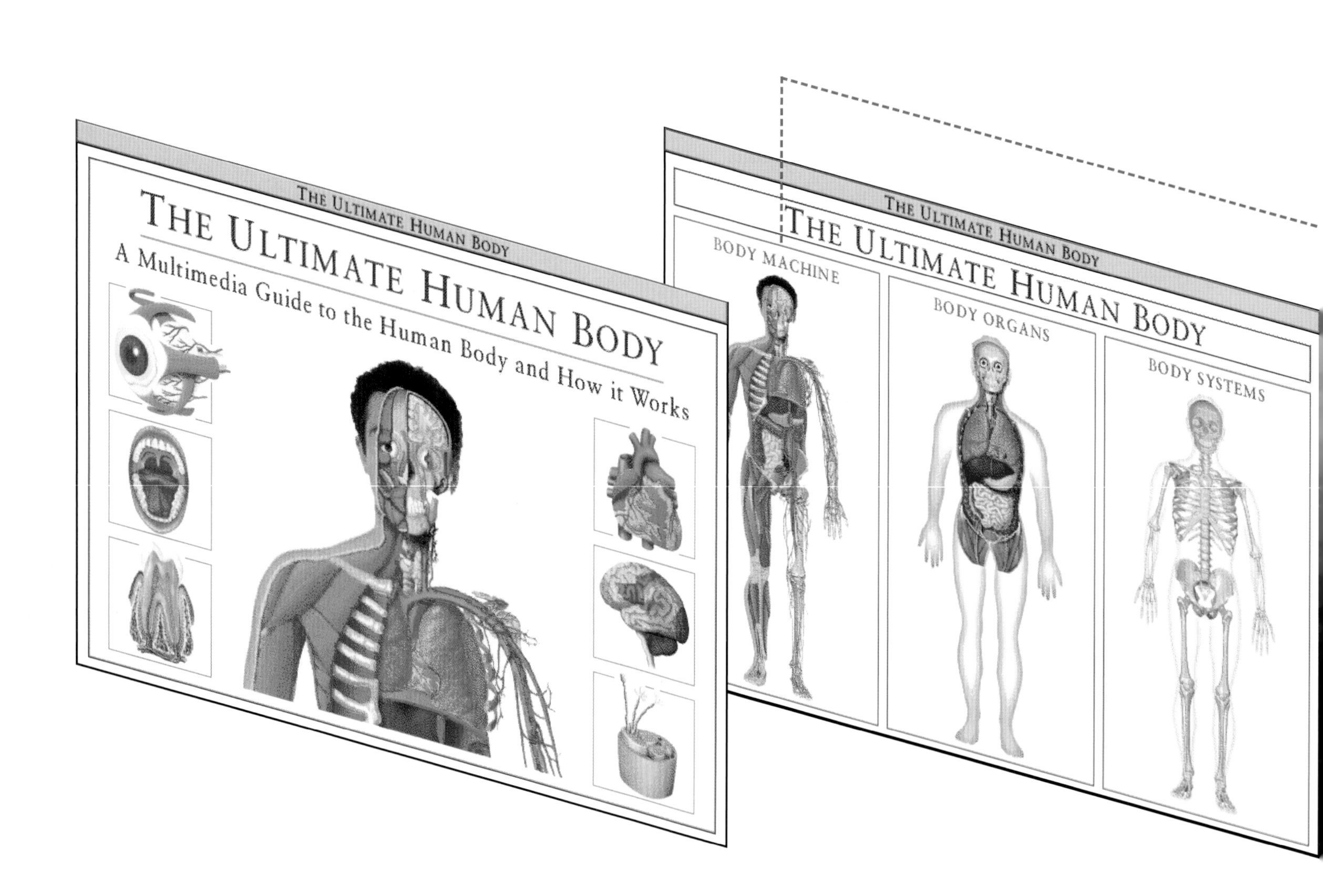

THE ULTIMATE HUMAN BODY

CLIENT / PUBLISHER Dorling Kindersley Multimedia

DESIGN Dorling Kindersley Multimedia, London, Great Britain. Andrean Pinnington, managing editor; Caroline Murry, design manager; Sharon Bambaji, technical lead; Emma Ainsworth, Des Plunkett and David Wall, design; Patrick Schirvanian, Salvatore Tomaselli, Richard Greenland, Lai Marsh, Patrizio Semproni and Paul Stefka, digital animation and imaging; Ruth Lingford, cell animation and illustration; Joanna Cameron, Lydia Umney, Simonne End, Tony Graham and John Temperton, medical illustrators; Sid Wells, Ian Hawkridge, Patch McQuaid and Tim McQuaid, audio; Roy Margolis, software manager; Katy Disley, Graham Westlake, Julian James and Philip Miller, software development; Isabel Whitfield, product testing supervisor; Kate Fox, Catherine O'Rourke and Christine Rista, picture research; Richard Walker PhD, Susan Sturrock, Diane Jakobson PhD, writers. Additional help provided by medical illustrators and medical consultants.

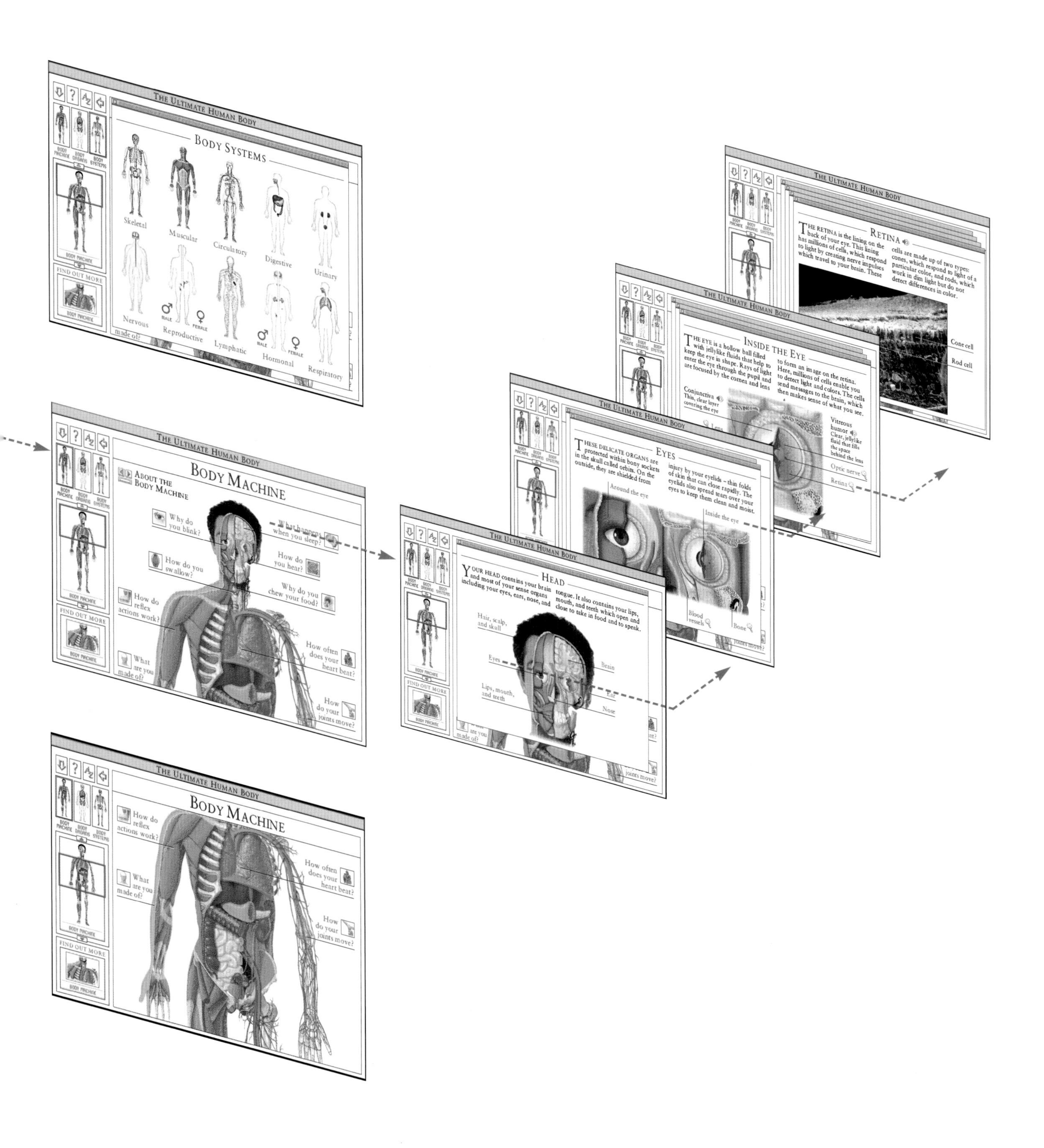

This title explores "the most complex machine in the world," —the human body. Though some information is highly technical, it rarely intimidates, owing to an elegant layering that allows viewers to dig deeper at their own pace. All the systems of the body—from the skeletal and the muscular to the hormonal and the lymphatic—are illustrated with eye-popping drawings and concise text. Navigation is fluid, with a zoom-in facility that increases granularity of detail from a full-frontal view of the body down to the cellular perspective provided by an electron microscope.

The unusual navigation construct of this title employs a compelling metaphor: the rings of a virtual tree represent passage to various epochs in the history of the Native Americans. Click on a ring near the center, and users are launched into a multimedia module discussing the Anasazi; click on an outward ring, and users will learn about the 7th Cavalry's massacre at Wounded Knee of more than 250 members of Big Foot's Mnikowoju band.

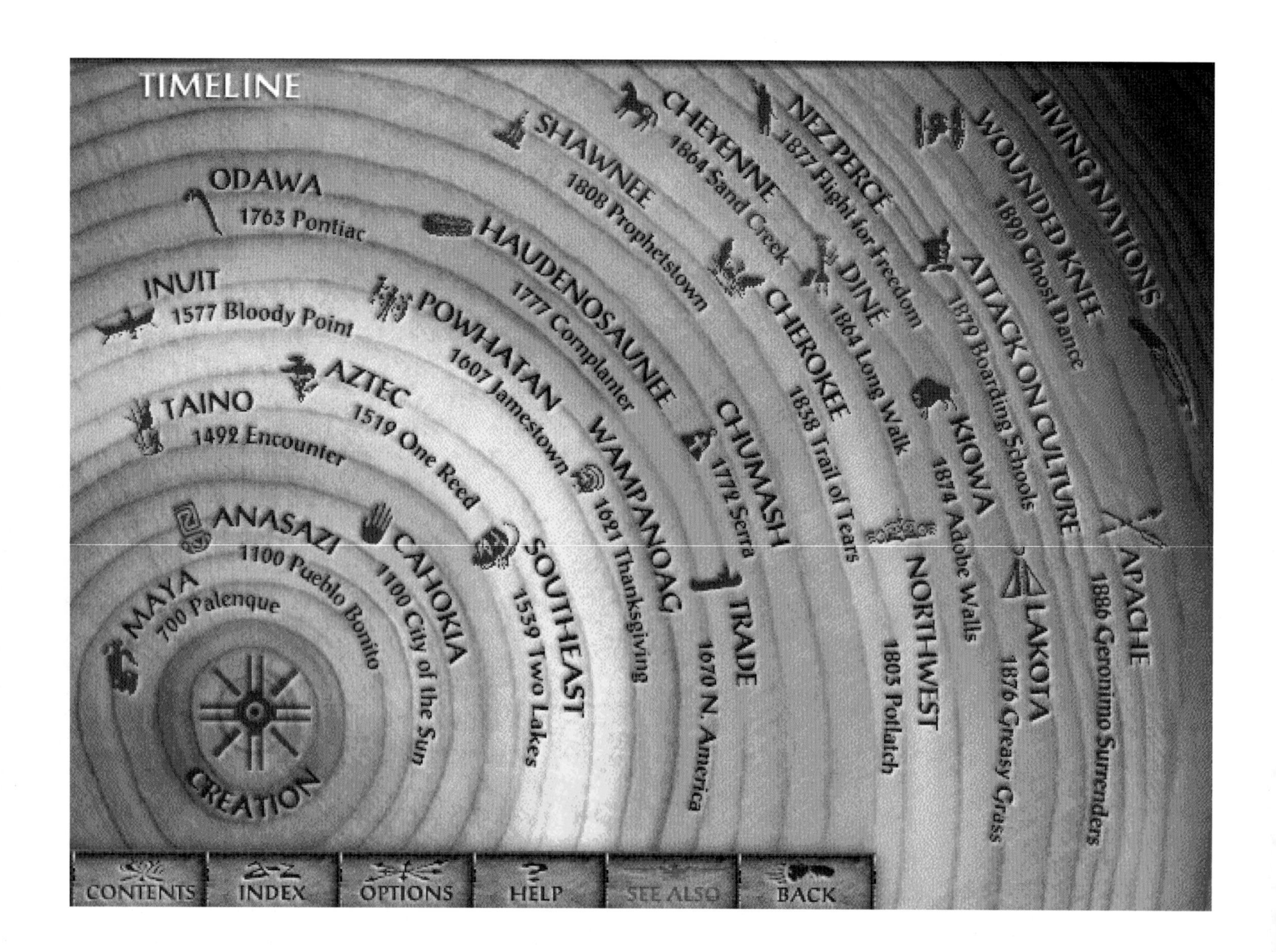

500 NATIONS 

CLIENT / PUBLISHER TIG Productions and Microsoft Corporation

DESIGN Mass Productions, Seattle, WA. Andreas Kronenberg, art director; W.T. Morgan, creative director; W.T. Morgan and Andreas Kronenberg, interface designers; W.T. Morgan and Roberta Grossman, writers; Ken Showman, Gordon Cox and Lise Depres, programmers; W.T. Morgan and Jack Leustig, video directors; W.T. Morgan, digital video director; Andreas Kronenberg and Peter Lloyd, graphic designers; Andreas Kronenberg, Audra Kronenberg, Mark Leaman, Matt Leclair, Connie Nakamura, Peter Lloyd, Don Dardett, and Bruce Heavi, illustrators; Randy Thorn, sound supervisor; James LeBrecht and Dennis Leondre, sound design; Peter Buffett, music composer; W.T. Morgan, producer/director; Jim Wilson and Kevin Costner, executive producers. Various, photographers. Santa Barbara Studios and Mass Productions, animators. Based on "500 Nations" a film by Jack Leustig. Kevin Costner, host.

N E W M E D I A

T O O L S

We use tools to explore and manipulate the world around us. The tools shown here were selected for their ease of use and accessibility. Some do a single thing really well, while others comprise the functions of an entire office and fit into a hand. They extend our reach and by so doing carve out their own category of inclusion. Consequently, these tools deserve to be judged as much for their utility as for their beauty.

ASSIST

CLIENT / PUBLISHER rae Technology

DESIGN Samir Arora and Dave Kleinberg, creative direction and programming; J. Otto Seybold, illustrator.

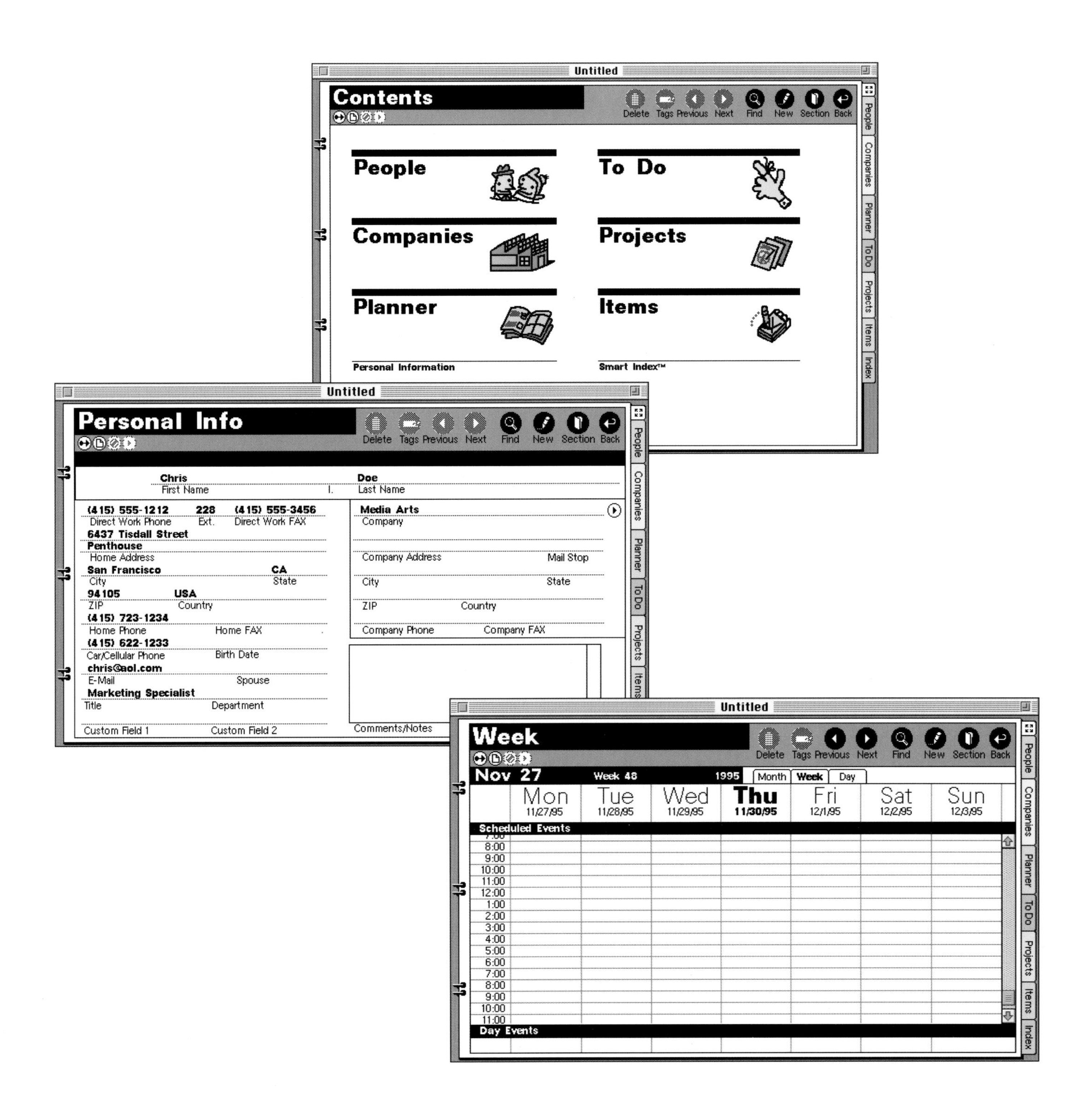

This Daybook organizer software is accommodating, nimble, and uniformly intelligible. Powerful and easy to use, *Assist* allows users to keep track of personal contacts, company information, and projects, and to freely link them together. It comes with a handy calendar for planning the week, as well as a flexible "notes and pictures" module. Sporting a bare-bones design, *Assist* provides an ever-present navigation bar in the upper right-hand corner of the screen for ease of roving.

This promotional disk effectively mimics the breezy environment of Apple's online service. The user-friendly navigational metaphors developed by Apple's operating system are employed here, which is a real plus for Web surfers who tire of learning new paradigms each time they use a service. The lighthearted graphics of this disk are unusual for what is essentially a customer service site, a category of interactivity that tends to inspire tearful yawns more than gape-mouthed awe.

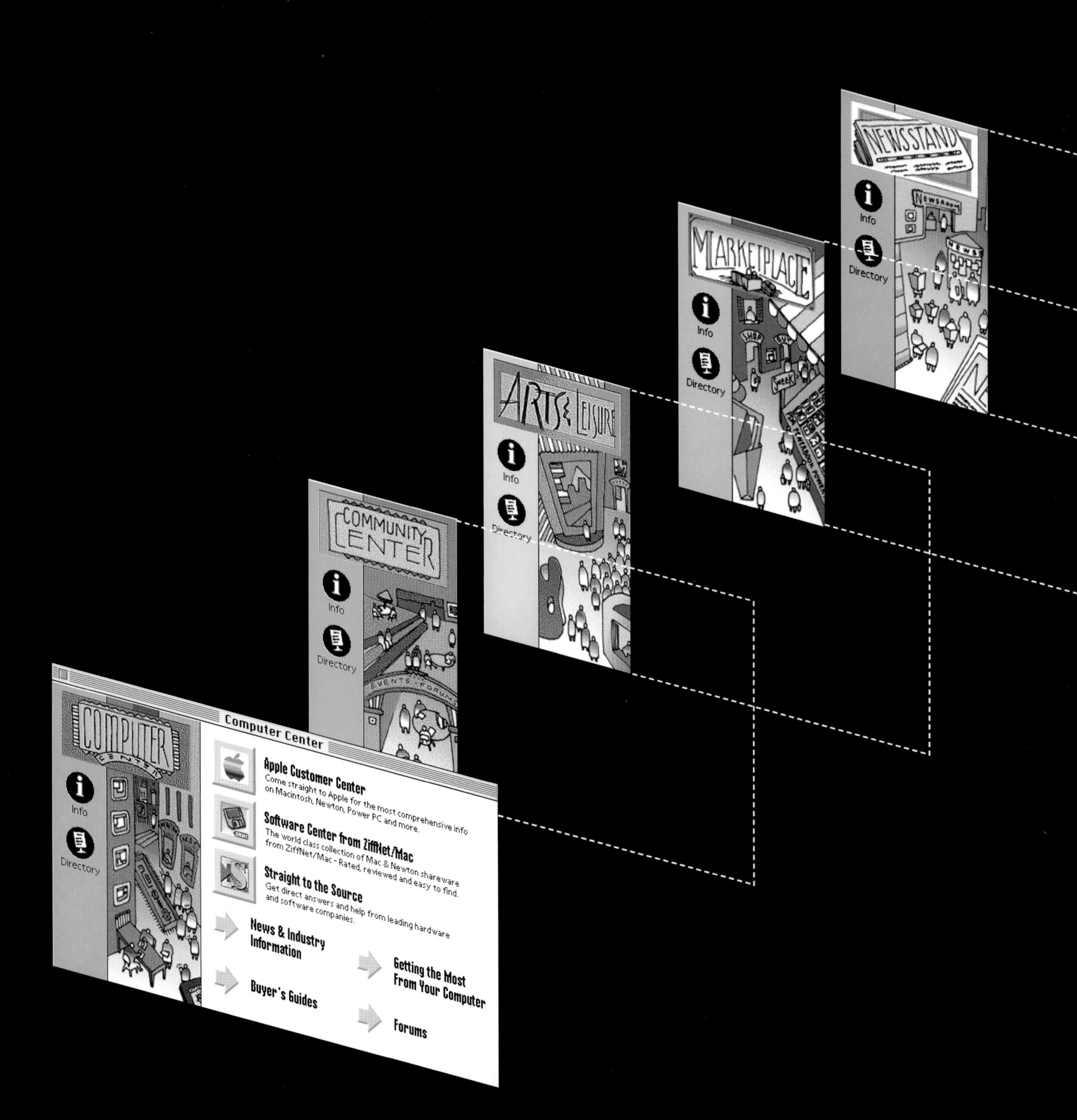

APPLE EWORLD SERVICE

CLIENT/PUBLISHER Apple Computer, Inc.

DESIGN Cleo Huggins and Mark Drury, art directors; Mark Drury, illustrator.

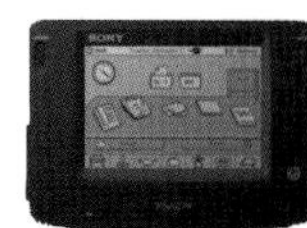

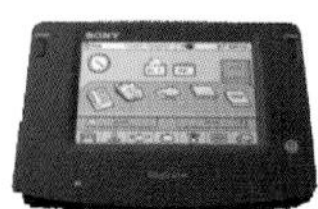

This demo has nearly magical powers. Users may rotate *Magic Link's* image in all directions by dragging the mouse and holding down the button. Stop dragging the mouse, and the image freezes. Click a hot spot on the image, and a call-out box appears with a brief blurb about the function of that area.

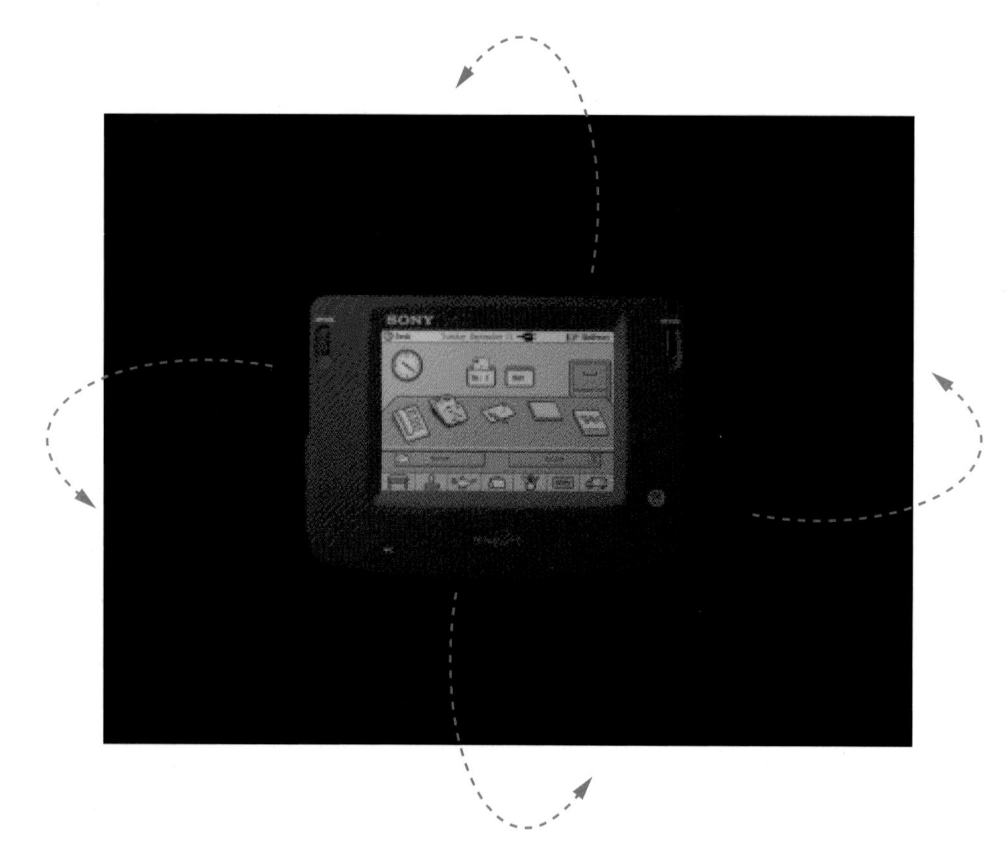

This demo of *Magic Link's* Personal Digital Assistant is as dandy as the gadget itself. Part information manager/part communications software, *Magic Link* is bundled with a calendar, Rolodex, word processor (with a virtual keyboard), project manager, clock, filing system, modem, and much more. A hand-held hybrid that would make Dick Tracy blush, *Magic Link* is a smoothly integrated package of hardware and software with an interface that effectively employs metaphors of the office environment. *Magic Link* itself deserves recognition as a cutting-edge New Media tool as much as its demo deserves acclaim as its inventive promotion piece.

MAGIC LINK INTERACTIVE DEMO

CLIENT / PUBLISHER Sony Magic Link™ Personal Intelligent Communicator

DESIGN Denise White, creative director; Ward Mulroy, art director; Jim Banks, copy supervisor; Adam Heneghan, Eric Heneghan, interactive directors/programmers, Linda Goldberg, sleeve designer.

Publishers of the perennial *Sunset Magazine* have come up with an impressive reference title that provides gardeners easy access to encyclopedic information on more than 6,000 plants grown in the western United States. ■ Curious gardeners have two ways to gather information. At any time, they can access an index of plants—complete with Latin and common names—and instantly locate a particular plant. They can also use the "Plant Selector," which allows them to prune back Sunset's vast database by entering their zip codes (which suggests an appropriate climate zone), selecting typical growing conditions (sun, water), and the types of plants desired (trees, ground cover). Gardeners then peruse the collection of full-color photographs and collateral information delivered by the database. ■ Gardeners may click on the "Pronounce" speech balloon, which prompts a voice that properly enunciates the Latin name of the pictured plant. Videos offer "QuickTips" on gardening, while a "Companion Plants" option allows gardeners to expand their planting options. A handy "Garden Notebook" allows gardeners to store and print out their customized lists and collected notes.

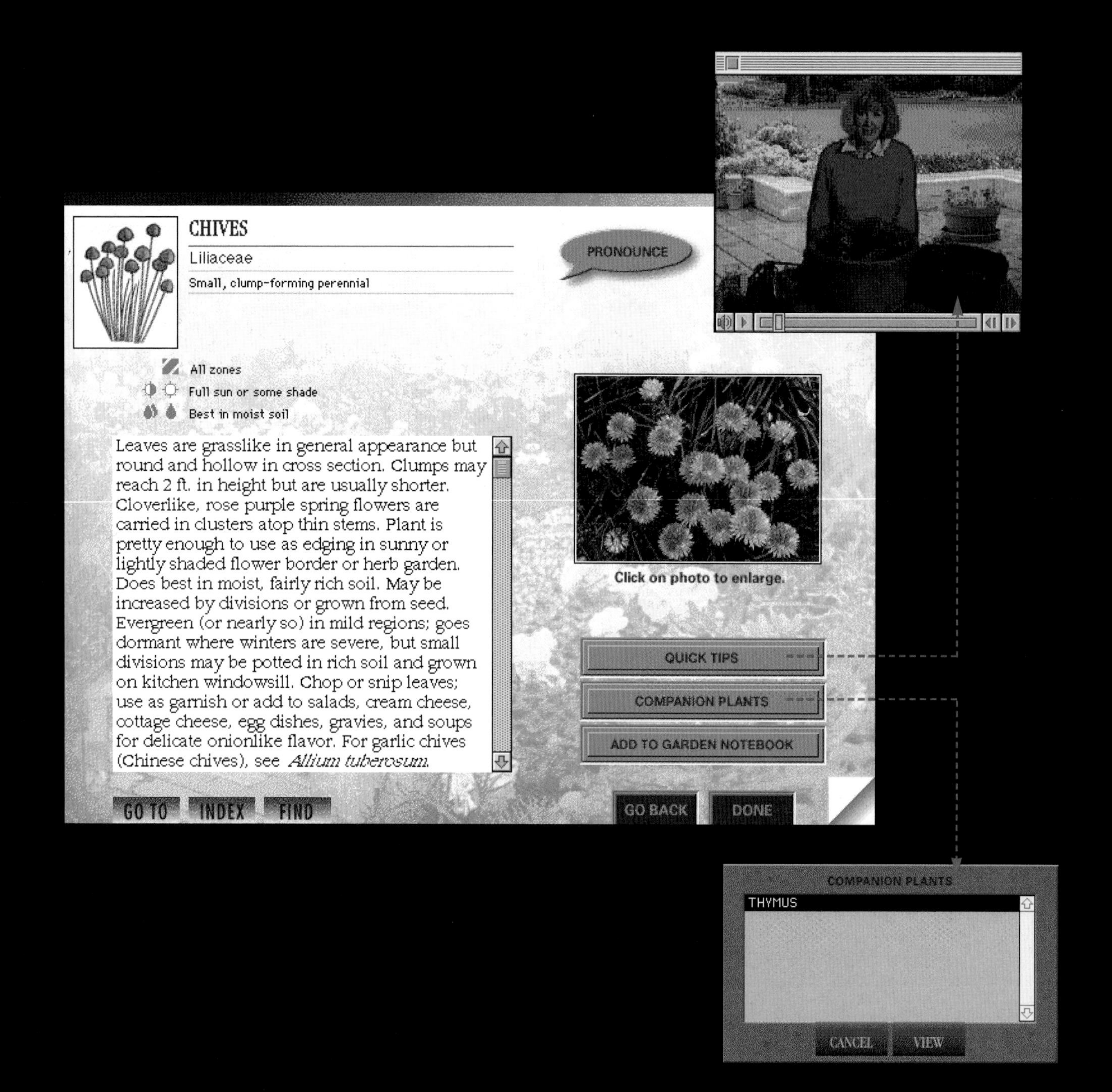

SUNSET WESTERN GARDEN CD-ROM 

CLIENT / PUBLISHER Sunset Publishing Corporation

DESIGN Medior Incorporated, San Mateo, CA. Medior Incorporated, design and production; Ken Winchester, executive producer.

NEW MEDIA

PROTOTYPES

Prototypes can shed light upon a phase of the creative process that is seldom visible outside the mind. Just as it is a rare and wonderful thing to look over the preliminary sketches made by a painter, watch a play as it matures in rehearsal, so it is helpful to view New Media prototypes. The ones included here were selected as much for the ideas they flesh out as for the design style they promote. Being works in progress, they often lack the polish their designers would ultimately bring to bear, and perhaps for this reason alone are important to consider.

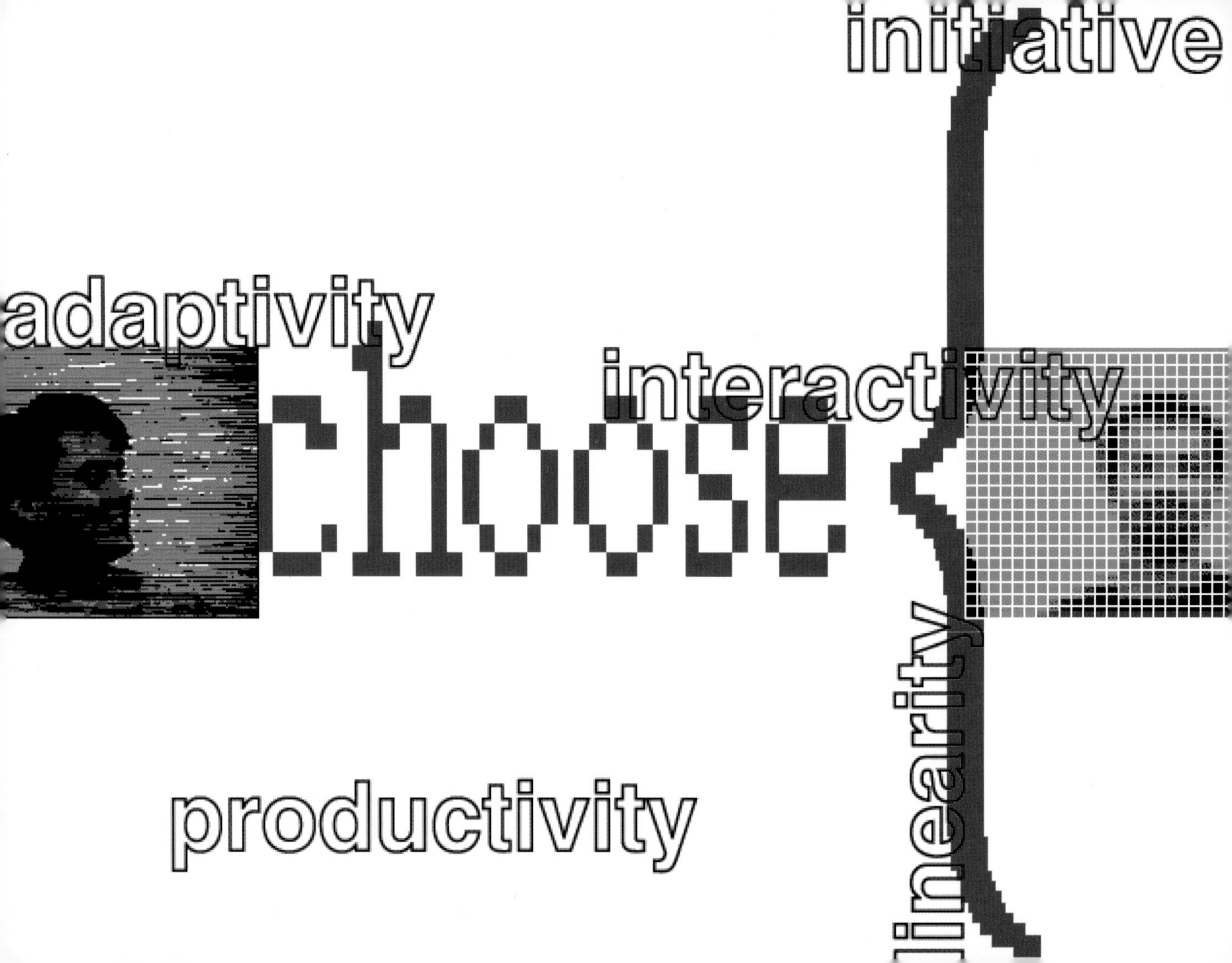
initiative
adaptivity
choose
interactivity
linearity
productivity

"Sounds like just about everything that has some sort of cause and effect is interactive."

"Maybe when we think of interactivity in other areas, like with people, there's something more substantial because the response is always unexpected."

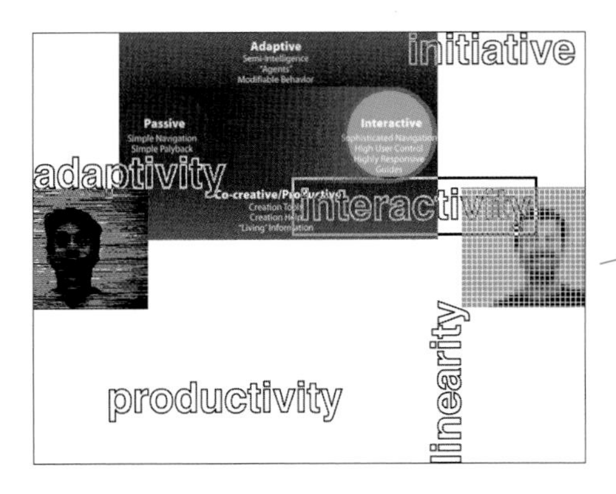

"Don't you make choices in your life all the time? Do you find these choices boring, are they in the way or are they helpful?"

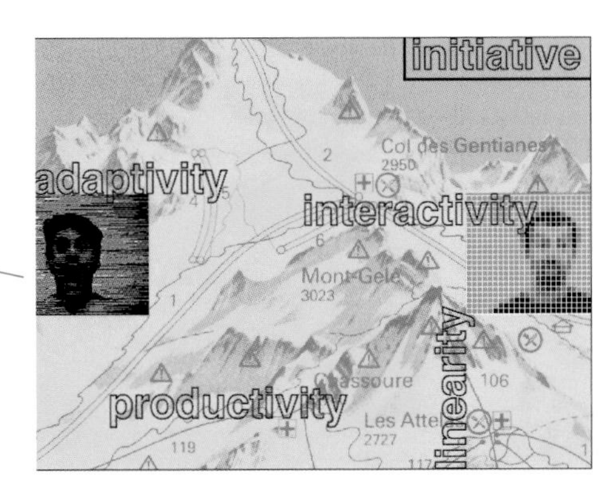

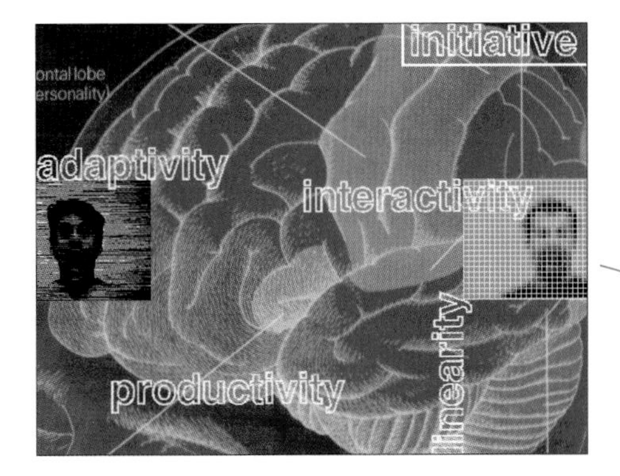

"Maybe what's useful here is that we want to give the user of this information a feeling of ownership over their path."

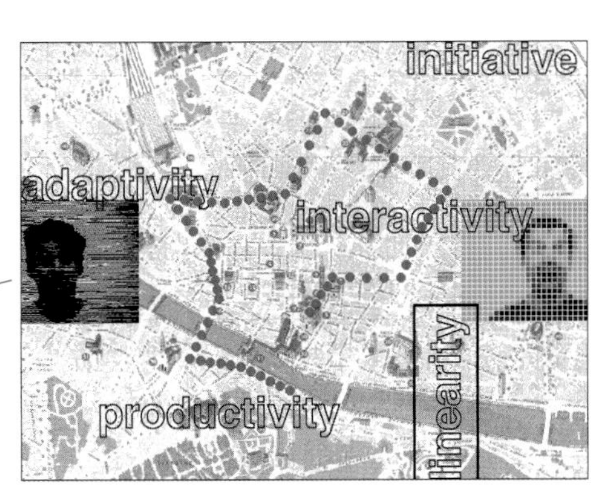

"We can think of a lot of experiences that we have as either linear or non-linear."

"It sounds like this was a vacation on which you could truly travel and experience serendipitously."

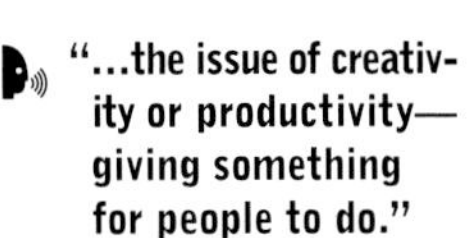

"...the issue of creativity or productivity—giving something for people to do."

"...which makes us call into question our traditional views of how these things are maintained—particurly copyright and patent."

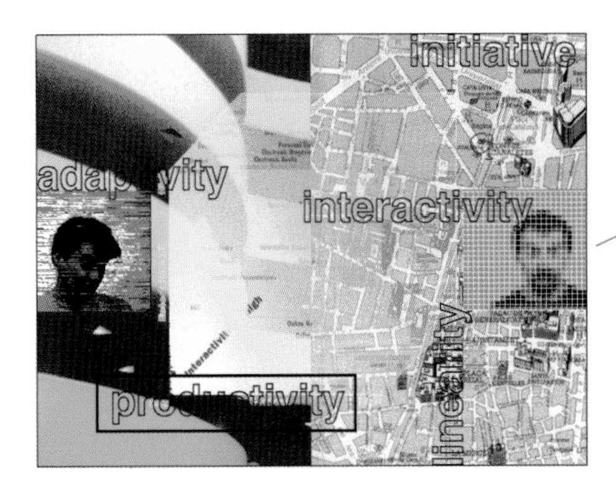

This disk offers the rare and valuable opportunity to listen, watch, and manipulate an interactive presentation of an interactive conversation about interactive design by two interactive design pros, Nathan Shedroff (the violet man) and Peter Spreenberg (the green man). ■ This cybernetic co-meditation manages to be as random as it is linear, as content-rich as it is stylistically barbed. When each man speaks his head violently jerks as if undergoing shock therapy; conversation, meanwhile, careens toward adaptivity, bounces off productivity, glances off linearity, and veers towards interactivity. (Users can control the flow of words and images by clicking on them.) The balance of the screen, meanwhile, transforms as the conversation "progresses." Provided users are patient, Spreenberg will ultimately take out the snapshots of his European vacation.

Marketed by the publishers of *Emigre* magazine, this is a random collage with loads of verve and lumps of attitude. *Throwing Apples at the Sun* is essentially a performance art piece for the computer. An unusually rich multimedia romp, it sports wily interfaces and navigation options, cursors that transform into dinner jackets, pictures of nude men with their private parts masked out, quirky dialog boxes ("This does nothing," one states), and agitated collages of video remnants. Laced throughout is a sharp soundtrack that blends a rap-style lyricism with Appalachian guitar-picking, shreds of poetry, and the occasional yelp and holler. A catalogue of custom fonts is also included should users wish to place an order.

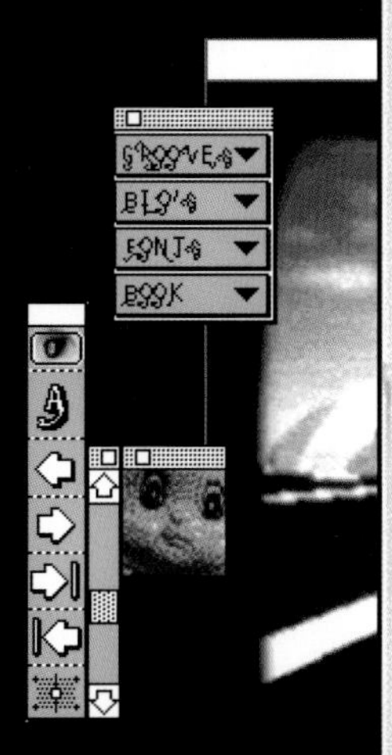

THROWING APPLES AT THE SUN

CLIENT/PUBLISHER The Apollo Program

DESIGN Elliot Peter Earls, art director, interface designer, writer, programmer, video director, digital video director, graphic designer, photographer, illustrator, audio, animator, music composer and sound editor; The Apollo Program, new media production company.

Designed by Guy Jeffrey Nelson for "drunk techy people," *DesignahSign!* is a toy for the font crazed. As inventive as it is charming, this floppy allows the user to create their own street signs, providing them with a mix-n-match assortment of whimsical and suggestive phrases and symbols. Though simple and to the point, this package also toys with the tension between the randomness endemic to interactive media and the designer's need to control certain sequences.

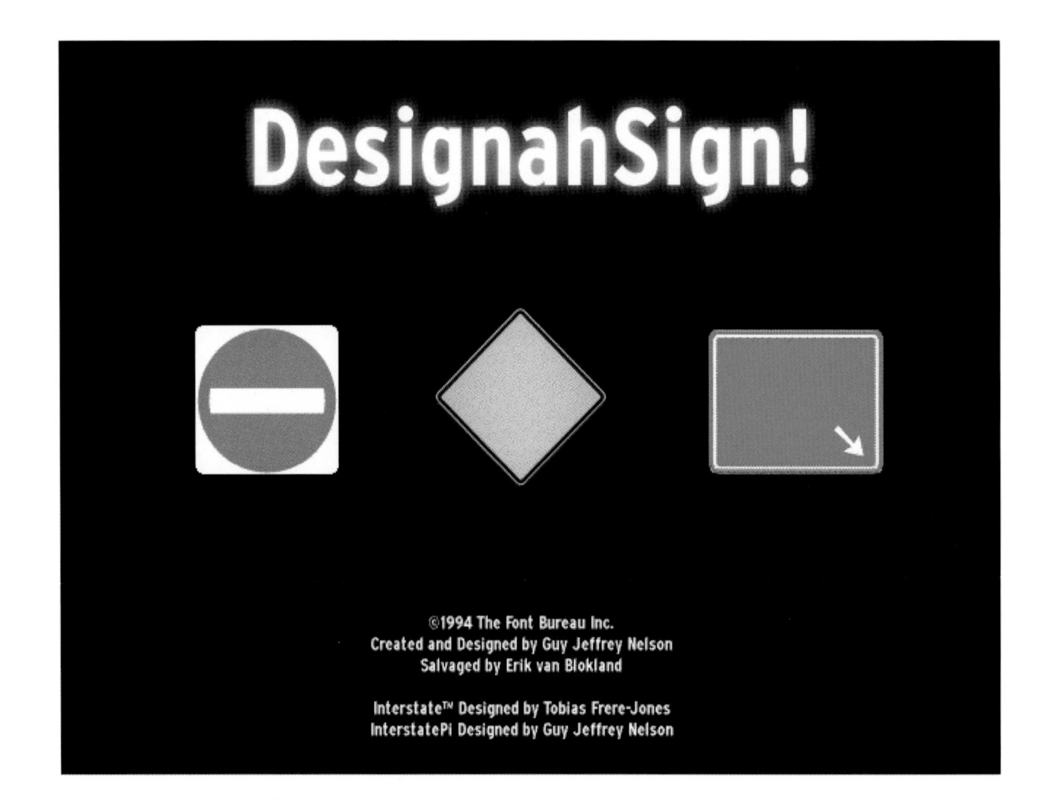

DESIGNAHSIGN!

CLIENT / PUBLISHER The Font Bureau, Inc.

DESIGN Guy Jeffery Nelson Design, Boston, MA. Guy Jeffery Nelson, art director, interface designer, writer and graphic designer; Eric Von Blockland, programmer; Guy Jeffery Nelson Design, new media production company.

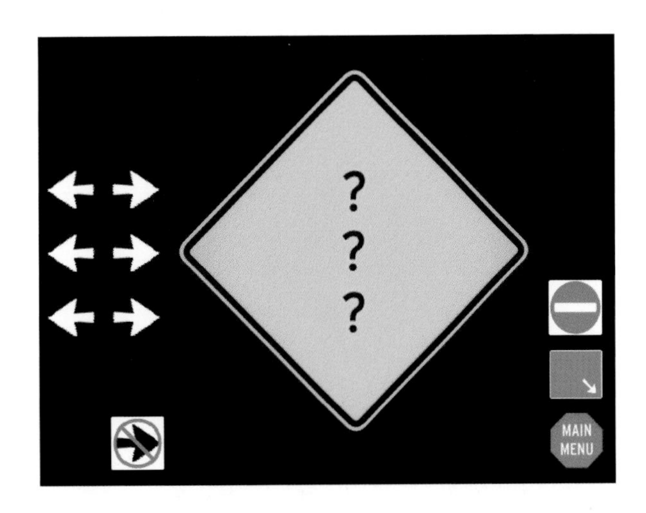
?
?
?
MAIN
MENU

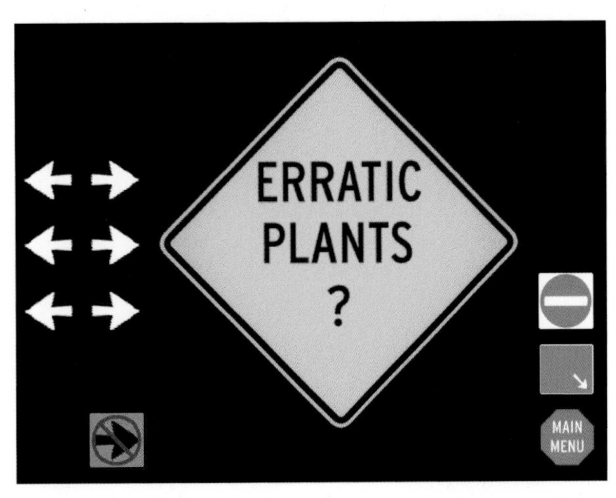
ERRATIC
PLANTS
?
MAIN
MENU

SAUCY
AFTERLIFE
2.5 FT
MAIN
MENU

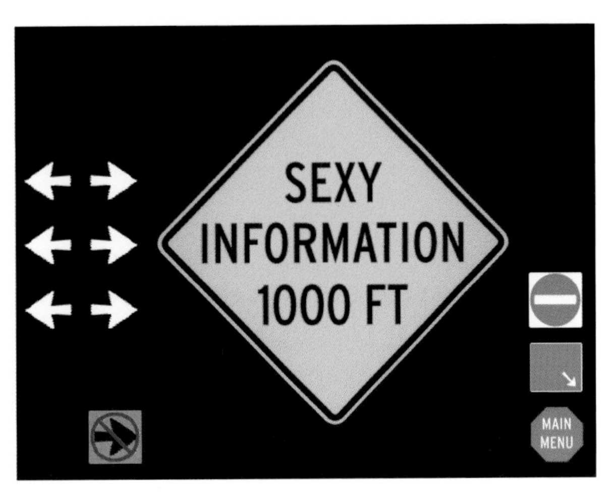
SEXY
INFORMATION
1000 FT
MAIN
MENU

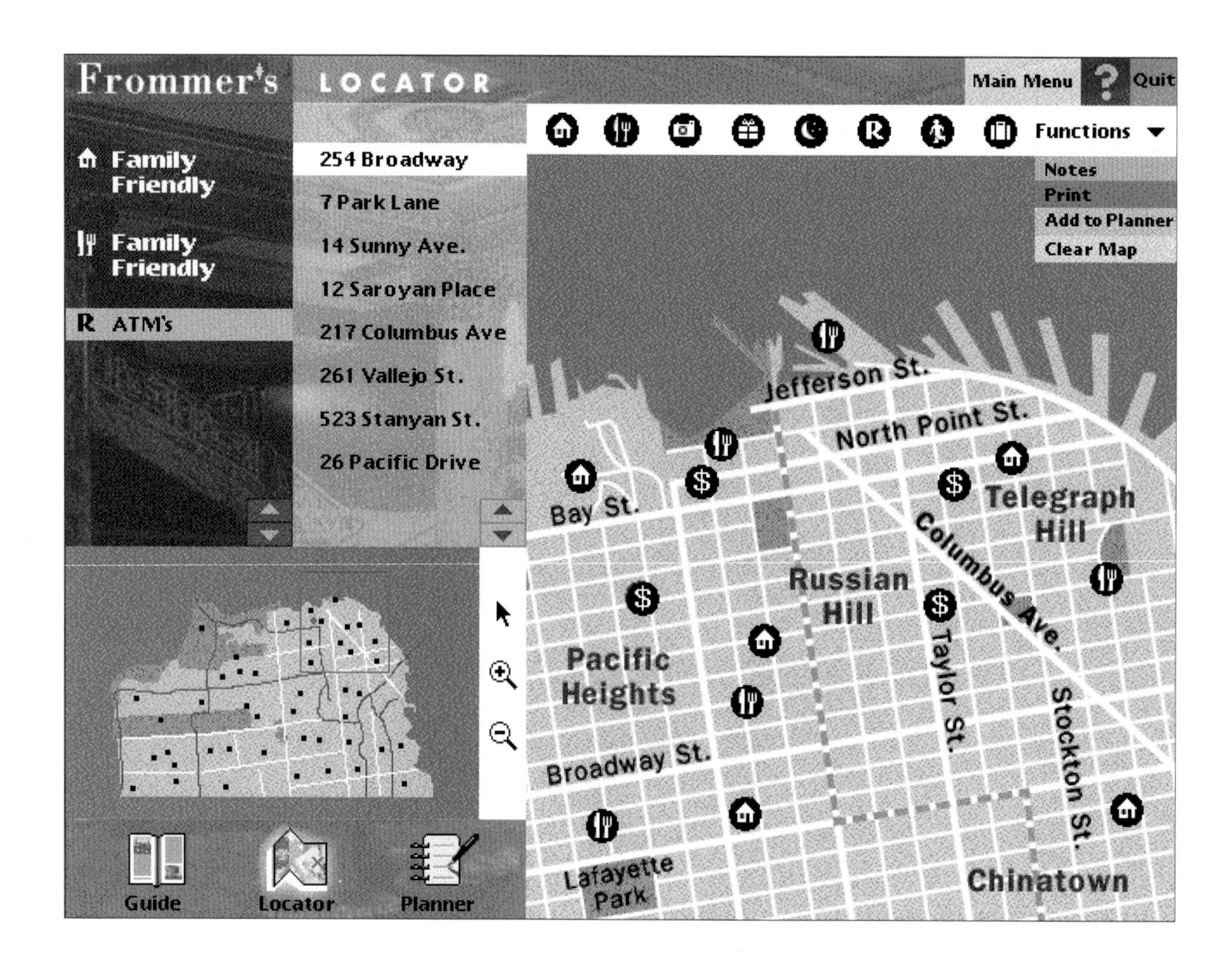

FROMMER'S INTERACTIVE TRAVEL GUIDES: SAN FRANCISCO

CLIENT / PUBLISHER Macmillian Digital USA

DESIGN Macmillian Digital USA, New York, NY. Janet Tingey, art director; Johnathan Fishel, producer. Geosystems Global Corp., programming. Tom Nicholson Associates, Guido Jimenez, Lesilie Dann and Ian Vantuyl, interface designers; Sarah Glickman and Maya Kopytman, graphic designers. Corbis Media, photography. Carta Interactive, new media production company/project management.

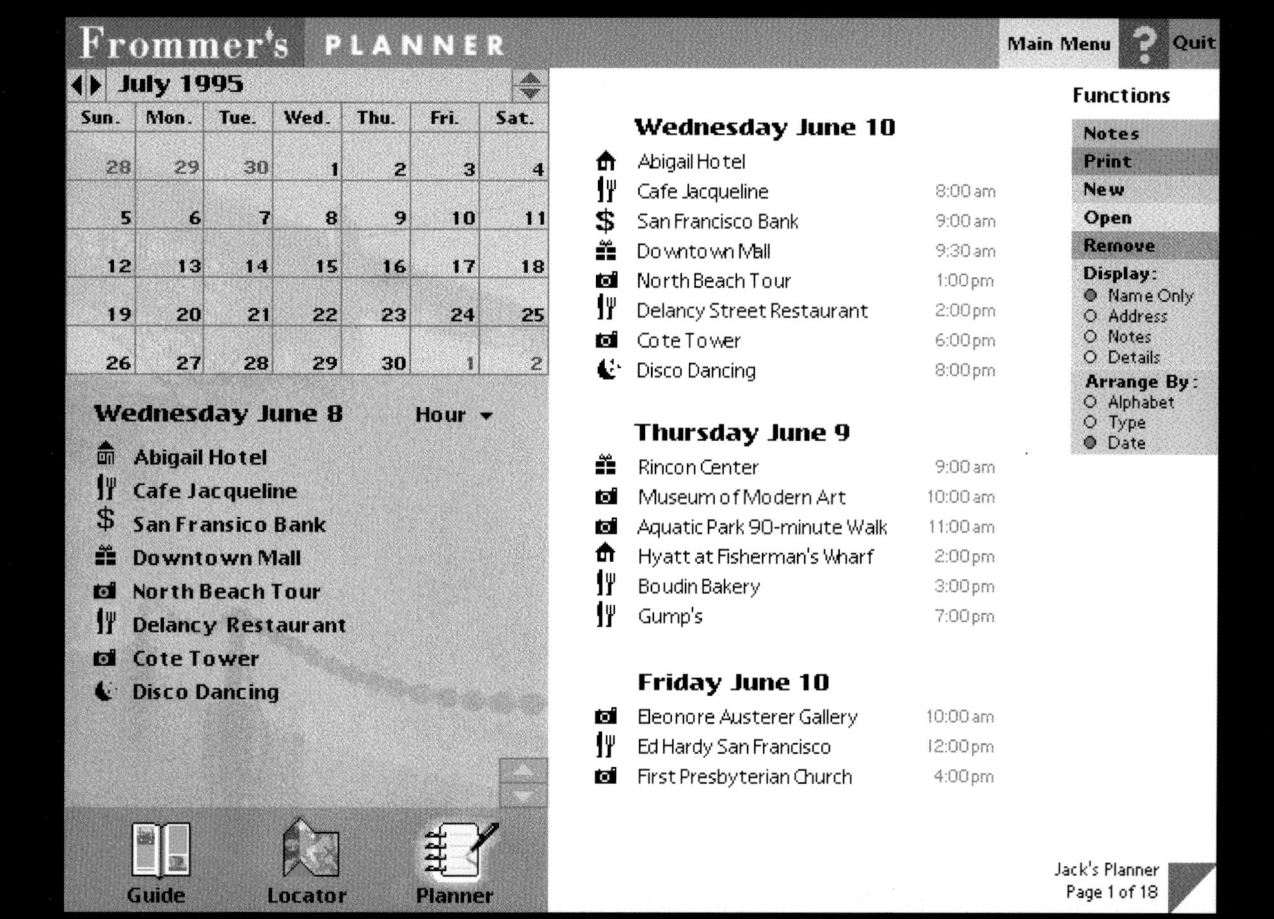

A fresh spin on the traditional Baedeker, the chief strength of the *Frommer's Interactive Travel Guides: San Francisco* is that it provides a handy trip planner and calendar as well as a printing function. With rich content and robust functionality, navigation through this guide of Everybody's Favorite City is simple and pathways among areas are both graceful and useful. The publisher promises that the guide will boast an online connection for ease of updates—a definite advantage over paper guides.

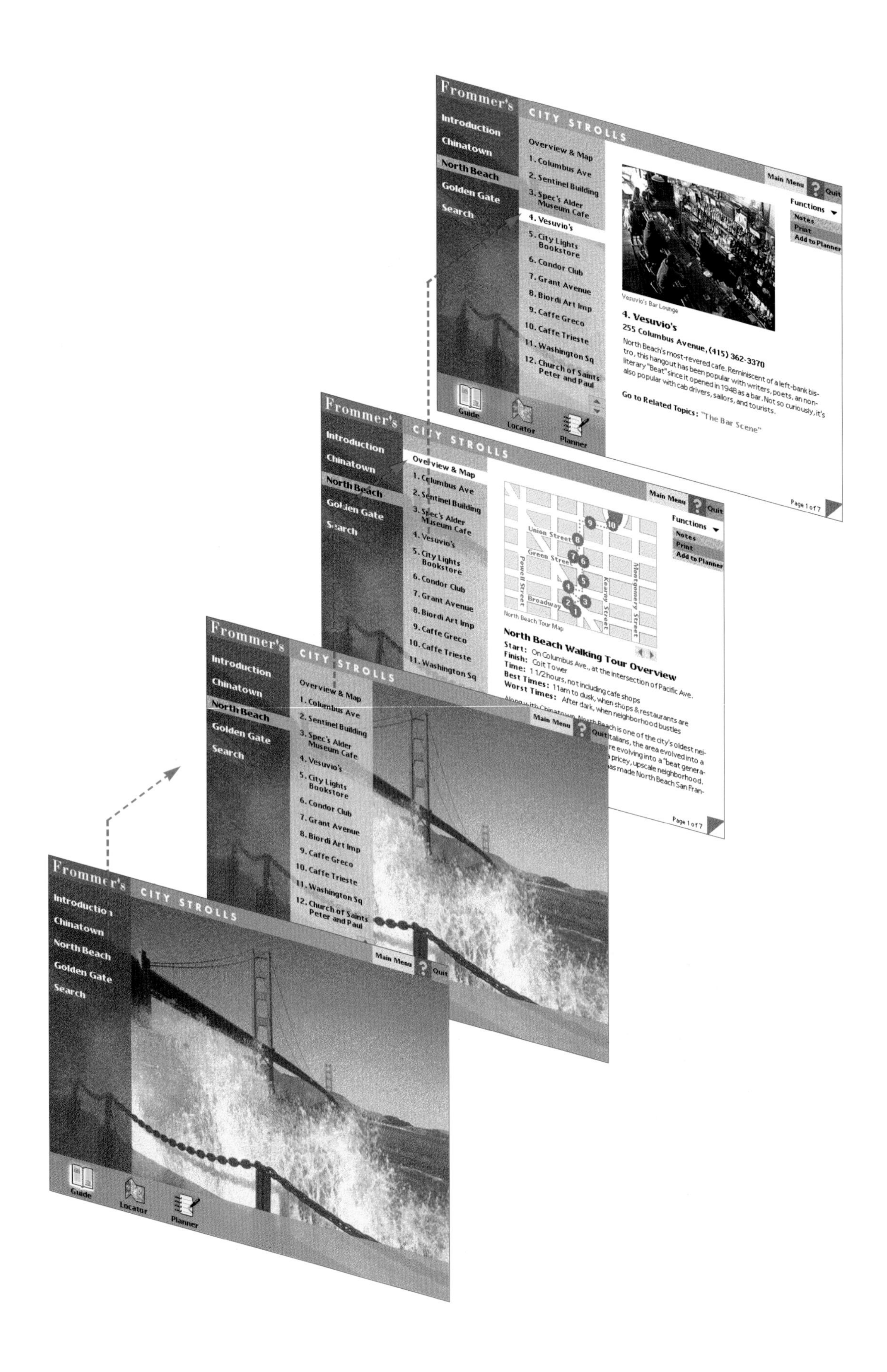

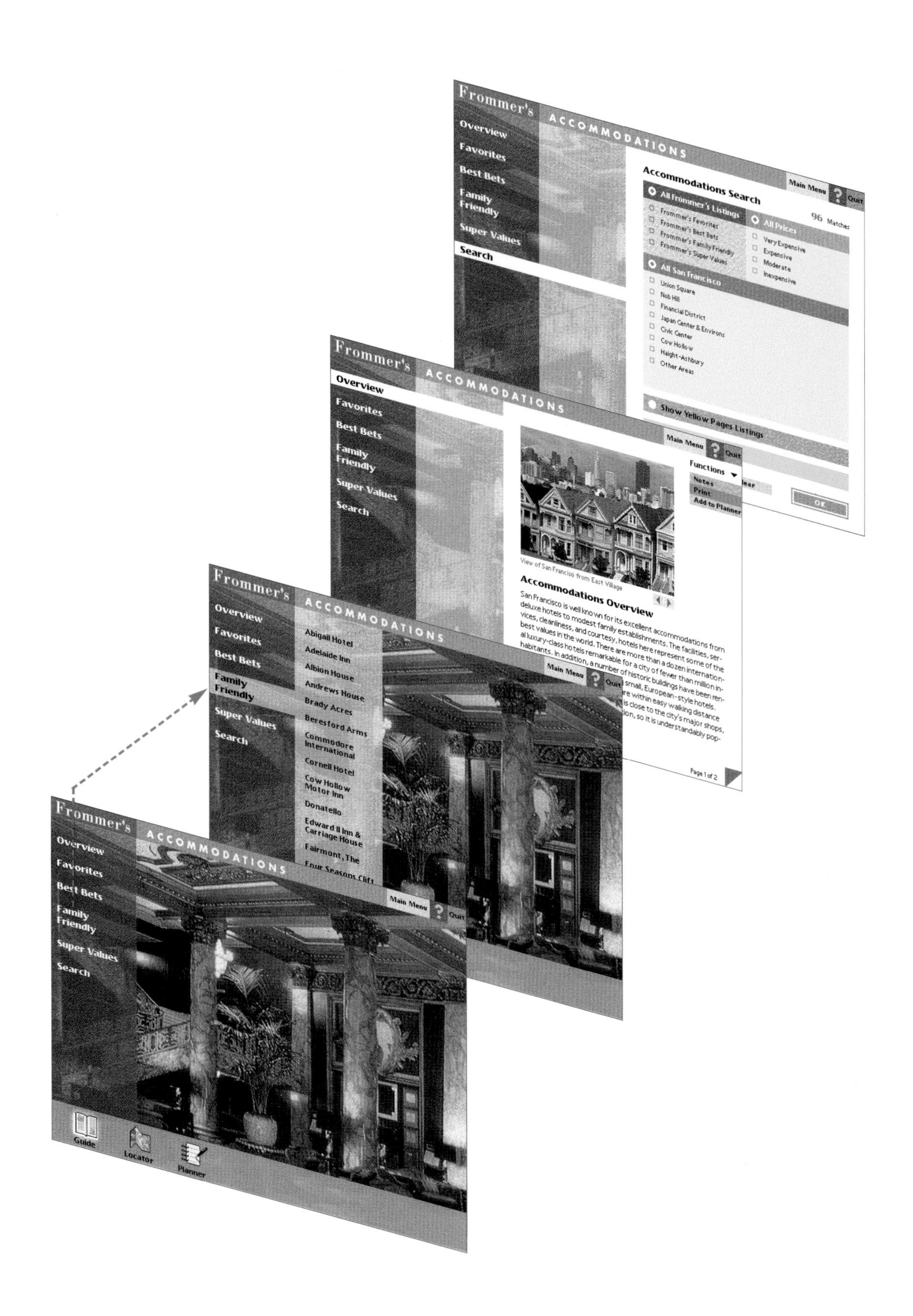
Frommer's
ACCOMMODATIONS
Overview
Favorites
Best Bets
Family Friendly
Super Values
Search
Accommodations Search
Main Menu
Quit
All Frommer's Listings
Frommer's Favorites
Frommer's Best Bets
Frommer's Family Friendly
Frommer's Super Values
All Prices
Very Expensive
Expensive
Moderate
Inexpensive
96 Matches
All San Francisco
Union Square
Nob Hill
Financial District
Japan Center & Environs
Civic Center
Cow Hollow
Haight-Ashbury
Other Areas
Show Yellow Pages Listings
OK
Functions
Notes
Print
Add to Planner
View of San Francisco from East Village
Accommodations Overview
San Francisco is well known for its excellent accommodations from deluxe hotels to modest family establishments. The facilities, services, cleanliness, and courtesy, hotels here represent some of the best values in the world. There are more than a dozen international luxury-class hotels remarkable for a city of fewer than million inhabitants. In addition, a number of historic buildings have been ren-
Page 1 of 2
Abigail Hotel
Adelaide Inn
Albion House
Andrews House
Brady Acres
Beresford Arms
Commodore International
Cornell Hotel
Cow Hollow Motor Inn
Donatello
Edward II Inn & Carriage House
Fairmont, The
Guide
Locator
Planner

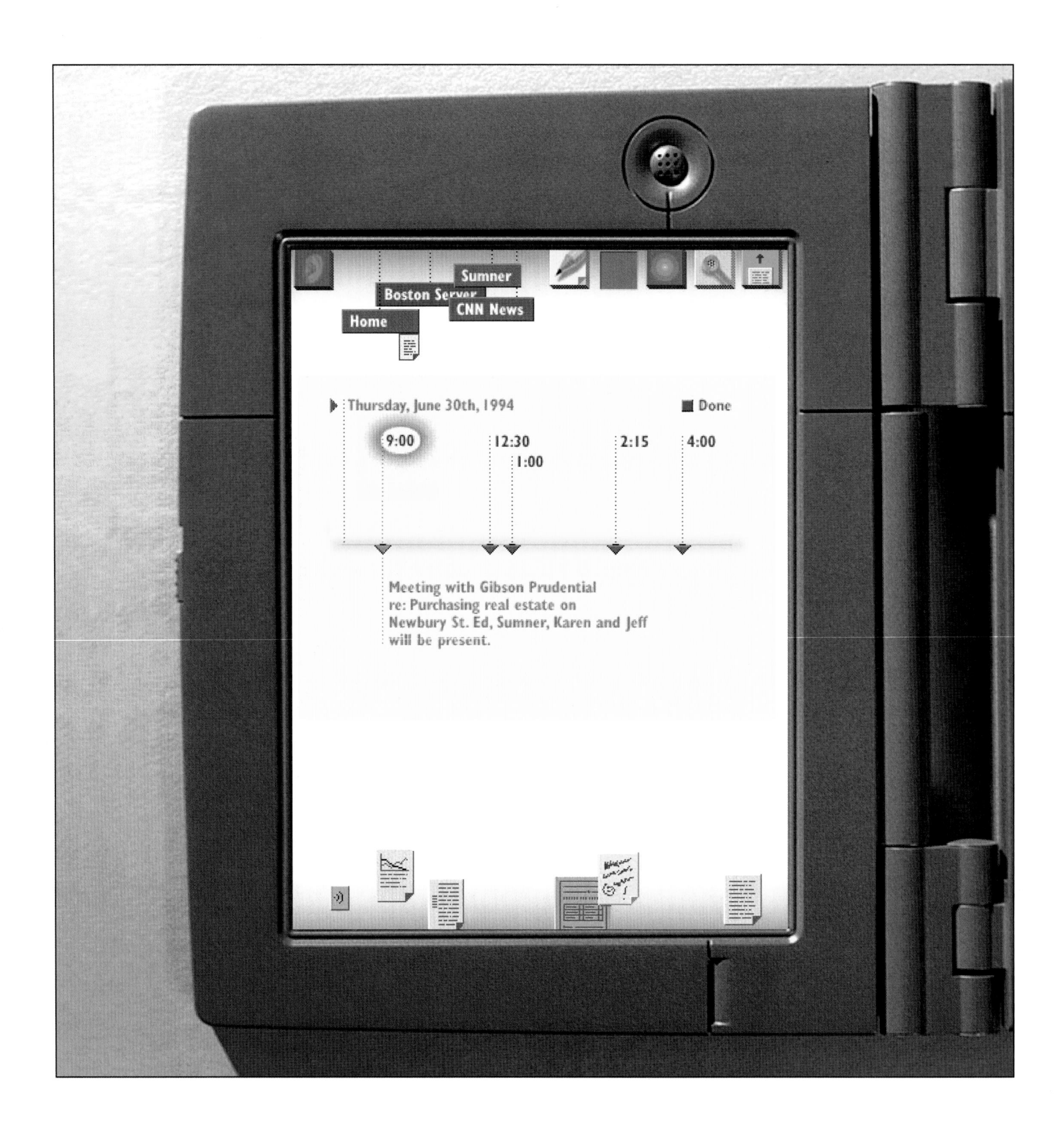

This demo for Digital Equipment Company's "next-generation" personal digital assistant (code-named "Dove"), offers a thrilling glimpse at the blue sky stage of an amazing gadget. Attempting to alter how we think about the computer desktop, the Dove interface smoothly blends real-world artifacts—"While You Were Out" slips, for instance—with those traditionally associated with computers, such as modems. The result is an interface whose form gracefully follows its many functions. ■ This hybrid contrivance is designed to combine the administrative and communicative roles of an entire office into a seamless system of hardware and software. Users communicate with this cyber-secretary primarily by speaking to it, though a virtual keyboard and data lines for fax, printing, and networking provide the input and output capabilities of a notebook computer, as well. Sound and animation enhance the meaning of various functions and tools, so that when Dove is in voice recognition mode, for instance, the screen shows animated soundwaves flooding into an open ear, whereas when it is delivering a message to the user, a speech balloon delivers that message as printed text. Regardless of whether Dove leaves its blue sky orbit for flesh-and-blood life on earth, its demo will help all designers visualize what it is to fly.

DOVE

CLIENT / PUBLISHER Digital Equipment Company

DESIGN Fitch, Boston, MA. Chris Pacione, art director; Alex Subrizi, Ed Chung, Glen Hoffman, interface designers; Sarah Weissinger and Mike Mooney, writers; Ed Chung, programmer; Mark Steele, photographer; Ed Chung and Chris Pacione, sound editors.

Reminder Note
Bring materials cost
folder to the meeting.

Citiplex
Sumner
CNN News
Boston Server
Home
6/30
6

his prototype reveals the promise of the documentary-n-a-disc genre, both in terms of design and subject natter. ■ Designer Lisa Powers initiated this project s a student, choosing to focus on the rich and some-imes tragic life of jazz vocalist Sheila Jordan. Viewers can tailor their exploration of the singer's life by clicking on icons that signify everything from her recordings to her personal and professional relationships. Viewers can then listen to Jordan's music (which included bebop, blues, duos, and "alternative music") and watch interviews with Jordan and those who have known her throughout her career. Portions of the work make effective use of scrolling text and animation. The beauty and moodiness of this work-in-progress is particularly well-suited to the subject.

NEW MEDIA

INDEX

G R A P H I S

M A G A Z I N E

B O O K S

Graphis 296
The Digital Revolution: R/GA Softimage Silicon Graphics European Mindscapes Multimedia
Graphis 295
Carson Chan/Day Apeloig Leith Agency Legorreta Gorham
Graphis 297
Ishioka Fletcher Arnett ABV Achilli & Piazza CD Boxed Sets

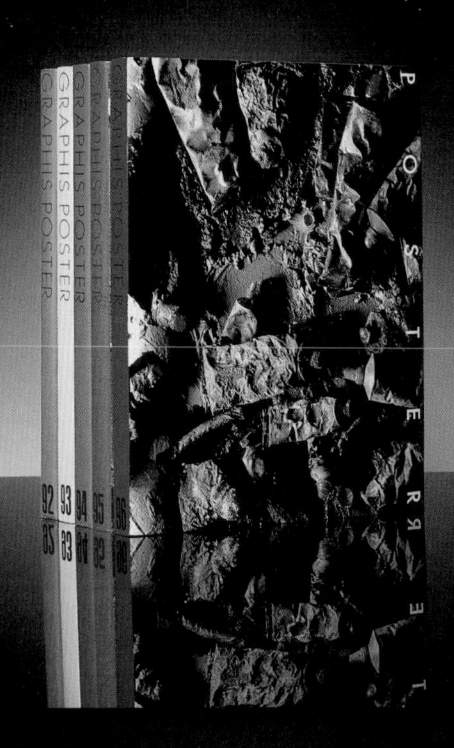

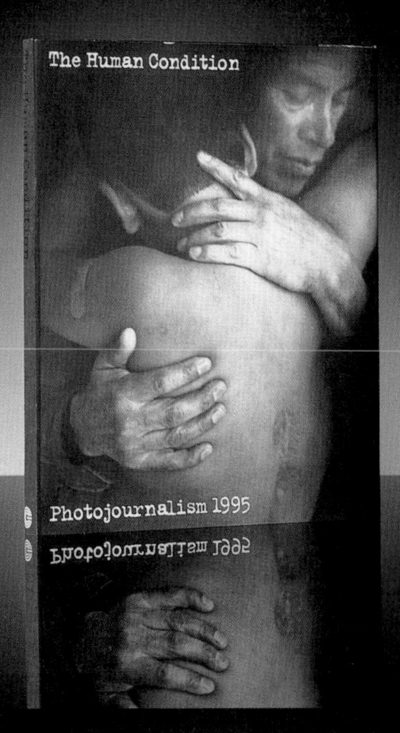

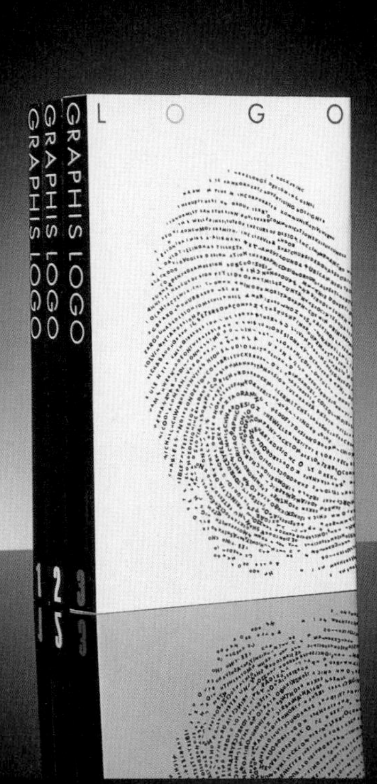

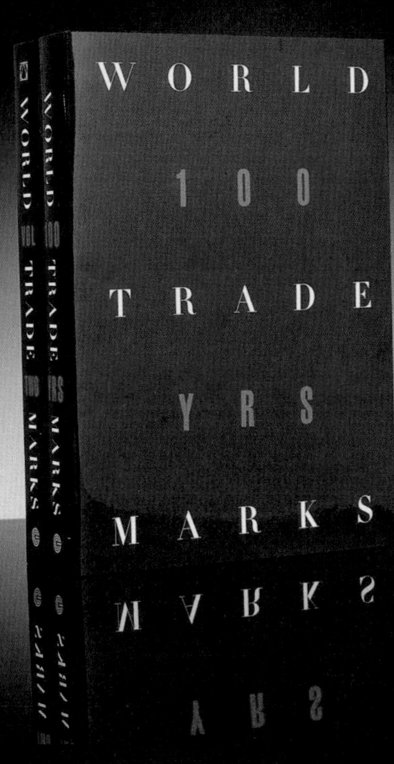

RICHARD SAUL WURMAN

INFORMATION ARCHITECTS

In·for·ma·tion Ar·chi·tect [L *infotectus*] n. 1) the individual who organizes the patterns inherent in data, *making the complex clear.* 2) a person who creates the structure or map of information which allows others to find their personal path to knowledge. 3) the emerging 21st century professional occupation addressing the needs of the age focused upon clarity, human understanding and the science of the organization of information. -In·for·ma·tion Ar·chi·tec·ture

PETER BRADFORD *EDITOR*

USA, CANADA, SOUTH AMERICA, ASIA, PACIFIC

MAGAZINE	USA	CANADA	SOUTHAMERICA/ ASIA/PACIFIC
☐ ONE YEAR (6 ISSUES)	US$ 89.00	US$ 99.00	US$ 125.00
☐ TWO YEARS (12 ISSUES)	US$ 159.00	US$ 179.00	US$ 235.00
☐ AIRMAIL SURCHARGE (6 ISSUES)	US$ 59.00	US$ 59.00	US$ 59.00

25% DISCOUNT FOR STUDENTS WITH COPY OF VALID, DATED STUDENT ID AND PAYMENT WITH ORDER

BOOKS	ALL REGIONS
☐ GRAPHIS ADVERTISING 96	US$ 69.95
☐ GRAPHIS ALTERNATIVE PHOTOGRAPHY 95	US$ 69.95
☐ GRAPHIS ANNUAL REPORTS 4	US$ 69.95
☐ GRAPHIS BOOK DESIGN	US$ 75.95
☐ GRAPHIS CORPORATE IDENTITY 2	US$ 75.95
☐ GRAPHIS DESIGN 96	US$ 69.95
☐ GRAPHIS DIGITAL FONTS	US$ 69.95
☐ GRAPHIS EPHEMERA	US$ 75.95
☐ GRAPHIS FINE ART PHOTOGRAPHY	US$ 85.95
☐ GRAPHIS INFORMATION ARCHITECTS	US$ 49.95
☐ GRAPHIS LETTERHEAD 3	US$ 75.00
☐ GRAPHIS LOGO 3	US$ 49.95
☐ GRAPHIS MUSIC CDS	US$ 75.95
☐ GRAPHIS NEW MEDIA	US$ 75.00
☐ GRAPHIS NUDES (PAPERBACK)	US$ 39.95
☐ GRAPHIS PHOTO 95	US$ 69.95
☐ GRAPHIS POSTER 96	US$ 69.95
☐ GRAPHIS PRODUCTS BY DESIGN	US$ 75.95
☐ GRAPHIS SHOPPING BAGS	US$ 69.95
☐ GRAPHIS STUDENT DESIGN 96	US$ 49.95
☐ GRAPHIS TYPOGRAPHY 1	US$ 69.95
☐ GRAPHIS TYPE SPECIMENS	US$ 49.95
☐ **GRAPHIS PAPER SPECIFIER SYSTEM (GPS)**	US$ 495.00

** ADD $30 SHIPPING/HANDLING FOR GPS

NOTE! NY RESIDENTS ADD 8.25% SALES TAX

☐ CHECK ENCLOSED (PAYABLE TO GRAPHIS) (US$ ONLY, DRAWN ON A BANK IN THE USA)

USE CREDIT CARDS (DEBITED IN US DOLLARS)

☐ AMERICAN EXPRESS ☐ MASTERCARD ☐ VISA

CARD NO. EXP. DATE

CARDHOLDER NAME

SIGNATURE

(PLEASE PRINT)

NAME

COMPANY

ADDRESS

CITY

STATE/PROVINCE ZIP CODE

COUNTRY

SEND ORDER FORM AND MAKE CHECK PAYABLE TO:
GRAPHIS US, INC.,
141 LEXINGTON AVENUE, NEW YORK, NY 10016-8193, USA

EUROPE, AFRICA, MIDDLE EAST

MAGAZINE	EUROPE/AFRICA MIDDLE EAST	GERMANY	U.K.
☐ ONE YEAR (6 ISSUES)	SFR. 164.–	DM 190,–	£ 68.00
☐ TWO YEARS (12 ISSUES)	SFR. 295.–	DM 342,–	£ 122.00
☐ AIRMAIL SURCHARGES	SFR 65.–	DM 75,–	£ 30.00
☐ REGISTERED MAIL	SFR 20.–	DM 24,–	£ 9.00

STUDENTS MAY REQUEST A 25% DISCOUNT BY SENDING STUDENT ID

BOOKS	EUROPE/AFRICA MIDDLE EAST	GERMANY	U.K.
☐ GRAPHIS ADVERTISING 96	SFR. 123.–	DM 149,–	£ 52.00
☐ GRAPHIS ALTERNATIVE PHOTO 95	SFR. 123.–	DM 149,–	£ 52.00
☐ GRAPHIS ANNUAL REPORTS 4	SFR. 137.–	DM 162,–	£ 55.00
☐ GRAPHIS BOOK DESIGN	SFR. 137.–	DM 162,–	£ 55.00
☐ GRAPHIS CORPORATE IDENTITY 2	SFR. 137.–	DM 162,–	£ 55.00
☐ GRAPHIS DESIGN 96	SFR. 123.–	DM 149,–	£ 52.00
☐ GRAPHIS DIGITAL FONTS	SFR. 123.–	DM 149,–	£ 52.00
☐ GRAPHIS EPHEMERA	SFR. 137.–	DM 162,–	£ 55.00
☐ GRAPHIS FINE ART PHOTOGRAPHY	SFR. 128.–	DM 155,–	£ 69.00
☐ GRAPHIS INFORMATION ARCHITECTS	SFR. 123.–	DM 149,–	£ 52.00
☐ GRAPHIS LETTERHEAD 3	SFR. 137.–	DM 162,–	£ 55.00
☐ GRAPHIS LOGO 3	SFR. 123.–	DM 149,–	£ 52.00
☐ GRAPHIS MUSIC CDS	SFR. 137.–	DM 162,–	£ 55.00
☐ GRAPHIS NEW MEDIA	SFR. 137.–	DM 162,–	£ 55.00
☐ GRAPHIS NUDES (PAPERBACK)	SFR. 59.–	DM 71,–	£ 32.00
☐ GRAPHIS PHOTO 95	SFR. 123.–	DM 149,–	£ 52.00
☐ GRAPHIS POSTER 96	SFR. 123.–	DM 149,–	£ 52.00
☐ GRAPHIS PRODUCTS BY DESIGN	SFR. 123.–	DM 149,–	£ 52.00
☐ GRAPHIS SHOPPING BAGS	SFR. 123.–	DM 149,–	£ 52.00
☐ GRAPHIS STUDENT DESIGN	SFR. 59.–	DM 71,–	£ 32.00
☐ GRAPHIS TYPOGRAPHY 1	SFR. 137.–	DM 162,–	£ 55.00
☐ GRAPHIS TYPE SPECIMENS	SFR. 75.–	DM 89,–	£ 37.00
☐ GRAPHIS TV COMMERCIALS (VIDEO)	SFR. 65.–	DM 78,–	£ 36.00

(FOR ORDERS FROM EC COUNTRIES V.A.T. WILL BE CHARGED IN ADDITION TO ABOVE BOOK PRICES)

☐ CHECK ENCLOSED (PLEASE MAKE SFR.-CHECK PAYABLE TO A SWISS BANK

FOR CREDIT CARD PAYMENT (DEBITED IN SWISS FRANCS):

☐ AMERICAN EXPRESS ☐ DINER'S CLUB

☐ VISA/BARCLAYCARD/CARTE BLEUE

CARD NO. EXP. DATE

CARDHOLDER NAME

SIGNATURE

☐ PLEASE BILL ME (ADDITIONAL MAILING COSTS WILL BE CHARGED)

(PLEASE PRINT)

LAST NAME FIRST NAME

COMPANY

ADDRESS

CITY POSTAL CODE

COUNTRY

PLEASE SEND ORDER FORM AND MAKE CHECK PAYABLE TO:
GRAPHIS PRESS CORP.
DUFOURSTRASSE 107, CH–8008 ZÜRICH, SWITZERLAND

Synergy Interactive, Haruhiko Shono, art director (see page 163 for further credits)

Robert Mapplethorpe, photographer (see page 96 for further credits)

Art